The Ultimate
Book of Darts

The Ultimate Book of Darts

A Complete Guide to Games, Gear, Terms, and Rules

By Anne "Sleepy" Kramer

Skyhorse Publishing

Skyhorse Publishing books may be purchased in bulk at special discounts for sales promotion, corporate gifts, fund-raising, or educational purposes. Special editions can also be created to specifications. For details, contact the Special Sales Department, Skyhorse Publishing, 307 West 36th Street, 11th Floor, New York, NY 10018 or info@skyhorsepublishing.com.

Skyhorse® and Skyhorse Publishing® are registered trademarks of Skyhorse Publishing, Inc. ®, a Delaware corporation.

www.skyhorsepublishing.com

10 9 8 7 6 5 4 3 2

Library of Congress Cataloging-in-Publication Data is available on file.

ISBN: 978-1-62087-785-2

Printed in China

For my best friend and love of my life, JK.
And to Stef, our greatest gift in life. I could not have done this without you both. Your love is what keeps me going strong.

TABLE OF CONTENTS

Acknowledgments . . . . *ix*

Foreword . . . . *x*

Introduction . . . . *xi*

Chapter 1-History of the Game. 1

Chapter 2-The Gear 5

Chapter 3-Form, Mechanics, and Etiquette. 19

Chapter 4-The Mental Game. 27

Chapter 5-Taking a Deeper Dive into Practice 31

Chapter 6-The Games to Play 45

Chapter 7-League & Tournament Play 51

Chapter 8-The Professional and the PDC .55

Chapter 9-The Television and Internet Influence. 63

Chapter 10-The Soft-Tip Revolution. 77

Chapter 11-The Progression of Darts in America 89

Chapter 12-History of US Tournaments 119

Chapter 13-History of World Tournaments 139

Chapter 14-The Old Timers. 157

Chapter 15-The Interviews. 161

Chapter 16-Advice from the Pros 201

World Record Attempts *233*

Darting for the Cause, More than a Game *235*

League and Association Information List *243*

Recommended Reading. *253*

Glossary of Terminology *271*

Appendix A: The Study of Practice Routines and their Effectiveness *277*

Appendix B: Battle of the Sexes. *293*

ACKNOWLEDGMENTS

If you had told me last year that I would be writing a book about darts with more than 75,000 words in it, I most likely would have laughed at you. Yet here I am with a finished product. There are so many people I need to thank in regards to this book. First and foremost would have to be my husband, JK, who spent many a lonely evening watching television while I tapped away on this keyboard. Second, all the people who took the time to provide me the information or content I was looking for, and finally, to all the people that have spent the last ninety days offering moral support as this journey progressed. I honestly could not have done this work without all the help I received and I dedicate this book to all the great dart players out there that truly are one, big, happy family. When it came down to it, we all had the same motto, which is the one I use on my website as well . . . "sharing your passion for the game."

FOREWORD
By "Dr. Darts"

It is always an exciting time for me when a new book about darts appears on the bookshelves (or nowadays on download too). I am rarely disappointed and *The Ultimate Book of Darts* is no exception.

I'm not being sexist but I have to say how refreshing it is that a well-known female darts columnist and darts player of over thirty years standing has put digits to keyboard to produce this book and bring a new perspective to the game we all love.

This is no general approach to the sport. This is a book aimed quintessentially at the North American market but will doubtless be of help and interest to a worldwide audience of darts fans.

Drawing from her own experiences and eclectic sources and with cooperation from darts stars of the past and present and established authors such as 'Dartoid' (Paul Seigel) and George Silberzahn, Anne has constructed a work which will be of value not only to those wanting to learn about the sport of darts for the first time but also established players wishing to hone their game.

I am very happy to be associated with and contribute in some small way to this exciting project.

Dr. Patrick Chaplin
Essex
England

www.patrickchaplin.com

February 2013

INTRODUCTION

There are many reasons why a book about darts would be well-received by the public. There actually are quite a few books that have been written about all aspects of darts in different parts of the world. Some have been written by historians, and some by World Champions. I am far from both, however, I wanted to bring a fresh and new perspective to the game: that of an everyday player. I wanted to keep it from being too technical or too intimidating. I also wanted to keep it related to the North American way of playing darts. I wanted to reach out to new players who really want to learn the game, but don't have anyone around to teach them and don't know where to go for the information they seek. This book is also for those seasoned players who wish to find the key to success and to take their game to the next level, but may not know how to get there. Full-time players who want to hear all the stories, and maybe share memories with other players, will also enjoy this book. And then there are the historians; they are longtime players who want to know everything there is about the game, its players, its equipment, its personalities, and its icons. There is also so much to be said about the journey of progress that darts has taken in America—and all over the world. There are many players in countries where one may not think the game of darts exists, such as Pakistan, Iran, Malaysia, Philippines, China, Mongolia, and Russia. Hopefully we have put together a product that will serve to satisfy all those readers and all those players, as well as reach out to the rest of the world and give them an opportunity to learn the history of what has become a beloved and popular game throughout the years.

While I am not a world-renowned player, I have been playing darts for more than thirty years and I have competed and continue to compete in major tournaments all over the United States. My husband has been playing darts for more than thirty-five years and has competed in major tournaments in the United States, as well as World events in Australia and England. He achieved a US number one ranking and was ranked one of the top ten players in the world. We've played darts together at different levels for twenty-eight years, and with all of his experience at such a high level of play, as well as being able to call many top players in the world our friends, I feel that I have heard stories and been able to experience things that your average dart player would never be able to hear or experience. I was blessed with a great memory; therefore, I can share these experiences with the public.

My story begins in 1981 when I started playing darts with my family at home. I have six brothers and one of them joined a league and needed to practice frequently. Being a competitive family, it was not long before the rest of us were hooked and playing every single night. For some odd reason, I excelled more than the rest of the family, to the point that I became one of the top female players in Arizona by the age of sixteen. Youth events did not yet exist back then, so I competed with the adults all the time. During this time, Arizona and Southern California were part of the same region, so I spent many times a year traveling to Southern California to play regional events and tournaments against some of the top players in the United States. Jump to 1984, the year my husband entered my life. What a whirlwind! By January 1985, I'd regained my composure and was an official Southern California resident and a member of that same group of top players. Witnessing my husband's quest to be the number one ranked player in the United States in 1985 was an awesome experience. That year, he also won a gold and silver medal in the 1985 World Cup. I loved hearing stories about (and eventually seeing the video of) the American team achieving the extraordinary and beating the British team 9-0 before going on to win the gold medal for the team event.

After I became an official Southern California resident, I was invited to take part in many events, one of them being an all ladies tournament in Northern California, in which a group of us drove to Northern California to stay at a friend's house. Upon arrival, it became clear that I was not part of the inner circle, as I was only nineteen years old, so I was directed to a couch in the guest house for the night. I was so exhausted that being banished to the guest house didn't even upset me; I wanted sleep and nothing else. The next morning, when the other ladies lined up for roll call, they were surprised to find themselves short one person and quickly realized that they'd left me at the guest house, fast asleep! Therefore, from that day forward, I was officially known as "The Sleepy One."

Years later, we entered into to the age of computers and the Internet. Email, chat rooms, instant messenger, forums, etc. To communicate online at any time, a screen name was required. I decided to morph my nickname and my real name together, and this is how the SleepyKramer name was born. As more forums were created for people to talk about darts, it became more popular and "all the rage," and the online persona with the screen name grew and grew. I spent day after day talking to many different people from all over the world and from all walks of life about darts. I would then meet these people at tournaments and instead of introducing myself by my real name, I would have to introduce myself as SleepyKramer. I spent two years sharing my stories and experiences with so many other players in online forums. Eventually, I decided to take the persona one step further and make a website to promote darts as much as I could. The website was also a way for people to know that my nickname was not only synonymous with me the person, but also with a website that shared their passion for the game.

So, SLEEPYKRAMER.COM was born. On the site, I tried to develop a place where anyone in the world could go to find information about darts and links to players, stores, manufactures, forums, leagues, books, and anything and everything related to the darting world. I also wanted it to be a place where I could introduce players to the world and give them a little extra exposure to help them advertise themselves as players and to help them in their quests to obtain sponsorship or to advertise their sponsors and sell their signature items. The introduction of Facebook has led to additional avenues for sharing information. It also helped me discover a few different websites where I began writing monthly articles about things going on in the world of darts. I would also offer commentary on topics that were being talked about in many different forums online.

Within a year of writing these online articles, I was contacted by this publishing company about writing a book about darts. It seemed like a great adventure to me and it also felt like a natural progression for the things I really enjoyed writing about: darts. But more importantly, this offered me the opportunity to give something back to the game and its players after all the years of fun the game has given both my husband and me.

CHAPTER 1:
HISTORY OF THE GAME

The game is quaintly referred to as the tossing of the arrows and more distinctly known as a game of skill. In some countries, the governing bodies have taken the initiative to have darts declared a sport, while in others, it is less culturally accepted and still considered just a game to be played in the local pub or at home. Regardless, the game at its grass roots level began in England and has always been known as a workingman's game. It is a relatively inexpensive pastime, in which setting up the equipment requires a small amount of space and special uniforms or padding is not required. Anyone can play regardless of age, size, and gender, and physical attributes have no effect on whether a player can be successful. It is a game that can be played by serious players at a very high level as well as casual players in living rooms, garages, or basements.

In the early 1900s, some considered darts to be a game of mere chance. At this time, betting was allowed on games of skill, but was not allowed on games of chance. A local inn owner was brought before magistrates because he was allowing betting on dart matches. Because the magistrates considered darts to be a game of chance, the inn owner brought in a local player to prove them wrong. The magistrates then declared that darts was, in fact, a game a skill and betting was then allowed and has been allowed ever since.

When it comes to determining the age and origin of the game of darts, it has been said that the game began as a contest between bored soldiers during their breaks from battle. The soldiers threw short spears into the upturned ends of wine barrels, similar to the act of knife throwing. As any competition progresses, more defined targets become a requirement to determine who has the most skill. It was said that this led to the use of the slice of a tree trunk as a target, as the natural rings of the tree made great scoring surfaces. Tree trunks also had radial cracks that would appear as the wood dried out; these would split the surface into different sections.

As time passed and technology progressed, so did the creativity of players. The missile (or dart) used evolved from a barrel-shaped piece of wood about four inches long with a metal point stuck in one end and feathers on the other to a patented all-metal barrel in 1906. We will continue further about the progression of the darts and materials used in the next chapter.

The toeline used in the game is called an "oche." It is the marker on the floor, set a specific distance from the dartboard and the players stand behind this line to throw their darts at the dartboard. It was noted that when the game of darts was standardized in 1920, the word listed in the tournament rule book was "hockey," which is derived from an old English word "hocken," which means "to spit." The rule book goes on to further explain that there were spitting competitions held in English pubs and there is a theory that the "hockey line" was determined by the length that a given player could spit from standing with his back to the dartboard. The word then progressed to "oche," with a silent H.

Some time during the last years of the nineteenth or the first few years of the twentieth century, wireworker Thomas Buckle of Dewsbury, West Yorkshire, England devised the numbering of the dartboard which is recognized around the country and around the globe today as 'standard'.

Buckle had in his possession a London 'Fives Board'; a dartboard comprising of twelve segments numbered (from the top and clockwise)

20, 5, 15, 10, 20, 5, 15, 10, 20, 5, 15, 10. The wireworker toyed with the board and then expanded it to twenty segments reading clockwise from the top, 20, 1, 18, 4, 13, 6, 10, 15, 2, 17, 3, 19, 7, 16, 8, 11, 14, 9, 12, 5. The board was marketed locally and sold so well that it eventually became known as the 'Yorkshire' or 'Doubles' board.

During the subsequent decade or so the board was 'exported' to London where a treble ring was added but the numbering sequence remained the same. In 1924 the newly-formed National Darts Association (NDA) declared the board and its numbering to be 'standard'. It was adopted by many darts leagues but only became truly standard in the 1970s in the UK.

After the Second World War the Buckle design did find its way across the pond to the USA and this eventually led to the establishment of numerous darts leagues in the country mainly playing to English darts rules.

Photo courtesy of Bryan Haraway/Professional Darts Corporation

Darts player Chris White.

CHAPTER 2:
THE GEAR

You should consider many factors when choosing your dart gear. Comfort is often the first thing players look for, from the dartboard set-up, to the darts you hold in your hand, to your physical comfort when throwing the dart. If you are not comfortable, you will continue to make changes and have less of a chance to develop consistent mechanics and practice habits.

The dartboards used today are divided into twenty equal sections. Circular-shaped wires divide each numbered section into single, double, or triple sections. In the 1970s, there was a board used that did not feature a triple section. This board was known as a Yorkshire board. Another form of board used was known as The Fives board. No matter the type of board used, different colors sub-divide the board even further and will alternate section by section. Hitting the larger black or white sections of the board will score a single of the corresponding number for that section. Hitting the alternating red or green sections in the inner narrow triple ring will score triple of the corresponding number for that section. Hitting the alternating red or green sections in the outer narrow double ring will score double of the corresponding number for that section. The inner section or center of the board, known as the bulls-eye, is divided into two sections. The outer section, known as the outer bull, scores a total of 25 points per dart and the inner section, known as the center bull or double bull, scores a total of 50 points per dart. Although not used in everyday competitions, manufacturers have also created what is known as a "quad" board, which features an additional quad

The Fives board

ring between the triple ring and the bulls-eye and each dart that lands in this section will score quadruple of the corresponding number for that section.

The traditional dart board used in competition today

Any darts that bounce out of the board during play or any darts that land outside of the outer double ring do not count, no score is given for those darts, and they cannot be re-thrown during the turn. If your dart lodges itself loosely in the board and drops out after the next darts hit the board, this dart does not count for score, as well. If a player hits the other darts and causes the dart thrown to be held in place by the other two darts in the board, this dart will only be scored if the point is touching the scoring surface.

Dartboards can be placed pretty much anywhere these days, as they only require the placement of a small wall-mounted bracket. When considering placement of your dartboard, there are a few details that should not be overlooked. It is recommended that you have a clear walking path to and from the board with no clutter or obstacles in your way and it should also be a low-traffic area. Because there is the danger of the darts bouncing off wires or falling out of the board, it is imperative that no items are placed around or below the dartboard and that you avoid them hitting a tile floor or hard surface, as this could cause irreparable damage to the darts. Carpeting or some type of dart mat that you can roll out is highly recommended if your floor is not already carpeted. Also remember that darts will stick in wooden floors and the points can also cause some chips in your tile. While the mounting bracket for a board can be placed directly onto a wall, it is recommended that new players place some sort of background behind or around the board to ensure that should a player miss the board entirely, you will avoid having holes poked into your wall.

It is also important to be as thorough and precise as possible when hanging your dartboard. While being off an eighth of an inch may not seem significant, consideration must be given to the dartboard itself. Since the width of a wire between a winning or losing shot can come down to mere millimeters, being off an eighth of an inch in the height of your dartboard can also mean an eight of an inch difference in what you hope to be your game-winning shot, which can then result in a miss and cost you the game.

Don't forget to leave yourself space for a scoreboard. There are many different sizes and varieties of scoreboards available on the market that range from ones that use chalk, grease pens, or dry erase markers. Obviously, the larger the scoreboard, the better visibility players will have for scoring the match. There are many electronic scoreboards available on the market today, as well, that are equipped to function in whatever game you choose to play, whether it be 301, 501, or cricket. Some may even be pre-programmed so you are able to compete against the computer.

For many years in the beginning of darts, the throwing distance varied from area to area and event to event. Some would be played at the 8' line, while others would play at 7' 6". Eventually, the World Dart Federation put together all the different distances and came out with the average throwing distance of 7' 9¼", which is now the universal distance used globally and was

Sample of a dry erase scoreboard

calculated using the Pythagorean theorem, $a^2 + b^2 = c^2$. This distance, however, does not apply to the electronic dart game, as the distance for this started at 8' and remains the same to this day.

To set up your dartboard, the official throwing distance to use is 7'9¼". The height of the board from the floor to the center of the bull is 5'8". The diagonal distance from the center of the bull to front of the throw line is 9'7³/₈".

Dartboard manufacturing has improved throughout the years. Before the First World War, pubs in the United Kingdom had dartboards made from solid blocks of wood, usually elm. The elm then had to be soaked overnight to heal the holes made by the darts, which was messy and smelly. A company called Nodor created the "no odor" board using sisal for the fabrication.

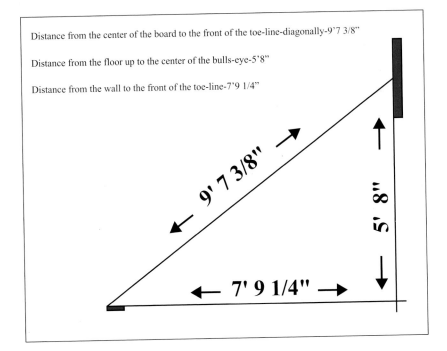

Distance from the center of the board to the front of the toe-line-diagonally-9'7 3/8"

Distance from the floor up to the center of the bulls-eye-5'8"

Distance from the wall to the front of the toe-line-7'9 1/4"

9' 7 3/8"

5' 8"

7' 9 1/4"

Boards today continue to be manufactured using sisal. Sisal is a fiber normally used to make rope. The manufacturing and the grooming of the sisal is a tedious process, and once it is cut into chunks, called "biscuits," it is then ready to be used in the fabrication of a dartboard. The outer steel band is placed, and then filled with the sisal biscuits. The amount of biscuits used controls the hardness or softness of the board itself. Once placed into the steel band, the biscuits are covered in glue on one side and placed onto the round wooden backboard. The next step in the process is to compress the sisal into a perfectly round shape. The sisal and board are then put through a machine to smooth them out for the colors to be printed onto the surface.

Sisal Plant

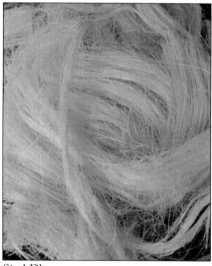

Sisal Fibers

The use of sisal was a great success; when the darts stuck into the board, it caused little or no damage, as the sisal fibers would separate to allow the dart to lodge itself between the fibers and the sisal would close and fill the

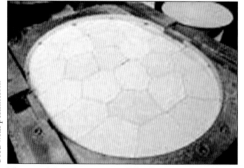

The sisal biscuit process. The biscuits have been placed in the steel outer band and are ready to be compressed into the circular shape of the dartboard.

hole once the dart was removed. A regulation board is 17¾ inches in diameter and is divided into twenty radial sections. The wires are then placed or the blade system is inserted. In older or less expensive boards, traditional round wires are used; however, in today's market, the use

Side view of the dartboard cut down the middle where you can view the bottom base board, the sisal biscuits, and the painting of the top layer of the sisal.

Images © The Winmau Dartboard Company. Used with permission.

of a blade system is more popular among the players. The blade system reduces bounce-outs of the darts and allows for a maximum scoring surface. It has been said that the new blade system used in dartboards today has accounted for the increase in players-per-dart average because the scoring surface has been increased.

The darts themselves have also progressed along with the technology used to manufacture them. Darts are made up of four components: the points, the barrels, the shafts, and the fletchings or flights. In the early days, darts were made of wood, and then progressed to barrels made of metals, such as brass, then copper/tungsten, and more currently tungsten blends. Tungsten in its original form is brittle; therefore, many darts are made from barrels that contain a combination of 80 to 95 percent tungsten mixed with other metals, such as nickel, which adds strength for the manufacturing and milling of the billets. When the barrels were made of wood, you were pretty limited in your choice of the weight of your

Parts of the dart

darts, but with the use of metals such as tungsten, the weight of the dart can now vary anywhere from 12 grams to more than 30 grams. There are certain parts of the United States where the traditional wooden darts, known as "woodies" or "widdy" darts, are still used in competitive play and the inclusion of plastic tipped darts used in the electronic dartboards are also prevalent.

Samples of shafts available, aluminum and nylon.

The choice of the length of shaft you use is also based on the dart you have and the way you throw. Shafts are made at different lengths to suit every style of player and every style of dart. They are manufactured from materials such as plastic, nylon polymer, or metals such as aluminum or titanium.

Longer shafts can shift the weight of your dart toward the back end, causing the dart to tilt backwards during flight and land at a downward angle. Shorter shafts make the dart more compact, reduce the drag on the back end of the dart, and more often than not, your dart will land at an angle tilting upward.

The feathers, wings, or fins, which were called fletching in the early days, are now known as "flights" and have progressed along with the darts throughout the years. In the beginning of the game, feathers (typically from turkeys) were used for the same reasons they were added feathers on arrows. An American patented a folded paper flight in 1898. For many years, the use of different blends of plastic materials, nylon, or foil has been prevalent in the manufacturing of flights, which also allows for the addition of multiple shapes as well as colors and print graphics. Today, technology has advanced so far that there are now machine-molded solid plastic flight systems being imported from Asia. The use of plastics now gives players the chance to

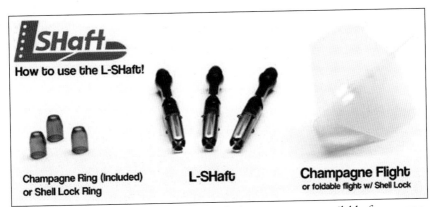

How to use the L-SHaft!

Champagne Ring (Included) or Shell Lock Ring   **L-SHaft**   **Champagne Flight** or foldable flight w/ Shell Lock

A sample of the precision molded plastic flight systems now available from manufacturers in Asia.

customize their darts with any type of design or icon of their choice or even their own names, as many top players do. The reasoning behind the use of feathers or a flight is to add drag to the dart, which prevents the rear of the dart from overtaking the point. The shape of the flight itself controls the amount of drag on the dart in flight and the choice you make will depend on your style of throw, along with the weight and length of your dart.

There are many differences in the flights that you can choose. "Hard" flights are made from a stiff, polyester plastic where the layers are permanently sealed together by heat during the manufacturing process. These flights do not tear as easily as softer flights, however, when they do tear, they are ruined and will need to be replaced. Hard flights also do not have as much flexibility as softer flights, which may cause the flights to pop off more often when throwing close groups and also may cause more deflections of your darts in that the barrel will careen off the flight slightly and veer away from its intended target.

Softer flights, otherwise known as "poly" flights are made of a more flexible plastic and then folded into the required shape with glue holding the layers of the plastic together. If the flight is slightly torn during use, it can be pressed back together. The softness or "give" in the flight will not cause as much deflections as with the hard plastic flights.

Other flights out on the market today are Dimplex, or Ribtex flights, which have an embossed pattern on them, as well as nylon flights, which are said to be amongst the most durable flights available.

Sample of a soft "poly" flight along with a textured "Dimplex" flight.

Choosing a dart that is right for you is an important step and can sometimes be a very tedious process. The shape of the barrel and feel of the grip of the dart, along with your consistent grip of the dart, is a large facet in maintaining proper mechanics during your throw each and every time. If you move your fingers

A tungsten billet before the manufacturing process

around to different spots every time you grip the dart, you will then be changing the way you release the dart during every throw.

Today there is a wide variety of dart manufacturers, and with the help of modern technology, they are able to use custom lathes that have computers built into them. This allows a manufacturer to program specific barrel designs into the lathe, for a more expedient and detail oriented manufacturing process. These machines have progressed to such an advanced stage that the exact design and dimensions of a dart can be added to the computer, which will then tell the lathe exactly how to cut and shape the tungsten billet with precision automation in minutes. Darts can now be machined with no grooves or grips all the way up to the roughest of textures.

Different styles of dart barrels

Because there are many varieties of shapes, designs, grips, and grooves to choose from, there is a type of dart that will suit everyone's needs. The shape of the dart that you choose should allow you a consistent grip, while the balance of the dart, whether it be pencil-shaped or torpedo-shaped, should be based on how hard or soft you throw. It is said that the best way to find a comfortable grip of the dart is to balance it on your index finger to find the center of balance, then add your thumb and additional fingers to support your grip.

The way a dart flies through the air and how it lands on the board can also be the result of the flights and shafts that you choose and is dependent on your form and how you release the dart, along with your mechanics. With so many varieties in a person's form, along with his or her height and arm length, which can change the release point from one player to another, you'll most likely choose your set-up based on a trial-and-error method. What may work for one player may not work for another and making changes and experimenting with other set-ups is always recommended until you narrow down your choices to what you feel is best for you. Once you decide on a set-up, you should stick with it for a determined length of time before deciding whether your set-up is appropriate.

Most people would not consider out charts to be a form of gear to be considered when getting yourself set up to play darts, but as you grow as a player, it is a fundamental component to your

★ OUT CHART ★

170 – T20 T20 DB	129 – T19 T16 D12	95 – T19 D19	61 – T15 D8
167 – T20 T19 DB	128 – T18 T14 D16	94 – T18 D20	60 – 20 D20
164 – T20 T18 DB	127 – T20 T17 D8	93 – T19 D18	59 – 19 D20
161 – T20 T17 DB	126 – T20 T10 D18	92 – T20 D16	58 – 18 D20
160 – T20 T20 D20	125 – T20 T11 D16	91 – T17 D20	57 – 17 D20
158 – T20 T20 D19	124 – T20 T16 D8	90 – T18 D18	56 – 16 D20
157 – T20 T19 D20	123 – T19 T14 D12	89 – T19 D16	55 – 15 D20
156 – T20 T20 D18	122 – T18 T20 D4	88 – T16 D20	54 – 14 D20
155 – T20 T19 D19	121 – T17 T18 D8	87 – T17 D18	53 – 13 D20
154 – T20 T18 D20	120 – T20 20 D20	86 – T18 D16	52 – 12 D20
153 – T20 T19 D18	119 – T19 T10 D16	85 – T15 D20	51 – 11 D20
152 – T20 T20 D16	118 – T20 18 D20	84 – T20 D12	50 – 18 D16
151 – T20 T17 D20	117 – T20 17 D20	83 – T17 D16	49 – 17 D16
150 – T20 T18 D18	116 – T20 16 D20	82 – T14 D20	48 – 16 D16
149 – T20 T19 D16	115 – T20 15 D20	81 – T19 D12	47 – 15 D16
148 – T20 T16 D20	114 – T20 14 D20	80 – T20 D10	46 – 6 D20
147 – T20 T17 D18	113 – T19 16 D20	79 – T13 D20	45 – 15 D20
146 – T20 T18 D16	112 – T20 12 D20	78 – T18 D12	44 – 12 D16
145 – T20 T15 D20	111 – T19 14 D20	77 – T15 D16	43 – 3 D20
144 – T20 T20 D12	110 – T20 10 D20	76 – T20 D8	42 – 10 D16
143 – T20 T17 D16	109 – T20 9 D20	75 – T17 D12	41 – 9 D16
142 – T20 T14 D20	108 – T19 19 D16	74 – T14 D16	
141 – T20 T19 D12	107 – T20 15 D16	73 – T19 D8	
140 – T20 T20 D10	106 – T20 14 D16	72 – T16 D12	
139 – T19 T14 D20	105 – T20 8 D20	71 – T13 D16	
138 – T20 T18 D12	104 – T18 10 D20	70 – T18 D8	
137 – T17 T14 D20	103 – T17 12 D20	69 – T15 D12	
136 – T20 T20 D8	102 – T19 13 D16	68 – T20 D4	
135 – T20 T17 D12	101 – T17 10 D20	67 – T17 D8	
134 – T20 T14 D16	100 – T20 D20	66 – T14 D12	
133 – T20 T19 D8	99 – T19 10 D16	65 – T11 D16	
132 – T20 T16 D12	98 – T20 D19	64 – T16 D8	
131 – T20 T13 D16	97 – T20 D20	63 – T13 D12	
130 – T20 T18 D8	96 – T20 D18	62 – T10 D16	

★★★

★★★

Sample of a 3 dart out chart

key to success in the 301 and 501 games. I recommend that every player obtain an out chart whenever they purchase darts and a dartboard. Many players consider it very intimidating because it then involves math, but knowing your out-shot combinations will boost your confidence and your game to a higher level. There are many variations available that include many different out-shot combinations, but my suggestion would be one similar to the one shown above.

American Dart Gear

American Darts, or "widdy" darts, is a variation of the traditional English darts game and is played mostly in the eastern parts of the United States around east-ern Pennsylvania, New Jersey, parts of New York State and Delaware, and as far south as Maryland; however, its grass roots come from the coal min-ing towns of northeastern Pennsylvania.

The traditional American "widdy" dartboard

The American dartboard is made of basswood, and the better-quality models will have a center that rotates so that the board will wear in a more even manner. There are thin metal wires imbedded into the board to separate the sections of the board for scoring. The scoring surface itself is slightly different than traditional English dart boards, as there is only one bull and the triple ring is on the outer edge and the double ring is just inside the triple ring. The rest of the board is a scoring surface for single points. The numeric sequence is the same as a traditional English board, however, the height of the board and distance thrown are much different. The center of the bull is at 5' 3" and the distance from the face of the board diagonally to the throwing line is 7' 3".

The darts used are the traditional "widdy" darts with wooden barrels. These barrels are fletched with turkey feather flights glued into place, the darts are 5¾ inches long,

Widdy Baseball board

and they weigh anywhere from 12 to 14 grams. There is a metal tip section that is bored into the end of the wooden barrel and a weight is inserted into the barrel to move the balance of the dart more to the center.

An American "widdy" dart

CHAPTER 3:
FORM, MECHANICS, AND ETIQUETTE

Form and Mechanics

One of the two things that appear to affect how people play is their individual mechanics and confidence in themselves and their game. Just like golf players, or baseball players, or anyone that has to perform the same motion over and over again to achieve a perfect result, darts demands repetitive motion, and being able to complete that same motion over and over again can be a great key to success.

Most players seem to think that when they start playing, they have to hop, jump, skip, or do a shot-put dance to get the dart to the board. They think they need to throw a dart like they are throwing a baseball, hard and fast, rather than employing any type of finesse. I remember meeting a young lady once, who was a new player, and she told me that because she was only 4' 10", she felt she had to put some extra effort from her body into her throw for the dart to reach the board. And she exerted even more energy when she had to throw at the top of the board. When we met, and she saw my mechanics and that I was only 4 inches taller than her, she realized she was jumping around far too much. There are no rules when it comes to size, shape, and gender for throwing darts.

Players should remember to find a stance that is stable and comfortable for them. They should not base their on stance on how someone else stands or how someone else tells them to stand. There is no law set in stone that says you need to stand facing the board at a 45-degree angle or at a 90-degree angle. It is important for you to be comfortable in your stance and to be steady and relaxed. Experimentation is also critical when determining your stance,

Darts player John Kramer

especially if you have any physical problems that keep you from standing or turning a certain way. You do not want to be uncomfortable or experience any pain in your stance, because this will cause you to make slight adjustments to compensate for pain or discomfort, which then can affect your throw. Many of the top players prefer to put the majority of their weight on their lead foot at the oche line and the rest of the weight on the back foot, which acts as a point of balance or the anchor for your stance. Center yourself with the dartboard, as many oche's can be placed offset from the center of the board.

Your grip of the dart itself should be stable and firm, yet relaxed without any tension placed on your fingers, while still being able to maintain control of the dart in the throwing motion. Some players are more comfortable gripping the dart with two fingers, some with three, and some with four. Do whatever you are comfortable with; however, the coordination of your fingers while releasing the dart can affect the direction of the dart once it leaves your hand. You should push your thumb against at least two of your fingers to grip the dart.

To set your arm for the throw itself, hold your arm at a 90-degree angle parallel to the floor. To set the dart in motion for the throw, bring your hand back toward your face, usually at eye level. This helps maintain accuracy and improve hand-eye coordination. The arm should then proceed to the forward motion of throwing the dart toward the board. While the entire process is not forceful, some impetus must be given to the projectile to get it to fly to the dartboard. The trajectory of

Before you throw bring your arm back to a 90-degree angle.

the dart will depend on the amount of force placed in the throwing motion and the arc of the dart as it travels to the board. A major thing to remember is that the more motion you have during your throwing process, the greater the chances that something will go wrong in that process. Your throwing motion should utilize your entire lower arm with minimal motion from your upper arm. On your follow-through, once the dart is released, you should continue following through with your arm and end with at least one of your fingers pointing at the target. The core of your body should remain balanced with little to no movement. The process is similar to taking a wadded up piece of paper and trying to toss it through a small opening, such as a basket. The finesse used in the motion is the same finesse that should be used when throwing a dart. Just because the object is heavier does not mean that finesse is not required. The process involves the use of hand-eye coordination.

As a new player, always remember that you are not going to be perfect. The darts you throw when first starting out will go everywhere, and this will only get better with practice. There is only one person in the world that I do not apply this to, and she happens to be my mother. At the time this happened, my brothers and I had been playing for about a year, and finally one day while I was practicing, she came in and asked me how to play. I explained the different scoring surfaces of the dart board and that we did not throw at the bulls-eye for score, but at the triple 20, since this would achieve the highest maximum score. With that explanation, we began mom's lesson on how to throw. I showed her the proper stance, showed her how to hold the dart, how to just use her arm and to use some finesse. Now mom was ready to take her first try at throwing darts. I stepped back and to my complete surprise . . . *thunk, thunk,* and *thunk* . . . three triple 20s for a maximum score of 180 on the first three darts she threw. And not only that, she did it with brass darts, which are a lot fatter in the barrel than the traditional tungsten darts of today. Needless to say, mom was forever banned from the dartboard since none of us had ever been able to hit a maximum score in practice or play. I wish we had video back then because the moment was priceless and is one that I will never forget. To this day, she has yet to pick up any darts again. And why should she? She was perfect on her first try; she doesn't need to improve on that at all.

The best practice for a brand new player is to focus on trying to get all three darts in a certain section of the board, like the larger section of the 20. If you try at first to hit smaller targets, your success rate will be lower, and you might experience some frustration, which you should try to avoid as a new player. As time goes by, and with more practice, you will be able to narrow down your target base. I received great advice from someone a long time ago when they told me that if a player could manage to hit three single 20s per turn, that player would win a majority of their matches against other players. Since I was a female player, this applied easily; however, with the men's game, a little more consistency with higher scoring is usually required. This mentality, though, will help take away a lot of the pressure in competition, as you won't be thinking that you have to hit big scores each turn to win a game. It also creates more confidence in you as a player.

Repetitive motion and muscle memory are also contributing factors for your form and mechanics. One sees players every day that will have one dart land in the area they intended, only to have the next two darts land in completely different locations that may be more than an inch away from their intended target. It has been said the repetitive motion leads to muscle memory, which in turn can allow a player to start to repeat the same motion over and over again with as little variance as

possible each and every time, resulting in the darts landing in smaller, tighter groups.

Etiquette

Darts has always been considered a gentleman's sport and a game that begins and ends with a handshake. Sportsmanship is a prevailing quality that a majority of players try to maintain from the beginning of the match to the end.

There are some aspects of the game that fall under etiquette or a code of conduct of sorts that seasoned players take for granted, but that new players may not be aware of. A new player may make an error to breach this code known to all the other players and could lead to many players being angry or frustrated with the new player. It is important to remember to educate all new players on some of the simple basics that we all have learned along the way.

Treat other players in a courteous manner. Distractions while a player is at the line concentrating on his shot can be very disturbing. Give the thrower plenty of room to throw and stay behind him when he is taking his turn at the line. Obviously, not all conditions will allow for a quiet atmosphere and most players are used to background noise, music, and general chatter. The sudden loud noises stand out, however, which can cause a distraction. Speaking to the player or speaking behind the player while he or she is throwing is frowned upon. This also applies to spectators in the area.

When your turn is completed, leave your darts in the board until the scorekeeper has marked down the correct score or you as the scorekeeper have written down the correct score. It is best to leave the darts in the board until completion of this task in the event that the opponent questions what score was thrown.

As a scorekeeper, you should not make any sudden movements, and you should remain as still as possible while the shooter is throwing. The scorekeeper should not announce any scores to the shooter unless the shooter asks.

If you have a question about what has been thrown, the scorekeeper is considered the official of the match and should be the only one relaying your score or a remaining balance of score left. Your teammates may also assist in this and can also tell you what to throw at next, however, the scorekeeper is not allowed to advise you on what should be thrown next.

The final aspect to remember also ends with sportsmanship and a handshake. Always remember that someone will win and someone will lose. If you are the winner, take the time to appreciate the efforts of the player who did not win. If you are not the winner, take the time to appreciate the efforts of the player who did win. We all want to be on the winning side, but it does not work that way, and learning to win or lose gracefully will go a long way with you and your career in darts.

Sportsmanship is best described as the direct actions of a person who exhibits qualities that are held in high esteem by many who participate in the same sport. Such traits as fairness, courtesy, good temper, as well as winning and/or losing gracefully are some of the many well-favored aspects of being considered someone who conducts themselves with good "sportsmanship."

Photo courtesy of Lawrence Lustig/Professional Darts Corporation

Professional darts player Jeff Smith, from Canada

CHAPTER 4:
THE MENTAL GAME

I t's a relatively unknown entity. It's hard to teach and even more difficult to obtain. Most people mistake it for arrogance. Only a chosen few are lucky enough to experience it. Once it is recognized, it can be intimidating to another player. It can sometimes mean the difference in the outcome of a game. What is this mysterious thing that so many crave? Confidence.

It's been my experience that the more confidence you have, the more dominating a player you can be regardless of your skill level because it can mentally intimidate your opponent. Obviously some skill is involved, but the trick is to be comfortable with your own skill level. You know what you can do and you know your own talent. This controls the nerves and your focus, which can improve performance.

We all often joke that darts is 10 percent talent and 90 percent mental. The mental aspect of your play can vary and affect your game in a multitude of ways and is a topic that is more difficult to address in a "how to" book—it's not always easy to teach mental toughness since people react to situations differently. The mental aspect tells you that you are nervous because you know that you have to hit a game-winning shot. Your brain transmits this to the rest of your body, and next thing you know, you are shaking like a leaf in a storm. So how do you overcome these physical obstacles to become more confident in yourself and your game? Practice is always a good start. Proper mechanics and being comfortable with the way you throw can also help. Being fluent on your out-shots to finish a game is another. You should not have to stop and think of what to shoot at. It is important to combine all these factors together for a complete package as a player.

Players also fail to understand the negative effects of, the dreaded board call. We've all been there: Your name is called against one of the top players. You moan and groan about the call. You think about what you are going to do for the rest of the afternoon once you are done with the match. You drag yourself to the board with the hopes that the top player doesn't beat you up too bad. And of course, it's no big surprise to you that you lost. Why? You lost the match as soon as you heard the board call. You never gave yourself a chance to give it your all. And don't think that that top player is not using this to their advantage. He knows his abilities, he has confidence! He knows he intimidates you in this situation because your body language has already given that secret away! He is holding all the cards and knows that he just has to play a steady match to beat you, while you are killing yourself to hit perfect scores on every turn because you think this is what it will take to beat this type of player. Meanwhile, the top player is doing the same as I would in this situation . . . hitting basic, solid scores per round without any added pressure on himself to win the match.

Of course, the easiest way to gain confidence in yourself as a player and your game and to take your first steps towards greatness is to dedicate yourself to practicing. While there is some natural talent involved, players are not born into greatness. They dedicate themselves to practice with the intention to improve their performance with repetition of their basic mechanics to achieve as close to perfection as they can with each and every throw.

For most people, practice is hard enough without pushing themselves even harder. Making the sacrifice and taking those extra steps can be challenging. Most will give up. This is where the heart of a champion is born. If great performances were easy, there would be many great

Though young, Joshua Demers knows the value of practicing hard.

players out there and their achievements would not be so rare. Greatness can be very demanding. The road to greatness is paved with an individual's commitment to excellence and their rejection of failure. Greatness isn't reserved for a select few or the chosen ones. It is available to you and to everyone.

Focus and concentration are traits that are elemental to being a successful dart player. It is a fundamental necessity to be able to tune out all outside distractions and direct all your thoughts to the task at hand, whether it is in a game or just routine practice. Many players develop this while looking at the dartboard, concentrating on a small speck or spot on the target with the aim to improve their concentration on the target. Reinforcing this concentration and ability to tune out outside distractions on a continual basis will help you when those random instances arise where you have no control of what is going on in your surroundings.

For some players, the mental aspect of the game can continue further by delving into the psychology of a player and how it affects them while playing. We'll explore more of this in the next chapter.

Darts player Darin Young.

Photo courtesy of Lawrence Lustig/Professional Darts Corporation

CHAPTER 5:
TAKING A DEEPER DIVE
INTO PRACTICE

Despite the amount of great players in the world today, there has been no determination made that any one player's practice routine is better than another's or that certain practice routines will make you a World Champion. While the time and dedication you put forth for practice may determine your fate, many players favor one practice routine over another and it is most often a reflection of what each individual player is comfortable with, since they have to do this on a daily basis to achieve any modicum of success.

Some players prefer to play games against opponents to play at a competitive level for their practice, while others prefer to play games by themselves. Some others believe that simply throwing at one target to obtain effective accuracy is the key, and some believe that practicing their triples and doubles is their path to success. Regardless of which way you choose to practice, it should be a guided, self-directed practice to establish routines and rituals that will build success incrementally. Proficiency at practice equals improvement in performance. A player will either choose to practice, or commit to practice. How do we know what level of proficiency is needed? Well, there are five stages to the learning process. 1. Novice 2. Beginner 3. Competent 4. Proficient 5. Expert. You can be self-directed in your learning process and as the old saying goes, "you get out of it what you put into it". What stage you end up in will depend on your dedication and commitment to practice.

While no practice routine has been set in stone as the proven method, the one that comes to mind the most for effective accuracy would be a player trying to ensure that they are following proper mechanics in their practice while trying to consistently hit specific targets on the dartboard. Many years ago, a top player used to tell newer players to just throw one dart at the board. Then with the next two darts, try to hit that first dart. This led to developing the consistency of throwing your darts at a specific target. Other players felt that throwing at the triple 20 all the time helped them to achieve scoring consistency, while others felt that going around the board with triples and doubles helped them become more consistent with moving around the board while still being able to throw consistent groups per turn.

If you are a current player and you feel that there is a gap in your performance, you should evaluate your current performance and establish what your desired performance level is, or what you feel it should be, then create the training that you need to bridge that gap. It will then be up to you to determine how your success will be measured. Darts is one the many forms of competition that can sometimes rely solely on your performance level to evaluate your success, however, the success of your opponent can also determine your final result. Only you can determine if your performance level was up to the standards that you have put forth for yourself regardless of the outcome of the match played.

Three times World Champion, John Part, has also produced a six-part feature, Part's Darts, to give tips on practice and development as a player. The information can be located on the website for the Professional Darts Corporation. Click on the "About the PDC" link and select "FAQ" in the dropdown. One of the questions listed is entitled, "How can I become a better player?" Clicking on this question will provide the link to access Part's Darts.

Professional darts player John Part

Photo courtesy of Lawrence Lustig/
Professional Darts Corporation

There have also been quite a few books written by experienced players and World Champions that explore the practice topic on all different levels that could apply to any player. One of those authors, a long time player from the east coast, has taken the time to write two books about the game of darts, and has also developed a very in-depth practice routine for players to use on a daily basis and has even created a developmental plan for any player, known as Flight School. George Silberzahn, who is from Gibbstown NJ, in the Philadelphia area, has been playing darts since the 60's and has written "How to Master the Sport of Darts" and "Darts Beginning to End".

The first time George Silberzahn picked up a dart was in 1960. George's career in darts has spanned many decades from the 1960s to today. He has had many experiences throughout the years and is fortunate enough to be able to turn what he has learned into words. His knowledge and insight into the sport is undeniable and his training techniques have proven results. He's a darter who can speak to other darters because he's been there. He is familiar with both the feeling of hitting it right on and losing it. He'll take you to the top of your game if that's where you want to be, and if not, maybe he can simply help you enjoy the game more. His satisfaction comes from the success of those he's helped in a sport that has given him so much.

While practice is a major component of how well you are going to compete, there comes a time when some players get to a certain point, or basically hit a wall with their progression, and do not know what else they could do for themselves to take their game to the next level. Here is where we delve more into the mental aspect of the game and its practice routines to help players take that step towards progress.

Many players who have been at the game/sport of darts for a long time and are not happy with how well they play have contacted George. They wish to rise to the next level. In fact, the people that mostly populate the dart game/sport would never think that reading about darts is required. My guess is that 95 percent of those who have made darts part of their lives do not take it seriously enough to consider studying as part of the game. I do not mean study in the sense of formal education courses, but far from it; after all I'm talking about a game here. There is nothing wrong with this mind set until and unless the person begins to think about getting better at it. The moment a dart player begins to think about becoming a competitor, a shooter, is when he or she runs into problems.

As an introduction to George and his Flight School Program, we thought that it would be best to have a little question and answer period to get a brief view into George's thoughts about darts, it's progression, and why he developed Flight School. The interview was completed and offered to me by David Sproull, who also promotes Flight School Canada.

1. I have been your student for a short while now and have already seen results. My wife has just joined up as well. So far the cost for both of us has been nothing. Just how many students do you have and why put all this time in to help all of us get better at darts?

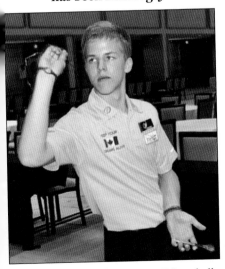

There are over eight hundred Flight Schoolers in over twenty countries and enrollment is growing every day. I spend from one to four hours a day answering questions and making suggestions and I consider this a "get to" rather than a "have to" do thing. It began when I switched from the American style to the English

Canadian darts player Dawson Murschell

style of darts and discovered the need for knowing out-shots and Cricket strategy—not needed in the American style. I was one of the originators, and president, of our first English darts league in New Jersey and wrote an out-shot chart for the league members. Soon after, I discovered that no one had a practice regimen that would let them learn control over the flight path of their darts to play the game well enough, to really maximize their enjoyment of the game, and wrote a booklet for the South Jersey English Dart Association members with tips on how I was practicing. Our original league roster had thirty-six members and of those, five eventually won National titles. That success prompted me to think that what I was suggesting worked. Over the next forty or so years that booklet turned into Flight School and *DARTS: Beginning to End* (B2E). The rewards of feedback from Flight Schoolers, telling me how their enjoyment of the game has increased as a result of my suggestions, puts a broad smile on my face nearly every day as I read emails from them. This is the stimulant that keeps me going. For me, and I maintain for everyone, Darts has never been about the money, it has always been about the enjoyment: Enjoyment from either winning or just taking part, depending on the person, and that is why I charge so much for Flight School: $0.00. Even for the very few who are able to make a living from it, money is really just a way to keep score of who is doing the winning. B2E gives me an opportunity to "spread the word" to many more people through a different means.

2. Could you maybe give everyone a brief description of what Flight School is, what it's all about and where people can find it, whom it is meant for and that sort of thing?

To steal from a real author: therein lies the rub: how to describe what I do. It covers every aspect of the game and is so broad, wide, and deep that

I have been unable to explain what it is in a short enough burst of words to get it across to the listeners/readers before their attention spans come to a halt. At lunch with a friend of mine for all these many years, Ray Fisher, himself a distinguished champion, I remarked "You know, Ray, B2E could only have been written by you or me because you have to have lived a darts life time in order to do it." I realize, as I now read what I just wrote, that sounds arrogant considering the worldwide scope of the game. But, considering the other books on darts I know, and the feedback I get, no it is not arrogant; it is more a statement of fact.

Find Flight School on www.howtodarts.com

Flight School is an online (email) tutorial. It is designed to help everyone interested in the game of darts and to derive more enjoyment from darts, while devoting only the time and effort of their choosing. Flight School is useful for those with the recreational level of interest and to those with professional aspirations.

Flight School enrollees receive help with organizing their efforts to become as good as they wish to be. They are supplied with methods and techniques proven to work. This help begins with identification of specific things that the person may wish to improve and specific things about which he or she wishes to know more, and then continues in his or her own solitary practice with Flight School drills which have been shown to work through practical use and continuing dialog on whatever the enrollee discovers a need to deal with.

Flight School practice regimens have a proven track record with hundreds of current Flight Schoolers worldwide. An alternative to Flight School online is a book: *DARTS: Beginning to End* which contains all the things for do-it-yourself Flight School. Support may only be needed for a bit of advice and is available through online enrollment in Flight School. Flight school is not just for beginners! There is a routine that will challenge the most accomplished player so don't think it's just for the beginner or intermediate player.

3. In the 1970s you were among the Top 10 American players. Have you seen or do you think you will see any of your flight school students reach that caliber that weren't playing that level prior to starting Flight School?

Oh, heavens yes. There are already many top ranked players who are Flight Schoolers, though mostly in North America. An odd thing though. When a person improves their game to a great extent they "own" that improvement and hold it close. The tools they used are only mentioned when asked, and even then not always.

4. Regardless of actual level of achievement do you have a Flight Schooler who you feel a little more pride in their progress than others? What was their story?

There are so many players who are enjoying their game more that I can't possibly single out one. Some, who are closest, are ones who have used the "Stroke 911" regimen (that's the emergency room "stuff") to regain their footing. Darts becomes so much a part of some people's sense of self-worth that loss of skill level devastates them. My experience with this most ugly phenomenon allowed me to put "Stroke 911" together.

5. Phil Taylor says he isn't a fan of so much beer at events. What's your take?

Darts is a pub/tavern/bar room game. That's where it came from and that is where it thrives. Efforts to take it away from its roots haven't worked out so well—yet. Soft tip is making a run at that, but so far the jury is still out. Enjoying "a tasty adult beverage" while enjoying the game still goes hand in hand although learning what moderation means soon becomes known to "serious" players.

6. And speaking of events, should darts be an Olympic sport, and does darts even WANT or need to be an Olympic sport?

Back to the roots of the game: Frequenting bars/pubs/taverns currently carries a stigma by "polite society," which has its effect on which games are viewed as acceptable. In America, the people zealous about reducing and eliminating consumption of alcoholic drinks have found like hearts with those concerned with injury and death that comes from driving while under the influence (DUI). All this combines so that I don't believe darts will be able get beyond the popular/political/social class negative view. There seems to be a group of games that can't break that barrier in America: pool (snooker), bowling, and even basketball to an extent are looked down on, which contributes to the axiom: the smaller the ball the more acceptable the game. All this makes me believe that darts will never be an Olympic sport.

7. If there were one thing you could do to improve the game of darts, what would it be?

Unify soft tip business with steel tip tradition.

8. Over the years, has the quality of darts gotten better or worse?

Oh, this is a no brainer. Like everything else, it has gotten much better. Just look at the way skill is measured—points per dart/darts per game. It wasn't all that long ago this measure didn't even exist!

9. I started my league play just this past summer, and it was very much a mixed league talent wise. I ended up playing against a pretty good shooter named Bill Nielson, who had actually played against Collin Lloyd. Needless to say I got soundly thrashed, but Bill was good about it and I enjoyed the experience. Afterwards with my teammates, I announced that I was going to play Bill again and that I would be able to beat him. Not that I had a burr in my saddle over the game, it was just a goal I wanted for myself. My teammates gave a response of "never in a million years." What do you think? I know it is impossible to tell what someone's upper limits are, but between gaining a little more playing experience and sticking with my Flight School drills and working on my stroke, is it possible? How far is flight school designed to take me realistically?

Flight School is a complete group of tools, which you can use to become "as good as can be or wish to be." You are limited only by your natural, intuitive ability and determination. I like to think in terms of milestones rather than goals. Goals infer an end has been reached and tend to encourage competing with your self—not good stuff. Bill Nielson may only be a stop on your way to where ever you go. Having played against someone of note is not a significant measure of your ability, how well you played is. I have never enjoyed losing to someone unless I forced that person to use every last one of his or her darts. And enjoy is still not a word I use to describe how I feel.

10. Anything else you would like to share or tell my readers about?

Enjoy the experience!

Flight School has been constructed to help dart nuts get the kinks out of their game and some of the kinks are above the shoulders. As many have pointed out, and wonder about, mind set and attitude has a lot to do with how well a person plays this game, so those things are important for someone who wishes to perfect their game beyond being a league player.

Many miss the point of practice. They think spending a lot of time in front of a dartboard will make them better at the game. This is true, to an extent, but as I point out in my book, with the results of a psychological study to support my view, once a person gets past the neophyte stage, practice gets more involved and the specific type of "practice" becomes very important. No less enjoyable, but critical to improvement. Missing this development element is what allows so many to stagnate at a certain level of play, which no amount of dedication seems to help. They never get any better.

Some become impressed with how much they've improved so quickly without doing anything but playing a lot, and this is what leads to stagnation at a certain level. They play well enough to win against most players and even some shooters and, therefore, become complacent about not needing to learn any more about practice or how to practice. They just believe they need to do more of it.

With Flight School, I try to instill a mind set about practice and short cutting to just a couple of drills seems to bypass that, which means an important part of Flight School is missed, so it is less likely to provide full effect.

How Flight School is a different way to practice darts:

- Flight School provides drills for learning how to control a dart's flight path.
- Flight School provides techniques for learning game strategies.
- Flight School provides guidance for competing at the game/sport of darts.
- Flight School does not teach a person how to play the game of darts.

Principle: Improve your practice to improve your game.

Explanation: Flight School practice isn't really practice, it is developing and perfecting delivery of a dart to a dartboard, but is named "practice" to avoid confusion.

Physical practice: Drills are tasks to be performed. Flight School is different from "practice games" because of the Flight School mindset. The Flight School mindset is like the one you have for taking out the trash. When taking out the trash, you don't analyze lifting, opening, tying, and closing—you just do those things and trash ends at the curb. That's the premise behind Flight School: Shooting a dart is mainly intuitive. The practice routines let you learn how to "shoot" a dart to where you want it without thought. The drill becomes one more task to be done during your day. Take out the trash then do the drill then do something else or see what's on TV.

Do not compete with yourself. A drill is not a contest to see how many targets you can hit, how many you can hit within so many minutes, which targets you finish first or last, or how many targets you have in your routine compared to someone else.

Psychobabble has limited application. Physical practice is to learn how to stick a dart into a target anywhere on the dartboard. It is not to find out how your body coordinates the actions needed to get the dart to stick where you want it. There is no need to know how you stand or lean or what your arm, wrist, and fingers are doing to get the dart to stick into the target. What your arm, wrist, and fingers are doing is none of your business.

You do not pit yourself against the clock or a goal or a previous accomplishment or some standard of performance. You just continue sticking darts into targets until it becomes taking out the trash. You can analyze yourself right out of the game.

There are four physical practice drills: A1, A2, A3, and A4 each one leads to the next. A4 is similar to A1, but includes grouping of darts where A1 does not. Your progression through the drills lets you see how your skill is improving. There are two other parts of Flight School that deal with the mental aspects (memorization) and competition aspects (emotional) issues of the dart game/sport.

Darts players John Kuczynski and Dylan Weikel taking aim

There is so much more information available regarding the Flight School experience and I truly recommend it for those that are looking for their own unique practice process that will suit them as individuals. If you wish to learn more about Flight School, you can contact George directly at his website http://www.howtodarts.com.

CHAPTER 6:
THE GAMES TO PLAY

501

The game of 501 is the most traditional game played today, with longer formats being added to extend the challenge to the top players. To begin the game, each player starts with 501 points. The object of the game is to score as many points as possible per turn, with three darts, and subtract each of your turns score from 501. Players alternate turns.

To win the game, a player must finish by hitting a double to win. Example: A player has 32 points remaining, and must hit a double 16 to win. If the player misses with the first dart and hits a single 16, the player then requires 16 points to win and will need a double 8 to finish the game. The game score can go no lower than 2 points, as double 1 is the lowest scoring double that can be used to win a game.

301

The game of 301 is less than traditional these days due to the challenge of needing to hit a double before you can start scoring. However, 301 was the game played at one of the most prestigious tournaments in the United States, the North American Open, which would draw hundreds of players in the singles event from all over the world. To begin this game, the same concept applies as when playing 501, however, the player starts with only 301 points, and the player is also required to hit a double of any number on the board to begin subtracting their score from 301. The double can be hit with any of the three darts per turn even if prior single numbers were hit. Any numbers hit before a double is hit are null and they do not count. Example: the player is throwing for a double 16 to start the game and hits a single 8 with their first dart, single 7 with their second dart, and a double 16 with their third dart. The player would then subtract 32 points for the double 16 hit from their starting score of 301 points for their turn. Subsequent turns would continue to subtract from their score until they get to 50 points or less, where a double is required to win the game. Again, the game score can go no lower than 2 points, as double 1 is the lowest scoring double that can be used to win a game.

Cricket

The game of cricket grew into prominence in the late eighties and continues today. The object of this game is that each player must hit three of each number for the numbers 20, 19, 18, 17, 16, 15, and bulls-eye. The outer bull counts as one bull and the center bull counts as two bulls. Doubles and triples on the board count as two and three of each number.

Hitting three of each number effectively "closes" a number to keep your opponent from scoring points on any of the numbers you have not closed. Players can score points on any number that their opponent has not closed as long as that player has already hit three of those numbers and "closed" that number themselves. The player that has closed all the numbers and has the higher amount of points is the winner.

There is a high level of strategy involved in this game, as your opponent's shots can dictate what your next shot will be. It is always important to stay aggressive, keep control of the match and to keep control of your lead. Once you lose the lead, you start to take defensive shots and mentally put pressure on yourself to make bigger shots to get the advantage in the game.

Marking the game, or keeping score of the match, requires more than subtraction. The board is shown below with some numbers marked and some scores added for reference.

The mark "/"is for one number hit. The mark "X" is for two numbers hit. The mark "X" with a circle around it is for three numbers hit, or the number is closed. The mark of just a circle can also be used when a player hits 3 or more of one number per turn to close a number.

In the example shown below, Player One has closed the 20s and scored 60 points, as well as hitting two 18s. Player Two has closed the 19s and scored 57 points. In order for Player One to stay the aggressor and keep the lead in the game, that player should close the 19s, which will keep Player Two from obtaining any further score on that number.

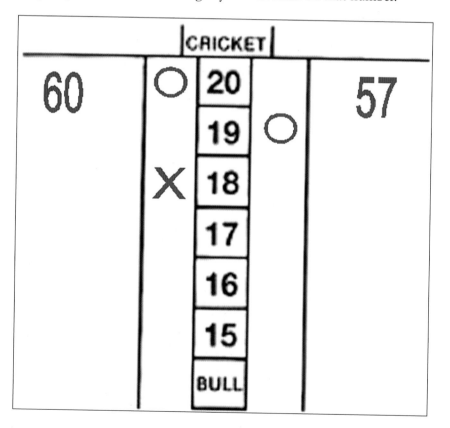

Cricket Count Up

This game is used more as a practice game or a warm-up game for players, and it involves taking one turn at each cricket number to see how many of these numbers you can hit per turn with three darts. Your score is cumulative until you end with the bulls-eye. Triples count as three, doubles as two, and singles as one. The highest score obtainable would be 60.

Darts player Gary Mawson releasing a throw

Photo courtesy of Lawrence Lustig/Professional Darts Corporation

Halve-It

This game goes by a few other names, but for the sake of reference and to avoid confusion, we opted to use this name. The game involves all the cricket numbers, but also employs a few more, along with doubles, triples, and three in a bed to make it a little more interesting. Each player starts with 40 points. Same rules are used, but the number sequence is changed. The sequence in this variation is 12, 13, 14, any triple, 15, 16, 17, any double, 18, 19, three in a bed, and bulls-eye. You only need to hit at least one of each per turn to be able to score points and you will throw three darts per turn at each one. If you miss any of the numbers, triples, doubles, or bulls-eye in your turn, your cumulative score is cut in half. If you hit any of the numbers, triples, doubles, or bulls-eye, these total points per turn are added to your score. The player with the highest score at the end of the game is the winner.

Round the World

The player begins with the number one and throws sequentially through the number twenty as well as the bulls-eye. The object of the game is to hit as many of each number per turn of three darts. Triples count as triples, doubles count as doubles, and singles count as singles. Scores are accumulated until every player has thrown at all numbers on the board. The game is also referred to as "Round the Clock" or "Around the World."

Darts player Ray Carver

CHAPTER 7:
LEAGUE & TOURNAMENT PLAY

Many cities and towns across the United States have leagues or associations set up for players to play weekly in singles, doubles, and/or team events, much in the same format that your local bowling, pool, or softball leagues may be run. Most times, the league is played during the week on a Tuesday, Wednesday, or Thursday night. The reason that most leagues adopt this format of a weekday match is for those players in the area that may travel to tournaments locally or out of state that generally take place on the weekends. Having weekday matches ensures that all players will be in attendance and no make-up matches will have to be played before the end of the season.

There is no set format put forth by the governing bodies of darts for league play and most leagues will adopt their own individual formats. Many leagues or associations also have their own websites to inform their membership about league schedules, league business, sponsors, and upcoming events. There are usually multiple locations involved that all have

teams, so the matches are scheduled accordingly so that not all teams are playing at home or are not playing away all the time. Some locations will have in-house leagues where play is at one location.

Generally, there is a membership fee for each player per season; however, most times this fee is for league operating costs and/or trophies at the end of the season of play. Most leagues are non-profit and are run by volunteers who may also be participating players. Many times the fees paid will go toward operating costs, printing costs, trophies, team shirts, etc. Many of the bigger, more prominent leagues will also use some of these funds to host a larger scale tournament to draw players from other areas of the country to play against their local players.

To find a league in your area, you can contact the governing bodies for darts in the United States at the American Darts Organization or the American Darts Association offices. Many of your local pubs that have dart boards placed in their location may also have league contact information. Another place to obtain league information would be a local dart store, which can generally be found in the yellow pages or through a website. To this day, one central location for league informa-tion has not been developed by any of the existing organizations. The Internet is one of the best sources for finding league information. One thing to remember when using the Internet to search for things is that it is a live and ever-evolving entity and websites and names are changing on a daily basis. This is in large part due to a league or association using different web hosting services and the fact that a domain name may not be available at the time they are looking to create their website. So while there may not be exact matches for your web searching, be creative and change the wording around to see what other key words may lead you to the correct information.

Tournament play in the United States can range from your local luck of the draw events at the neighborhood pub all the way up to a calendar of events that have prize purses from $5,000 to $35,000 or more. These events are open to all players and are located in different cities all over the country. Sometimes, the leagues or associations that you may be involved will host an event once a year to provide a competitive atmosphere for top players along with local players. There is generally no seeding for these events, and any player at any level can sign up to play each event offered.

There are many tournaments available all over the world, as well. I have seen events as far away as South Africa and Australia, as well as Asia, Europe, the Middle East, and Russia. If you happen to be looking for tournaments, the first step to locating them would be to contact the governing body for darts in your country. If they do not have the information, they could most likely lead you to sources that do.

Photo courtesy of Lawrence Lustig/Professional Darts Corporation

Canadian darts player Ken MacNeil

CHAPTER 8:
THE PROFESSIONAL AND THE PDC

There has been a long-standing debate for many years on just what classifies a player as being a professional. Some people say that if a player has any sponsors and receives money from them, they are considered a professional. Others state that if a player spends a majority of his or her free time competing and is ranked according to the governing body, they are then considered a professional. While there are still others that believe a true professional is someone who must not have any other source of income other than what you receive from your sponsors, from your winnings, and from any other events from which you might receive a monetary prize.

A person can be considered a professional if he or she is paid to perform a specific job and complete that job for monetary compensation. When referring to sports, a professional can be someone who is paid just for participating, whereas an amateur does not get paid at all for participating. A professional can also be a person who earns a living in a sport that is more frequently engaged in by amateurs or an expert player serving as a teacher, consultant, performer, or contestant.

An amateur can be a person who engages in a sport or other activity for pleasure rather than for financial benefit or for professional reasons. An amateur can also be known as a person who has never competed for any form of payment or any type of monetary prize. There is also the combination of professionals and amateurs now known as "pro-ams" who take part in amateur events, but pursue them to professional standards. However, it can also be considered an event where professionals and amateurs compete together.

There are many players today, mostly those from England, who are considered professionals in the true sense of the definition. Their entire livelihood comes from monetary compensation for appearing and competing at darting events, being paid for personal appearances, merchandising,

book writing, marketing, and
sales of themselves as players, their names, and their
merchandise.

Regardless of the classifi-
cation, the players themselves,
once they exceed a certain level
and are deemed a top player of
they game, they tend to gener-
ate a fan base or a following that would also put them into the category of
"professional." Just like with any other sport, darts does have its icons who
are loved and respected, along with the players that everyone loves to hate.
The game has its fans and followers and players at a lower level who look
up to their top players as role models and inspirations for them to try to
achieve a higher level for themselves.

As for actual rankings of the players themselves, whether they are
considered amateur or professional, there are a few different ranking systems in effect today. Which one to use depends on what country you live
in or what event you are playing in. The British Darts Organization, or
BDO, has its own set of rankings, as well as the World Dart Federation,
or WDF. These are generally used for all WDF world-ranked events in
Europe. These points are earned based on finishes in the singles events
in WDF ranked events. Events hosted by the Professional Darts
Corporation, or PDC, follow a ranking system based on an Order of
Merit where prize money is counted on a rolling two-year basis. The
Unites States has it's own ranking system administered by the American
Darts Organization, however, the only thing that these rankings are
used for is to determine the US Ambassador team members and the US
number one ranked player for the ladies and the men. Canada also has

its own ranking system administered by the National Darts Federation of Canada, or NDFC, and these rankings are obtained by finishes in singles events in Canada and are used to determine the national ranking for Canadian players. Rankings are obtained by playing at NDFC sanctioned tournaments. Almost every tournament in Canada that has a decent prize structure counts. Because the NDFC is affiliated with the World Dart Federation, players receive invitations to many events in England and the highest ranked players are named to the Canadian World Cup team.

Quite a few other countries also have their own ranking system; however, there does not seem to be on universal ranking system for all the different events. The NAPDA (North America Professional Darts Alliance) Order of Merit and NAPDA PRO Order of Merit recently introduced, a ranking system based on prize money won in tournaments in North America; these events must award prize purses of $8,000 and greater. The point structure is taken from Men's and Ladies '01 and Cricket singles in NAPDA Ranked, Sanctioned, and Pro events. These rankings are then used for seeding NAPDA Sanctioned and NAPDA Pro Tour events in North America. NAPDA's mission statement is "to establish a Professional Tour in North America by establishing the only true and best North America ranking system and to bring darts into the main stream of public awareness as more than a bar room game."

Seeding is often a topic of discussion when considering the participation of professional players in competitions. It is often asked, "What is seeding? What is it supposed to accomplish? Is it only for the professional level, or should it be applied at the amateur level as well? What is its purpose and what are we hoping to achieve with the seeding process?"

These questions and many more are often the topic of online discussions. Many think seeding is only a way to cater to the higher ranked players, or professionals, to guarantee them money. Many think that the more experienced top players prefer seeding because they are selfishly trying to ensure themselves a place in the finals. We see seeding used in many competitive fields, but for example, we will use the Professional Darts Corporation (PDC). The product that the PDC has created is a showcase for their players. The seeding process is used to try to guarantee their stars end up in the finals. This gives added incentive for their television coverage and sells tickets at their venues. We all know that there is nothing more exciting than seeing an underdog beat a premier player. The whole process is a marketing machine aimed to drive the success of their event to new and higher levels. Seeding is nothing more than a marketing tool. It is a tool used very well by the PDC and their success shows it.

The history of the Professional Darts Corporation goes back to 1992, where the original World Darts Council was created by sixteen of the top professional players, along with a few managers. Dick Allix, Tommy Cox, and John Markovic made the decision to break away from the long-standing British Darts Organization (BDO) to form their own professional corporation and take the game of darts to a new and higher level. The players themselves were unhappy with the British Darts Organization and felt that they were not doing enough to promote the game. The players wanted to attract new sponsors and obtain more television coverage than one event per year. The 1993 Embassy World Championship was the last time there was one unified World Championship in darts and this was the last year that the WDC players participated in the event, as the BDO would not recognize them and threatened to ban players. The first WDC event, the UK Masters, took place in 1993 and the first World Championship was played over the 1993–94 holiday season.

Eventually, a court dispute was filed and the two bodies reached an out-of-court settlement in 1997 in the form of a Tomlin Order. The details of the order were that the British Darts Organization would recognize the World Darts Council and agreed that all players would have the freedom of choice as to which open events they wanted to play. The World Darts Council discontinued its claim to be a world governing body and renamed itself the Professional Darts Corporation. The PDC agreed to accept and recognize that the World Darts Federation would be the governing body for the sport of darts worldwide, and that the British Darts Organization would be the governing body for darts in the United Kingdom. The stated purpose of the agreement was to promote the freedom of individual darts players to participate in open competition. An additional condition of the Tomlin Order was made so that the top sixteen players, and any Home Country players ranked between numbers 17 and 32 in each year's BDO Championship, and the top sixteen players in each year's PDC Championship shall not be permitted to enter the other competition in the immediate following year, however, there have been a few players that have since breached that clause in the contract and made their respective moves over to the PDC after winning the BDO events.

The Board of Directors decided to step down in July 2001 and the PDC was placed under the guidance of Promoter Barry Hearn, who was named chairman and who is still manning the controls of the organization to this day.

The goal of the PDC was to create a show to attract younger audience members and market the events as more than just a sporting event, and throughout the years, many dignitaries and celebrities have been spotted in the crowd. The show included players entering the venue to their own walk on music while being escorted by security and female models. Smoke, light, and pyrotechnics were used to create elaborate scenes in the show similar to the ideas used today in boxing and wrestling events. The matches are relayed to the crowd via giant video screens and a caller is present to shout out the scores of the match. The players themselves now all have their own nicknames for the marketing of themselves in this arena. The PDC has created a marketing machine for themselves with these shows and now has the reputation of being the leading innovator in terms of staging a professional dart tournament.

The PDC also has made arrangements with a few different affiliated organizations worldwide to obtain additional qualifiers for the World Championships. The most notable groups involved are the DPA in Australia, the SDC in Scandinavia, as well as obtaining qualifiers from North America, Japan, and South Africa. The PDC has also expanded across Europe with a European Tour, which is a series of five tournaments held in Germany, Austria, and the Netherlands that offers the top players in these areas an opportunity to complete at the top level, as well.

The PDC also created the PDC Unicorn Women's World Championship, which was open to all female darts players from both the BDO and PDC. The thirty-two qualifiers played down to the last two in a floor tournament and the final was televised live on Sky Sports after the final of the World Matchplay. The two finalists were also invited to become PDC ProTour card holders for 2011 and 2012 and received sponsorship from Rileys Dartzones, which were the PDC's staging partners in the event. They were also were invited to compete in the 2010 Grand Slam of Darts. However, the PDC Unicorn Women's World Championship event has since been discontinued.

The goal of the Professional Darts Corporation is to continue to leverage its strengths and ensure that the sport receives the recognition and respect that professional dart players deserve. The creation of the

Qualifying School—where a player can earn their Tour Card to compete on the PDC tournament circuit full time—as well as the introduction of the PDC Unicorn Youth Tour and World Youth Championship offers a guaranteed opportunity for aspiring players to compete at the top level.

The PDC also entered into a partnership with DARTSLIVE International. Their agreement offers the winner of THE WORLD soft-tip darts championship a qualifying spot to complete at the PDC World Darts Championships in December.

CHAPTER 9:
THE TELEVISION AND
INTERNET INFLUENCE

The game of darts made its first appearance on television in England in 1962 with the airing of the Westward TV Invitational. In 1972, ITV began airing the News of the World Championship, along with the Indoor League, which featured a darts event that was won by American player Conrad Daniels. Conrad had many titles and achievements throughout his career, but he will forever be known as the first American to win an event on English soil with his win of the London Indoor League.

Television broadcasting companies such as ITV and the BBC continued to air different darting events throughout the 1970s and 1980s, but it was the formation of the WDC/PDC (now the Professional Darts Corporation) that catapulted the game back onto the television screens when Sky TV aired the newly-formed organization's World Championship, as well as their World Matchplay events, starting in 1994. To date, the PDC's major events such as the World Championships, World Matchplay, World Grand Prix, Premier League, UK Open, and Grand Slam of Darts are still all aired by Sky Sports.

Many other stations in other countries have since joined into the mix of airing PDC darts events on television. The PDC had also ventured into television broadcasts in the United States with the help of ESPN for the 2006 World Series of Darts event. ESPN had previously attempted broadcasting darts in the United States back in the mid-1980s with the airing of coverage for the Lucky Lights Challenge of Champions, however, they did not obtain the ratings numbers that they had hoped for in either the Challenge of Champions or the World Series of Darts, and thus the Challenge of Champions lost its coverage and the World Series of Darts was removed from its peak airtime after only a few weeks.

The British Broadcasting Company, otherwise known as the BBC, expanded its coverage of darts events in 2001 with the airing of the

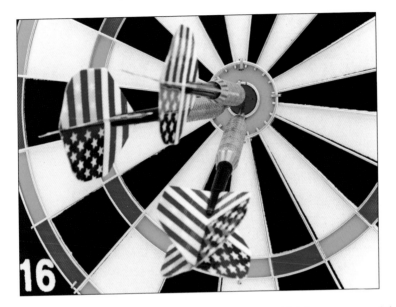

British Darts Organizations (BDO) Winmau World Masters event. The coverage was minimal, and viewers were not able to actually see every dart thrown live at the BDO World Championship until 2005. Eurosport covered the broadcasts for the Lakeside World Championships, along with a few other BDO major events.

The 2007 Grand Slam of Darts marked the return of ITV to major darts tournament coverage, and ITV4 now broadcasts the PDC Players Championship finals and the European Championship. In 2012, the BBC shared its coverage of the BDO World Championships with ESPN's pay-TV sports channel.

Many of these old events that had previously been televised are now archived on video streaming channels such as YouTube so that the general public can view the history of darts in the comfort of their own homes whenever they want. This in itself has led to an increase in the popularity of the game in the mainstream population of the world, as people who have never before seen a darting event are finding these videos.

When it comes to the television influence for the sport of darts in America, the instances are very few and far between. L. David Irete has been in the television broadcasting industry for more than forty years. He is also a dart player that has taken the time to infuse his experience in the television industry into the darting world. The celebrities know him as "The Dart Guy." The dart players know him as "The Video Guy." In the 1980s, David brought the darting world video productions of many different finals events from all over the country. Some have since made the transition to live streaming video and are available online now. David has a lot of knowledge and advice to share regarding the quest to get the sport of darts developed in the United States to enter the television level.

One of the main points of contention that was prevalent thirty years ago and is still present today is that even though the sport is rather well organized, given the lack of combined energies among its leaders and developers and the lack of self-discipline among some of its players, it has not progressed much over the past thirty years. The darting industry wants respect like that accorded to other sports. But it is David's opinion that darts suffers from a classic case of too many chiefs and no real camaraderie among its tribes. Verbal bickering and behind-the-scenes backstabbing are doing more to hold back the development of the sport than any barroom brawl (the kind we so humbly pride ourselves on avoiding) could ever do. There are many groups taking things in too many different directions because they think that their idea is the winning ticket, and in the meantime, no one is banding together as one entire group to achieve the greatness that they would be able to achieve with a solid core of sharing the same ideals and making things happen.

David's thoughts and ideas center around prescribing television to achieve the kind of exposure needed for the sport for it to get noticed, as well as attracting newcomers, but one thing that everyone needs to remember is that the television camera does not lie. What it sees, it tells . . . all of it. As television producers, they can polish the stage, put make-up on the finalists, splice in the music and color commentary, throw in an audience, but the end result today is still about a sport that is not totally together. The bottom line being that acceptance of darts by a national television audience and corporate sponsorship of a television broadcast on a regular basis (not just the occasional tournament "special") lies in your hands. No one can improve your appearance and performance but you! And after all, isn't that what television is all about—appearance and performance?

To see yourself on TV is to see the truth. To conduct an honest appraisal of that truth and to make appropriate changes will not only make us all better dart players, but also better competitors and more complete individuals on all levels. David says he receives emails inquiring about the equipment needed to be able to broadcast live events. Generally, the first questions he will ask these people are "Do you have an actual set made for the event?" "Do you have a guaranteed audience to be in place?" and "Do you have a required dress code for the players being filmed?" More often than not, the people interested in doing the broadcasting have not taken the time to put together an actual package to be presented to the public. The technology is available and the idea is ready to grow, but we have to get past the point of wanting to use the recorders on our cell phones to capture random moments of reality television and actually put a package together that is marketable and would be attractive to sponsors.

Many people say the reason the English perform so well under the lights is because they are more experienced with television. It's true. The British players have been playing darts in front of 10 to 20 million people on live television for the past twenty-five years or longer. American shooters are now gaining experience with the television experiences, but one time where that came to mind most for David was at the '85 World Cup, the US Men's Team performed incredibly-nearly taking the World Cup title for the first time ever all while under the lights of the television camera.

Photo courtesy of Lawrence Lustig/Professional Darts Corporation

Professional player Paul Lim has become used to playing in the spot light.

So how does all this relate to television? Think about it. For the past twenty-five years, TV cameras have been showing up at more and more tournaments worldwide with every passing year. And whether the cameras are ours, the BBC's, or anyone else's, we're seeing our pros handle the media pressure (like that found at the World Cup) with more poise and confidence every time out. Our people are playing better, looking better, and winning more. They must be feeling better about themselves for these accomplishments. It's important to remember that we're not just talking about the same top players over and over. We're talking about you: you who are represented by these players in competition. With continued effort, you'll soon find yourself in their shoes.

So what about American TV and darts? When will darts be televised nationally on a regular basis? For darts to be accepted by the national viewing public, and even more important, the sponsors, we must prove that darts is a whirlwind sport—a description most darters would agree with. But the problem is, our whirlwind is spinning as many people out of the sport as it brings in.

Dart players are subject to early burnout if they aren't careful. The atmospheric conditions—often featuring heavy smoke and alcohol— can really take their toll, and contribute to the large turnover of members in associations, clubs, leagues, etc. New membership and introduction of people to this sport are absolutely crucial to its growth and development—not only for TV, but also for dart manufacturers, stores, wholesalers, leagues, associations, and venue owners. The Professional Darts Corporation has taken the steps needed to remove the alcohol from the television viewer. They have also instituted mandatory drug testing of the players to take the game to the professional level and introduced the youth players of today, as well as the viewing public, to a much better example of what the sport of darts is all about.

The regular televising of darts nationwide will be both a result of, and a reason for, growth. Sooner or later, TV will happen. Making it happen sooner is going to take the efforts of every individual involved in the sport. Darts is no longer in its infancy in the United States, but when we talk to prospective sponsors, we do not have the experience needed to sound to them like the old, experienced men on the block.

One of the biggest efforts that can take place now that will pay off in many ways later is the introduction of the sport to the youth of the world, along with the rules and etiquette, which will increase the chances of the sport to grow to a much higher level. We also must continue to develop the players, create a platform for showing them off, and teach them how to entertain an audience.

In plain English, if people like David take the time to negotiate airtime for dart programs in cities across the country, he has to prove to stations and sponsors that he will have viewers. That proof can happen only with your commitment to the sport, its image, and its future.

So, let's say you have taken the next step and invited a cameraman and reporter out to cover your event. David wrote an article for *BullsEye News* regarding this exact situation and rather than altering it to suit me telling the story to you, I am going to share the article as it was written:

Cast of Characters

Joe Reporter: Your basic TV reporter, complete with his "I had no idea this many people played darts" attitude.

Cameraman: Your basic TV cameraman complete with his usual "Shoot anything that moves . . . anytime" aggressiveness.

You, the reader: Just be yourself.

Setting: A dart tournament in U-Name-It, USA

The Plot: Reporter Joe is assigned to cover a local dart tournament for . . . U-guessed-it, the local TV station.

The time: Is running out for the reporter, who has to meet his DEADLINE.

As we begin our story, we see a reporter and his cameraman coming into the tournament area, wide-eyed and open-mouthed. You, the tournament host, notice their arrival, but you are going crazy from organizing the event and you have failed to note their expressions, which indicate the two have no idea what the whole dart scene is about.

As you invite Joe Reporter to take a look around, you're taken aback by the boldness of his partner. The cameraman has already made himself and his bright lights quite at home, zooming in on the nearest top player for a close-up, blinding the player and all of those other players on that same bank of boards. And you get bet that all the players on those boards will be ogres to deal with later, especially the losers.

Meantime, Joe Reporter, having closely studied the action for all of 45 seconds, has come to two brilliant conclusions about the dart players and their game: (1) These people aren't very good at hitting the bulls-eye (like he knows they are supposed to) and (2) They sure like to drink.

Looking at his watch, Joe sees DEADLINE approaching. Time for a "head bite," he says. That means interview all who speak English. "Let's have the best local player say a few words to our viewing audience about the sport. Oops. He's not feeling too well right now: he just lost to a big shot from PA and is taking it out on a double scotch and rocks. "So much for the interview," Joe thinks. "Well, maybe we could do a quick demonstration."

You, the host, have since disappeared, tending to tournament duties and leaving Joe on his own to figure out how to create a darting demo. (And this is where the golden opportunity for darts to receive "accurate" publicity goes down the tubes.)

The reporter can't find you, has busted trying to get an interview. So he does what comes naturally: he throws the dart himself, bad form and all, aiming at the bulls-eye and totally misrepresenting the object of the game. Joe then looks to the camera and says, "Players from all over the country are here, playing for big money, and that's not bull. . . . Back to you at the news desk, Jim."

Here's the moral. Joe Reporter—in his speech to his viewers—has taken the attention away from darts and directed it to himself because he wasn't given the information he needed to report a proper story. His audience now thinks "What a cute, clever reporter that Joe is" instead of having learned about our sport. And the sport is left with yet another negative image to combat with corporate America and the public perception of the game and it's players.

While the initial idea was a great one, it failed miserably in the end. The organizer did a great service to the sport by contacting the local media for his event, which in my opinion should be done by every event organizer for every single event. But the organizer failed to be organized. The organizer should have at least dedicated him/herself to the visitors from the moment they entered the room until they left the room. The object was to advertise the event and then the person in charge did nothing to follow through to make sure the advertising was beneficial to the event, let alone beneficial to the sport itself. It is said that it takes ten times more initiative to recover from something negative than it does from something positive. While the good intentions of the event organizer were there, the misrepresentation that took place was broadcast to a public audience that didn't have a clue about the sport to begin with and now has perceived a negative image because of this one incident.

In the meantime, what else is there that you can do as an event organizer to promote the sport to the television level? Consider this. Most US cities have some sort of cable television service. According to the Federal Communications Commission (FCC) regulations, these cable services are obligated to reserve a frequency (channel) for general public use. Hence why it is given the name "public access."

Most cable companies offer public time slots ranging anywhere from fifteen minutes to one hour. You supply them with the tape, and most cable outlets will provide producers, directors, etc. and will offer the studio where your show will be taped. The cost for these services is extremely low and often free, but may vary from city to city, so it's best to get this information quoted to you directly from the cable company.

What does all this have to do with darts? Everything. Your club, association, dart team, or even just you—ham that you are—can expose the sport of darts to thousands of people through Public Access programming. You can appear on existing shows or create your own. The bottom line is to get on TV and tell people about our sport. Remember, you are entitled to that airtime. If you're involved with a tournament, a charity shoot, or are on a promotions committee for your club, this could be a way of obtaining exposure.

So, what's your first step?

Call your local cable company and inquire about their Public Access Programming. In most cases, they will send you, by mail, the information you need. If you are in the dark about producing a show of your own, ask if there are producers available in-house (many are interns working for the experience only), who can help you develop a program or book you on a show already airing on the cable. Take the time to find out more about Public Access in your area as soon as you can. You will be surprised at how easy it is to get the new people interested in the sport of darts.

Don't forget to also contact your local newspapers whenever you have an event scheduled. There are many people that read the newspaper and even just one small article could entice a reader to show up at your event to see what it is all about. Or maybe it happens to be someone who likes to just play darts in their garage or basement and never realized that there actually are organized events out there for him or her to compete in. With just a little of the right organized effort, the positives of the sport can be exposed to so many of the non-playing public that will raise awareness to the sport and eventually its events and players that the sponsors are looking for. It's not the few, random players we have that we need demanding to see darts on television, it is a public outcry that is needed to let the broadcasting companies and corporate America know that the general public wants to see these events on television as well.

The Internet Influence

There are so many factors that can be attributed to the growth of darts in the world today; however, the one aspect that has to be given the top title for it has to be the influence of the Internet. Instant information and communication, as well as streaming video, have taken players and events to a much higher level. In the past, you had to wait an entire week to view the paper on which the results of league matches were posted. Today, you can find out the results later that night—or even in an instant, if the score-keeper has a smartphone. Tournament results are up to the minute with people posting or tweeting their finishes even before the event may be over. Data can be compiled and used for research for future events at the click of a mouse and the sorting of a spreadsheet. There are so many different things going on right now that I felt I had to share them all with you.

The first aspect that is new to the darting world and making excellent use of the World Wide Web would be the podcast. A *podcast* is a type of digital media consisting of an episodic series of audio or video files subscribed to and downloaded through web syndication. Podcasting is a converged medium bringing together audio, the web, and portable media players to create a show to be broadcast over the Internet.

The pioneer podcast group, *Darts Around the World*, was formed in August of 2010, and is made of founding members, Evan Waterman, John Ronnholm, and David Hascup. The show began with what seemed like morning radio shock jocks hyped up on caffeine with the overwhelming need to upstage each other. Adam Smith, author of *The Thorn Report*, joined on as a travel writer giving listeners insight into the travel side of darts. L. David Irete joined shortly after, taking on the role as Director/Producer of the weekly podcast, bringing a much-needed balance and direction. The show today is setting a whole new standard for the level of communication amongst the darting community by offering a voice to anyone who wishes to speak. The formats range from roundtable discussions with top minds in darts to on-site coverage of major events, including exhibitions and tournaments. The show also travels to cities to tour and cover local darts and brings an in depth narrative to the masses. *Darts Around the World* can be listened to live at home or on the go thanks to revolutionary streaming technology. With smartphones widely adapted

around the world, the show can be heard on demand anytime, anywhere. David says that his goal is to eventually have local pubs streaming their local events every week.

Dart Talk is a radio program created and hosted by fellow dart player, Stephen Panuncialman and is a weekly discussion of different dart topics that happen to be popping up in the darting world today. Subjects can range from interviews with players, questions from fans, or specific commentary on subjects such as player sponsorships, seeding at tournaments, practice routines, and what people can do to bring a higher standard to the game.

The fastest growing and most amazing influence to the growth of darts over the last two years has been the influence of social networking websites. Together with tech savvy players, FaceBook and Twitter have expanded the ability for players to interact and communicate with each other on an entirely new level. Instead of having to make a bunch of phone calls to find a doubles partner, a player can post the same information in real time on Facebook and receive responses posted immediately. It also impacts how events are reported.

Another important aspect that is growing the game online is the invention of downloadable software

to play competitive games via the Internet either against other players in different locations all over the world or against the computer itself. To play against someone in another location, players will set up webcams and microphones on laptops close to the dartboard area. This allows players to play a match at any time, with anyone in the world, in the comfort of their own home. Many groups are being formed just like league teams that now take place in the virtual world.

The final introduction to the darting world that I see making a huge impact is the addition of live streaming video of events going on all over the world. Many of the events being played in England and Asia have cameras set up to record the event to show live anywhere in the world via the Internet. This allows people everywhere to enjoy the same experiences as those in the live audience, most times with a much better view. Archived footage can be found everywhere, as well as shorter video clips available on websites such as YouTube. The addition of on-demand video and live streaming video has created a new genre of spectators and fans of the game that normally would not get this level of exposure.

CHAPTER 10:
THE SOFT-TIP REVOLUTION

In the mid-1980s, a new revolution in darts was born with the creation of the electronic dartboard. Today, the game is known as "soft-tip"
darts; it uses an electronic board made of plastic that features pre-formed
holes instead of bristle where the plastic point of the dart sticks in the
holes. When the dart enters a hole, the scoreboard electronically counts
the points. The darts themselves are required to be lighter in weight due to
the durability of the plastic, thus only darts 20 grams or less are allowed.
Each hole in the board is the same size to fit the dart point and the edges
are beveled for the point to enter. Sensors and circuits behind the face of
the dartboard note the impact of the dart and will send the message to
the central computer processor. The electronic scoreboard is incorporated
into the machine itself and auto-populates or subtracts the scores as the
darts stick into the board and can populate the marks needed to score a
cricket game.

Sample soft-tip dart with plastic point

The machine itself has the appearance of a video game machine, as it
accepts coins for play and is equipped with visual graphics on the scoreboard monitor as well as a variety of sounds for effect. The latest technology
has also involved the Internet using the same brand of machines; it allows
players to connect to the company server and a network of dart machines
to play matches against each other regardless of where in the world they
are located. Membership cards are provided so players can keep track
of their stats. Almost all the events and tournaments use the available

data to keep per-dart averages, rank players, and use seeding in their events, as well as using the ranking process to group certain levels of players together for tournament play.

DARTSLIVE screen

Soft-tip tournaments use this data for

DARTSLIVE board

rankings and seeding to pair players of certain levels together to, in essence, even out the playing field. It also will provide handicaps for league matches where you may have to allow your opponent who is a lesser player to take a few turns for score before you are able to. However, the handicapping and seeding systems used are not a foolproof methodology, as some players will "play down" in prior matches to achieve a lower seed than they actually are, also known widely as "sand bagging."

During a recent trip to Asia, longtime darting pundit Paul Seigel, also known as Dartoid in the darting world, visited one of the newest soft-tip companies making great strides for the soft-tip game. Paul was gracious enough to allow me to use his commentary in this chapter because it is an accurate reflection of how many people feel about the growth in popularity for this aspect of the game.

Dartoid's Column: "Plastic gives me a rash," I once wrote. "Never in a million years will I drop a quarter to play a child's game." "Oversized doubles, and triples, and bulls—give me a pool table with pockets the size of basketball hoops and I'll be world champion by dinnertime." Handicapping, the freeze rule, bounce outs that count ("Give me a rock and I'll score a maximum every trip to the line"), machines that flash and beep ("like gaudy Vegas slots") and tell you where to throw, tips that bend and break . . . my criticism was incessant.

I have been wrong. Dead wrong.

Despite the marketing genius and deep pockets of the Professional Dart Corporation's (PDC) Barry Hearn and Company and the brilliant 100+ averages of the top handful of steel-tip professionals in the world, they and all steel-tip purists worldwide are living in the past and the present—and completely missing the future that is now.

Short format or long format, there is a monumental difference between hitting what you throw at the majority of the time, as the top professionals do, and winning—and missing just once, and losing. The former is the past and present—the legacy of Eric Bristow, John Lowe, Phil Taylor, and the rest. The later is the reality of soft-tip. It isn't easier. It's more difficult.

It's time to wake up and smell the plastic. The future is the soft-tip game.

I'm so guilty of missing the obvious—of being so caught up in my own quarrel between the past and present—as I prepared recently to travel to Bangkok to check out DARTSLIVE honcho Steve Ngu's newest iDarts Club (Shop A123, Park Lane, Sukhumvit Soi 63, Ekkimai) I found myself ill-prepared. Although, thanks to DARTSLIVE's Rob Heckman, I own a set of soft-tip darts, I discovered that I had only the three tips that came with them. Being that it was a Friday and I was to depart on Sunday I was in a jam.

So I called the Horizon Darts ladies. Without hesitation they graciously Federal Expressed a small bag of L-style tips. What incredible service.

I arrived at the iDarts Club at 9:00 p.m. the following Wednesday. *Never* in all my years in darts, stops in seedy bars in some ninety countries, and seventeen years of writing about my experiences have I encountered such a mesmerizing darts environment? The club packs all the energy and pizzazz of a world championship final in a relatively compact, shiny, neon-accented two-story restaurant-sized room. Music pounds, beer flows, the crowd is young and new to the sport—anxious to learn. The contrast with the past and present is overwhelming.

My friends Johnny Witkowski, Jayke O'Reilly, and Damian Hardy were greeted at the door by DARTSLIVE Thailand's CEO, Andy Ho. Ho is friends with the founder and CEO of DARTSLIVE Asia and DARTSLIVE International, Steve Ngu, who I met in Sacramento in February. After two days of presentations and long conversations with Heckman, Scotty Burnett, Scott Kirchner, David Irete, and Paul Lim, I left the west coast mind boggled with the

DARTSLIVE system, high-tech SEGA-driven machines that are networked globally so you can compete against friends all over the world—and which maintain individual statistics and leader boards—plans for iDart clubs in numerous countries, The World and Dragon tournaments, and so much more.

But most of all I was struck with the DARTLIVE philosophy . . .

Darts should be fun, said Ngu. Simple. But profound.

Darts enthusiasts talk constantly about what's wrong with the game, why it's been in decline, why Americans (and pretty much anybody outside of the United Kingdom) can't compete on the world stage. We need sponsorship. We need to be on television. We need sex appeal. We need characters. We need new blood. We need to run things like a business.

Well, Steve Ngu and his crew and their growing stable of DARTSLIVE sponsored players—from Paul Lim to three-time world champion John Part to Ray Carver, Darin Young, Randy Van Deursen, Benjamin Dersch, Burnett, Kirchner and Heckman—and probably others I have forgotten or am unaware of—are bringing *all of this* to the sport *and* they are *bringing the fun back*.

It's working. It's working because these guys understand the sport, understand that it's changing, and understand that it's *been* changing, have earned their way, know what is needed and what will attract new blood. They remember when they began. They remember when darts was *fun*.

The DARTSLIVE system isn't based on some old school marketing scheme. They aren't trying to grab headlines and sell product by sponsoring Manny Pacquiao, as Target Darts has done, or by promoting a rigged tournament, as did the PDC in 2006 with its so-called World Series of Darts. The pairings were set up to ensure that no American had a chance in hell of winning the highly promoted $1 million prize (although John Kuczynski—good for him—gave them a first round scare by knocking off John Part).

The DARTSLIVE *darts should be fun* philosophy permeates the iDarts Club in Bangkok. From Ho's enthusiasm to the helpfulness of his staff to the young crowd that burgeoned as the night became late one couldn't help but be caught up in the rhythm. The joint's *alive*. It has a *pulse*. It's like a *drug*. My friends and I couldn't pull ourselves away.

We played Count Up for hours. For a score of 700 or more one of the staff wandering among the dozen darts machines would present you a beer.

Laughter would frequently erupt as a brand new player landed a scoring dart. I could feel the beginning of their addiction. Just like a two-dollar instant Lotto win leads to another small gamble, as the machine winked and whistled brand new players were pulled back to the line, over and over—and they'll be back tomorrow and the next day and the next.

More than any youth darts program, any filthy old bar where the established players trounce those giving the game a first try (and often don't help them learn), and any televised or streaming Internet coverage of a tournament featuring the same couple of dozen players competing against each other

just as they did the week before and the week before that, the iDarts clubs—and the machines in particular—*sell* the sport to the new blood the sport so desperately needs.

The DARTSLIVE system and crew *understand and speak the language of a new generation.*

But what the system also does—most notably via The World tournament and qualifying events—is speak to the professionals and professional hopefuls. Not all of them yet but there's money to be made and rumors of massive amounts to be on offer in the future—and where there's money the professionals will follow. The DARTSLIVE guys understand this too.

Last year John Part and Adrian Lewis competed. Despite five-world steel-tip championships between them neither won.

The big names from Asia competed and most scored high in the 2011 point standings—players like Royden Lam from (Hong Kong) China, Laurence Ilagan and Roland Briones and Jaypee Detablan from the Philippines, Natthakhom Daochan-ngan from Thailand, and Yuji Eguchi and Mitsumasa Hoshino and Sho Katsumi from Japan—just to name a few. All of these players are as well known in their own darting communities and region as the likes of Taylor, James Wade, Raymond van Barneveld and the boys are elsewhere.

But they aren't ranked among the top in the world. Why?

It isn't because they aren't capable as being as competitive on the world stage as those who top the rankings. It's because the system, which is pretty much centered within a short radius of England is stacked against the players who don't live and compete week in and week out within that radius. Unless a player like Canada's John Part or Australia's Simon Whitlock makes the commitment to travel or move to within that radius a player outside of Europe, no matter how capable, doesn't have a prayer. Of course, this applies not only to the Asians, but also to Americans like Larry Butler who shocked the pants off Dennis Priestley and all the Brits when he won the 1994 World Matchplay in Blackpool in 1994 (taking out the late Jockey Wilson among others en route).

It applies to Tom Sawyer, Chris White, Chuck Pankow, Robbie Phillips, Gordon Dixon, Steve Panuncialman, John Kuczynski, Darin Young, and many more.

But enter DARTSLIVE. They have cracked this unfair system to bits. While developing new players from all around the world who are just learning the game they are offering legitimate opportunities to the more accomplished players from all around the world—from the chance to compete on equal terms within a fair system to decent paydays to sponsorship.

Will the best in the steel-tip world heed Winston Churchill's advice and Mr. Maguire's advice to Benjamin Braddock, stop looking down on the soft-tip game and enter the plastic fray? I suspect they will—when the prize funds increase. Currently it's not to their advantage because they can pocket oodles week after week in their own backyards.

Will the best in the world dominate when they do compete? Time will tell but I doubt it. The world is bigger than just England. There's massive talent all across this planet. Finally, all players have a *fair* chance to show what they can do.

From amateur to professional, from Asia to America—DARTSLIVE has brought the fun back and created a new paradigm for our sport.

My bet is that it will be the *standard* in five to ten years time.

From the field,
Dartoid

Recently, the Professional Darts Corporation and DARTSLIVE International entered into a new partnership to unite the steel-tip and soft-tip dart worlds. The following is the actual press release announcing the new partnership"

PDC and DARTSLIVE NEW PARTNERSHIP

For many years there has been an invisible divide between the steel and soft darts industry. A silent misunderstanding that has kept the growth of our sport from reaching its true potential.

Now, that divide can finally be slowly erased, with a new exclusive partnership. A partnership between two of the most recognized companies in the darts industry today! Both companies have great vision, ability to change the image and platforms to take darts from a "Bar Game" to a Professional "Sport."

We are extremely excited to announce, that the PDC (Professional Darts Corporation) and DARTSLIVE, shall work to bring the best of both worlds together.

With this combined effort, together we can change the face of our industry. We will have the strength to create something never been done before, we can unite our fans and players into one common direction—the GROWTH OF OUR SPORT!

CHAPTER 11:
THE PROGRESSION OF
DARTS IN AMERICA

While the game of darts has always been a part of the culture in England and a workingman's game for everyone to play down at the local pub, darts did not become even a small part of the American culture until the 1960s. It was a popular pasttime for US soldiers stationed in England, and when those same soldiers returned home, they brought their new hobby with them. By the mid-'70s, it became apparent that the game was growing by leaps and bounds in many areas of the United States. It was during this time that the American Darts Organization, which is the governing body for darts in America, was developed.

In 1975, there were no known networks for dart organizations, but there were hotbeds of activity in Philadelphia, New York, Cleveland, Chicago, Dallas, Detroit, Los Angeles, St. Louis, Washington DC, New Jersey, and Virginia. While there may have been more, these were the places that were known at the time, and that was the crux of the matter.

Tom Fleetwood of Bellflower, California, and Ed McDevitt of Philadelphia had tossed around the idea of a national organization and decided this was the time to act. An invitation was sent to known organizations to attend an informal meeting to discuss the formation of the American Darts Organization. That meeting, which was held on October 17, 1975, in conjunction with the Michigan Open Dart Tournament in Detroit, laid the foundation for the organization. On October 18, the first official ADO board meeting was held where dues, a logo, and operations were established.

The ADO began operation January 1, 1976, with 30 charter member clubs and a membership of

7,500 players. The First Annual ADO Men's All-Star playoffs were held and Nodor became the office dartboard of the ADO. Today, the ADO has a membership that averages 250 clubs on a yearly basis representing roughly 50,000 members.

The 1970s

1977: The ADO was incorporated in the state of Massachusetts and the first annual ADO Men's World Masters competition was held.

1978: The first tournament calendar was completed, tournament-sanctioning procedures were adopted, and the first Double Eagle was published. The standard throwing distance of 7' 9-1/4" was adopted by the World Dart Federation and ADO.

1979: The championship point-ranking system was put into place and the National Points Champions were Dan Pucillo and Lois Miller. The WDF World Cup II was hosted in Las Vegas, Nevada, which was the first major international darting event outside of Great Britain. The United States' adopted Thai Cowboy, Nicky Virachkul, won the gold medal in the Men's World Cup Singles event.

The 1980s

1980: The first Pacific Cup playoffs were held, the ADO Associate Membership option was established, and a darts handbook was written and published. The National Points Champions were Dan Pucillo and Sandy Reitan.

1981: The rules for sanctioning tournaments were standardized and approved and the first 180 certificates were issued. The National Points Champions were Dan Pucillo and Sandy Reitan.

1982: The first ADO computer was purchased and the first honorary lifetime membership was awarded to Barry Twomlow. US players Judy

Campbell, Andy Green, Wade McDonald, and Sandy Reitan won the gold medal in the WDF Pacific Cup team event. The National Points Champions were Jerry Umberger and Sandy Reitan.

1983: Cricket rules for sanctioned tournament were standardized and adopted. Sandy Reitan won the gold medal in the WDF World Cup Ladies Singles event, and honorary lifetime memberships were awarded to John Ross and James Miceli. The National Points Champions were Rick Ney and Sandy Reitan.

1984: New organizational and playoff structures were implemented and Area Managers were added. The WDF Pacific Cup III was hosted in Honolulu, Hawaii and the US team of JoAnn Anderson, Kathy Karpowish, Jerry Umberger, and Nicky Virachkul won the gold medal in the team event. The National Points Champions were Rick Ney and Sandy Reitan.

1985: The ADO adopted standardized modified round robin formats and points awarded for playoff events. The US team of John Kramer, Rick Ney, Tony Payne, and Danny Valletto defeated the English team 9-0 in the semi-finals of the WDF World Cup in Brisbane, Australia, and went on to defeat Australia in the final to win the gold medal. The doubles team of Danny Valletto and Rick Ney also placed third in the Men's Doubles event and took home a bronze medal. It was noted that the fate of the World Cup came down to the Men's Singles match between Eric Bristow and Tony Payne. Sadly, Tony missed one winning dart at double 16 and the US team lost the World Cup. (To this day, this is noted as the highest finish that a US men's team has ever achieved.) The Lucky Lights Challenge of Champions was first broadcast on ESPN. The National Points Champions were John Kramer and Kathy Maloney.

1986: The ADO championship point system was revised and the ADO reached 300 member clubs with 70,000 members. The National Points Champions were Tony Payne and Kathy Maloney.

1987: The ADO Youth Program was introduced and the first National Youth Manager, Ken Friend, was appointed. The first East-West All-Star match and National Youth Championships were held and a record number of 207 tournaments were sanctioned. The first ADO Youth Championship was held and the title of Youth Champion was given to B.J. Preston. The National Points Champions were Tony Payne and Kathy Karpowich.

1988: The US team of Jim Damore, Katy Hopkins, Paul Lim, and Lori Branthwaite won the overall WDF Pacific Cup silver medal, the Lucky Lights Challenge of Champions was again broadcast on ESPN, a regional realignment was completed, and longtime sponsor from Watney's, Frank Dickens, was presented with an honorary lifetime membership. The ADO Youth Championship was held and the title of Youth Champion was given to Bethel Strode. The National Points Champions were Paul Lim and Melanie Rice.

1989: Area playoffs were eliminated and salaried positions in the ADO office were established. A record number of 342 clubs had since joined the ADO and MasterCard and Alamo Rental Cars were added to membership benefits. The US team of Eva Grigsby, Paul Lim, Kathy Maloney, and Tony Payne won the following medals at the WDF World Cup VII: bronze medal in the Ladies Doubles; Eva won the gold medal in the Ladies Singles; Tony won the bronze medal in the Men's Singles; and the bronze medal in the Men's Doubles. The ADO Youth Championship was held and the title of Youth Champion was given to Albert Mendoza. The National Points Champions were Gerald Verrier and Eva Grigsby.

The 1990s

1990: The US team of Eva Grigsby, Kim Kellar, Dave Kelly, and Paul Lim won the overall gold medal at the WDF Pacific Cup VI. It was Kim

Kellar's first international competition and She nailed a double 16 on her third dart to seal the victory and the overall gold medal for the US team. The ADO Memorial Scholarship Fund was created with $5,000 and the National 501 Championship Playoff was launched. Len Heard reached the quarter finals of the News of the World tournament broadcast on Sky TV and Paul Lim threw a perfect 501 game at the Embassy World Professional Championships. The first ADO 501 National Championships were held and the titles of 501 National Champion were given to Rick Ney and Kathy Maloney. The title of ADO Youth Champion was given to Albert Mendoza. The National Points Champions were Paul Lim and Eva Grigsby.

1991: There was a record 136 tournaments listed on the ADO tournament calendar. Sandy Reitan won the Ladies Singles event at the Winmau World Masters and the WDF World Cup; she was the first woman to win both events in the same year. The ADO 501 National Championships were held and the titles of 501 National Champion were given to Rudy Hernandez and Kathy Maloney. The title of ADO Youth Champion was given to Albert Mendoza. The National Points Champions were Paul Lim and Stacy Bromberg.

1992: The US team of Sammy Cruz, Sean Downs, Kathy Maloney, and Sandy Reitan won the overall silver medal at the WDF Pacific Cup VII and the team of Sandy Reitan and Kathy Maloney won the gold medal in the Ladies Doubles event. The ADO Operations Manual was completed and Southern Comfort was announced as the sponsor for World Cup IX, which was to be hosted by the ADO. The ADO 501 National Championships were held and the titles of 501 National Champion were given to Dave Kelly and Stacy Bromberg. The title of ADO Youth Champion was given to Albert Mendoza. The National Points Champions were Larry Butler and Stacy Bromberg.

1993: A Marketing Section was added to the ADO Operations Manual. The ADO Welcome Party was first introduced in conjunction with the East-West All-Star event. The US team of Stacy Bromberg, Kathy Maloney, Larry Butler, Dave Kelly, and Tony Payne won the over-all bronze medal in the WDF World Cup, Kathy won the gold medal in the Ladies Singles event, and Stacy won the silver medal. The ADO 501 National Championships were held and the titles of 501 National Champion were given to Jim Watkins and Sandy Reitan. The title of ADO Youth Champion was given to Kevin Luke. The National Points Champions were Larry Butler and Kathy Maloney.

1994: The ADO presented an honorary lifetime membership to Ken Edelson, of General Sportcraft, Co. Ltd. This same year, Tom and Della Fleetwood retired from as ADO board members. Larry Butler was the first American to win a PDC event with his defeat of Dennis Priestley for the World Matchplay title. The ADO 501 National Championships were held and the titles of 501 National Champion were given to Jim Watkins and Kathy Maloney. The title of ADO Youth Champion was given to Barry Russell. The National Points Champions were Larry Butler and Sue Qualls.

1995: The US team placed fifth in the WDF World Cup X and Roger Carter won the bronze medal in the Men's Singles event. Stacy Bromberg was the runner-up in the Winmau World Masters Ladies Singles event and Tom and Della Fleetwood were presented honorary lifetime member-ships. The ADO 501 National Championships were held and the titles of 501 National Champion were given to Rudy Hernandez and Lori Verrier. The title of ADO Youth Champion was given to Kevin Luke. The National Points Champions were Larry Butler and Sue Qualls.

1996: The ADO celebrated its twentieth anniversary with 292 member clubs and 60,000 members and the *ADO Book of Brackets* was published. The Minute Man Dart League's John Innegan threw a perfect 501 game in tournament singles play. The ADO 501 National Championships were held and the titles of 501 National Champion were given to Jim Widmayer and Lori Verrier. The title of ADO Youth Champion was given to Brian Watson. The National Points Champions were Mitch Payton and Stacy Bromberg.

1997: The US Ladies Doubles team of Stacy Bromberg and Lori Verrier won the overall WDF World Cup and a gold medal in the Ladies Doubles event. The first cricket singles playoffs were held, a new qualification system for the World Cup team was launched, and the Pacific Cup was disbanded and combined with the Asia Cup. US youth player Kevin Holden reached the top four of the Winmau Youth World Masters and Glenn Silva threw a perfect 501 game in tournament play. The ADO 501 National Championships were held and the titles of 501 National Champion was given to Paul Lim and Stacy Bromberg. The title of ADO Youth Champion was given to Kevin Holden. The title of Cricket National Champion was given to Paul Lim and Marilyn Popp. The National Points Champions were Steve Brown and Stacy Bromberg.

1998: For the first time in ten years, the regions were realigned and the youth program was revised and expanded to include eighteen-to twenty-year-olds. Stacy Bromberg was the first player to break the 1,000-point mark in the ADO Championship Points System. For the first time, the prize of $10,000 was offered for the first perfect game at the Cricket National Championships. Round of nine and Deadeye certificates were added and a proposal was submitted for the new international regional cup competition, the America's Cup, which would launch in 2002. The ADO 501 National Championships were held and the titles of 501 National Champion were given to Steve Brown and Stacy Bromberg. The title of Cricket National Champion were given to John Finnegan and Stacy

Bromberg. The title of ADO Youth Champion was given to Jason Jarvis. The National Points Champions were Steve Brown and Stacy Bromberg.

1999: For the first time, the prize of $10,000 was offered for the first perfect game at the 501 National Championship; East-West All-Stars and International Programs were revamped; and the realignment of the regions was completed for implementation in 2000. Cyberdarts became the office website of the ADO and a new sponsorship contract with Nodor/DMI was signed. The ADO 501 National Championships were held and the titles of 501 National Champion were given to Jerry Umberger and Stacy Bromberg. The title of Cricket National Champion were given to Steve Brown and Doreen Berry. The title of ADO Youth Champion was given to Adam Cable. The National Points Champions were Paul Lim and Stacy Bromberg.

The 2000s

2000: The twenty-fifth anniversary road show was announced. Through the year 2000, 173,721 "180" certificates, 509 Deadeye certificates, 8,694 Round of Nine certificates had been issued and 3,882 tournaments have been sanctioned. Stacy Bromberg was the lone dart player named to the *Sports Illustrated* "Greatest Sports Figures of the Century" list for the state of Nevada, and Singapore native Paul Lim named one of the top fifty athletes of the twentieth century by the Singapore Sports Commission. The ADO 501 National Championships were held and the titles of 501 National Champion were given to Luis Martinez and Stacy Bromberg. The titles of Cricket National Champion were given to Tim Grossman and Lori Verrier. The title of ADO Youth Champion was given to Kirt Johnson. The National Points Champions were Paul Lim and Stacy Bromberg.

2001: The ADO 501 National Championships were held and the titles of 501 National Champions were given to Chris White and Carolyn

Mars. The titles of Cricket National Champion were given to Paul Lim and Lori Verrier. The title of ADO Youth Champion was given to Jimmy Coon, Jr. The National Points Champions were Ray Carver and Stacy Bromberg.

2002: The ADO 501 National Championships were held and the titles of 501 National Champion were given to Ray Carver and Carolyn Mars. The titles of Cricket National Champion were given to Shane Meeks and Marilyn Popp. The title of ADO Youth Champion was given to Jay Moore. The National Points Champions were John Kuczynski and Stacy Bromberg.

2003: The ADO 501 National Championships were held and the titles of 501 National Champion were given to Dieter Schutsch and Stacy Bromberg. The titles of Cricket National Champion were given to Steve Hertzfeld and Stacy Bromberg. The title of ADO Youth Champion was given to Seth Page. The National Points Champions were John Kuczynski and Stacy Bromberg.

2004: The ADO 501 National Championships were held and the titles of 501 National Champion were given to Scott Wollaston and Stacy Bromberg. The titles of Cricket National Champion were given to Chris White and Stacy Bromberg. The title of ADO Youth Champion was given to Ryan Mahaffey. The National Points Champions were John Kuczynski and Stacy Bromberg.

2005: The ADO celebrated its thirtieth Anniversary. The ADO 501 National Championships were held and the title of 501 National Champion was given to Marilyn Popp. The title of ADO Youth Champion was given to Ashley Stewart. The National Points Champions were John Kuczynski and Stacy Bromberg.

2006: The ADO 501 National Championships were held and the titles of 501 National Champion were given to Tim Grossman and Stacy

Bromberg. The titles of Cricket National Champion were given to John Kuczynski and Marilyn Popp. The title of ADO Youth Champion was given to Mike Scarborough. The National Points Champions were John Kuczynski and Stacy Bromberg.

2007: The ADO 501 National Championships were held and the titles of 501 National Champion were given to Chris Helms and Stacy Bromberg. The titles of Cricket National Champion were given to Gary Mawson and Marilyn Popp. The title of ADO Youth Champion was given to T.J. Jaques. The National Points Champions were Darin Young and Stacy Bromberg.

2008: The ADO 501 National Championships were held and the titles of 501 National Champion were given to Brad Wethington and Christina Medina. The titles of Cricket National Champion were given to Darin Young and Paula Murphy. The title of ADO Youth Champion was given to Dan Lauby, Jr. The National Points Champions were Brian Blake and Stacy Bromberg.

2009: The ADO 501 National Championships were held and the titles of 501 National Champion were given to Tim Grossman and Stacy Bromberg. The titles of Cricket National Champion were given to Darin Young and Paula Murphy. The title of ADO Youth Champion was given to Robert Ham. The National Points Champions were Steve Brown and Andrea Taylor.

2010: The ADO celebrated its thirty-fifth anniversary. The ADO 501 National Championships were held and the titles of 501 National Champion were given to Darin Young and Stacy Bromberg. The titles of Cricket National Champion were given to Chris White and Andrea Taylor. The title of ADO Youth Champion was given to Miles Gallagher. The National Points Champions were Steve Brown and Stacy Bromberg.

2011: The ADO 501 National Championships were held and the titles of 501 National Champion were given to Robbie Phillips and Stacy Bromberg. The titles of Cricket National Champion were given to Larry Butler and Marilyn Popp. The title of ADO Youth Champion was given to Kyle Gaulthier. The National Points Champions were Larry Butler and Stacy Bromberg.

2012: The ADO 501 National Championships were held and the titles of 501 National Champion were given to Larry Butler and Stacy Bromberg. The titles of Cricket National Champion were given to Darin Young and Shea Reynolds. The title of ADO Youth Champion was given to Austin Adams. The National Points Champions were Larry Butler and Cali West.

Many of the international competitions and results after the year 2000 are also covered in the History of World Tournaments section of the book. After the retirement of Tom and Della Fleetwood from the ADO, many changes occurred in the personnel involved in running the organization and the overall operations of the organization has undergone many changes. As time progressed into the twenty-first century and we entered the digital age, the history of the organization was left in the twentieth century in paper format and has yet to reach the modern digital age. However, the most notable occurrences that should be mentioned were the events that took place in 2001. The US team withdrew from the WDF World Cup event, as it occurred three weeks after 9/11. Two weeks after 9/11, and ADO National Playoff was scheduled to take place in New Jersey. I remember we took a flight to Newark for this event. The pilot made a point to fly over Manhattan and we could still see the clouds from the smoke and debris over the area where the World Trade Centers were located. It was a very eerie and somber moment for everyone on that plane. I also recall that many of us visited the hotel gift shop and purchased many items in memory of the World Trade Centers.

Tournament play in America progressed to its highest level of participation in the 1980s. The tournament calendar listed events throughout the entire year with a total prize combination value of more than $1 million. Dedicated players could travel weekend after weekend attending different events in different states. It wasn't until the mid-1980s that an actual pro-tour was established with the addition of the Lucky Lights cigarette company as a main sponsor. City after city would be sponsored by Lucky Lights and would change their event format so that all events had the same format. At the end of the year, all the men's and ladies singles winners would compete at the Lucky Lights International Challenge of Champions in December.

As we progress to the 1990s, lower participation slowed the growth of the game and large corporate sponsors such as Lucky Lights soon disappeared. It is also said that the introduction of the soft-tip darts game also influenced the decline in steel-tip participation because rankings were used, the machine kept score for you, and people enjoyed all the bells and whistles associated with play on the new machines. However, there was also an increase in travel expenses that went along with the decrease in prize money, which resulted in fewer traveling players.

The Professional Darts Corporation (PDC) also started experiencing growth in its endeavors and kept many of their players in England to play rather than venturing over to America for a holiday to play in a few tournaments. They were experiencing the chance to finally make some real money at the game and their growth has continued so much that many players can now earn a full-time income from their winnings alone.

Many say that for the sport of darts to grow at a steadier pace, it should be exposed to the youth of America, so they can begin training at an early age to compete, as with many other sports. Many years ago, the ADO established its own Youth Dart Program with the assistance of a group of people who had created a youth dart program in Georgia. Fellow player Ken Friend Sr. wrote the quote about the creation of his program and the later creation of the ADO National Youth Program. It is filled with great information and details a set format to be shared with others on how anyone can create a youth program in their own area.

"A hundred years from now, it will not matter what our bank accounts were, the kind of homes we lived in, the kind of cars we drove... but that the world may be different because we were important in the life of a child"
—*Ken Friend Sr.*

This simple yet eloquent statement formed the foundation for organized youth dart activities in Savannah, Georgia, and ultimately in the United States. These subtle beginnings have blossomed into much larger programs that have dramatically influenced the lives of many young people and those who have served as mentors. Others who benefited from the efforts of the original programs generally agree that Savannah is considered the birthplace of organized youth dart programs in the United States. The continued development of the original programs by the US dart community and the American Darts Organization has also carried the influence far beyond US borders. So, how did it all start? The year was 1982, and it all began with a phone call.

After moving to Savannah, Georgia, in 1981, I was asked if I would like to join a newly formed dart league called the Savannah Area Darting Association. Since my family was still living in Shreveport, Louisiana, and wouldn't be coming to Savannah for another three months, I thought it would be a good way to keep me off the streets. When my family was finally able to complete the move, my children, Ken, Jeff, and Shannon had no friends yet, and little to do with their time. So, guess what?...We hung a dartboard! The kids used the summer months to hone their skills, and before long we found the Florida room full of neighbor kids playing imaginary games against the best in the world.

The adults played regularly at a local pub called Cheers. Children were not allowed in bars, but there was a dance studio above Cheers that the owner said we could use for small tournaments for the kids. Each week my wife and I would go to the local trophy shop, buy small trophies, and head for Nick's Dance Studio. Each Saturday we had a simple luck of the draw tournament for our children, the neighbor kids, and various strays that wandered in. The original interest was high, but when school started the number of participants dropped dramatically. I told my wife that I would keep coming until we brought only our children. One Saturday, we brought our children and one of the neighbors. . . . I told my wife "that's it, we can't do this anymore." She said "but you promised the kids"... and then came the phone call.

Barbara Johnson, recording secretary of the SADA, asked if we would be interested in starting a youth league with the help of the SADA. She had been contacted by several members of the SADA who also had children interested in playing darts, but didn't know about our Saturday sessions. We decided to give it a go, and held a meeting with those who were interested. Luke and Linda Sims, Guy and Carol Jervis, Sherri and Jerry Rowell, and all our children sat down together and hammered out a plan to start the Savannah Junior Dart League in January 1983. The insight of the kids was extremely instrumental in league development.

We were fortunate to have young folks that wanted to learn how to play darts *and* run their league. It was decided to have a clinic/signup for the program, and to hold elections for the Junior Board of Directors. Adults were assigned as mentors for each position on the Board, but the task of running the league fell squarely on the shoulders of the young folks. Signup produced fifty-three players! Officers were elected, rules, regulations, and Bylaws drawn up, and the league was established as a non-profit organization. The SJDL was born.

Due to the obvious age differences that were involved, the juniors decided that there should be some sort of handicap system in place. The following system was adopted:

- "A" level players: free—in, double—out 01 games.
- "B" level players: free—in games, but after 5 turns at the double out, may shoot any combination of numbers that will attain zero (0) exactly.
- "C" level players: free—in games, not required to shoot doubles in a 301 match.
- "A" level players: three (3) Bulls in CRICKET.
- "B" level players: two (2) Bulls in CRICKET.
- "C" level players: one (1) Bull in CRICKET.

The competition between skill levels was really good and much closer than one might think with the age differences. (8–18)

- "A" Skill level players won 61 percent of their games.
- "B" Skill level players won 67 percent of their games.
- "C" Skill level players won 41 percent of their games.

Players wanted to earn their "A" credentials in the worst way, but had to endure a "test" that was conducted by the adults. The test consisted of accuracy and knowledge of the dartboard. Three adults would ask the player to shoot at a specific number, then at specific "outs" without the aid of an out-chart. Once they had satisfied the judges that they could hit what they were aiming for and could do the math, they were asked to go to the dart board, turn, and face the judges. They were then asked to point in the direction of specific numbers on the dartboard. To this day, those young players who have joined adult leagues say the "A" evaluation was the toughest thing they had to do as an SJDL player. Many of them studied for a week before their test. However, most admit it was one of the best things they could have learned.

The interaction of the parents and the young players changed over the course of a season. At first, parents came in to watch and/or coach. We actually discouraged the adults from coaching in favor of having the junior team captains handle match chores. Somewhat disgruntled, the parents began dropping off their kids and going on their way until the end of the matches. About mid-season they started coming back and staying the whole day. We used to joke with the kids by commenting on how well behaved their parents were. I was curious about the change of heart. Time and again, I heard a parent say, "You wouldn't believe how well Johnny/Suzie is doing in math at school and how well they are getting along with other kids. I just had to come learn more about this." It was obvious the sport had taught some young folks that there is actually an application for mathematics in the real world. The adults were learning that a little time spent with their children actually DID have positive consequences.

As with any organized youth sport activity, the art of sportsmanship was taught at every level. League members, both adult and junior, voted each season for those they thought most typified the ideals of the league. This award was considered the "Oscar" of SJDL awards, and awarding the "Sportsmanship Award" at the end of each season was always a heart-warming and emotional event.

The skill of the players grew, and they became hungry for more/better competition. At that time, the only venues for competitive darts outside their league were luck of the draw tournaments or larger, sponsored tournaments. An initial "trial by fire" test was created to get a better understanding of just how the young players could handle adult tournament competition. The SJDL formed "All-Star" teams based on singles competition from the previous season. The SJDL All-Star team then played a match against the reigning SADA City Champion team. Those adult players who participated swear those matches generated the worst pressure they had ever seen; not only from the competition, but also from also not being able to establish that "killer" instinct they would normally show against another adult. The matches were always close, and generated fun and fond memories for everyone.

There was a lot of resistance to the youth program from some of the adults. Visions of young players buckling under the pressure of endless rounds of competition and/or child-like emotions kept the adults from warming up to having young people in a sport previously considered a sanctuary for parents and adults. There were also concerns about exposing young people to the world of dart bars. I sometimes think they were also leery of letting their children see how they acted when the kids were not around. We encouraged the "naysayers" to come to the Saturday league sessions and to talk with/compete against the kids. Once the skeptics got involved, their perceptions quickly vanished. Some bars would allow young players to compete in their establishment if accompanied by a parent or legal guardian. Once again, the young folks stepped up and made a decision that only "A" level players could compete in adult events, and only when a bar owner agreed they could do so.

Everyone was impressed with the skills and sportsmanship of the young players. Emotional outbursts were rare, the kids were always sober, and their endurance was second to none. Even after long tournament days we found the kids either off in a corner practicing with each other or hunting down an adult to give them some competition. And when they got back to the house, they did it all over again.

The kids would not let up, and it was decided to go to the "big leagues" to see how well the young players could do. That decision was viewed as a "make or break" situation for the future of youth darts. The only way to push the limits of their skills was in major competition; against each other, and against the adults. In early 1984 the SJDL joined the American Darts Organization as the first ADO affiliated league in the United States dedicated to young players. This paved the way for the young players to compete at all levels in ADO competition.

The Area IV-3 Regional was to be held in Ocala, Florida. Entry was $100 per player (there were no special provisions for youth players at the time). When it was announced that SJDL players were going to go to the Regional, contributions came pouring in: even from some of those originally opposed to the program. All-Stars were selected from the best winning percentages of the previous season, and twelve young players packed themselves into a van and a car and headed for Ocala. The adult players were stunned by the audacity of the youth invasion until they started losing games to the kids. Although none of the kids earned their way to the Area level, it took a 142 out in the final round robin leg to keep Mike Rowell from advancing. At the end of the day, the kids had earned the credibility and respect required to set future youth activities and programs in motion:

- The newly formed Georgia Dart Association consisted of leagues from throughout the state of Georgia. The President, Lewis Wells, suggested that the SJDL become a part of the association so the kids would have a chance to compete in the State Championships.
- Youth events were added to sponsored tournaments in cities throughout the United States.

- Adults started to ask young players to be their partners in local and out of town tournaments.
- The *Bull's Eye News* ran articles on the Savannah League, the Immortals program in Southern California, and other youth dart activities in cities around the country.
- Local TV stations ran special segments on youth dart activities.
- The ADO became interested in the creation of a National Youth Dart Program.

After joining the ADO, a tournament dedicated to young players was sanctioned by the ADO. It was a controversial sanctioning request because it focused on the young folks. However, sanctioning was granted because it was also "open" to adults for the adult/junior events. This was the first junior tournament sanctioned by the ADO, and highlighted the efforts of the ADO to form a youth program. The "Spotlight" tournament had all the trimmings of a regular tournament; it was held at the Savannah Moose Lodge, sponsored by Southeastern Wholesale Darts and Laserdart, and special rates for lodging were provided by Days Inn. Kathy Maloney skipped another tournament to come spend the weekend with the kids! The tournament was one of the first to enforce the no smoking rule, and had a "cuss box" that generated over $75 for the Moose Lodge charities (at 25 cents per cuss!).

The tournament was held again in 1985, but two weeks before the tournament the trophy sponsor backed out. The Georgia State Championships were held the weekend prior to the youth tournament. While at the State Championship Lewis Wells and the Atlanta Dart Association came to the rescue by donating over 50 trophies that players had contributed when they heard of the difficulty we were having. It was a totally unexpected surprise, and became a prime example of the support and acceptance the kids were receiving from the dart community. Several nights of shaving/replacing plaques generated some of the best trophies we could have hoped for!

While at work one day late in 1984, I received a phone call from ADO Area IV Manager, Jay Tomlinson, asking if I would be interested in helping the ADO to establish a National Youth Dart Program. I was honored, but terrified. It was a clean sheet of paper with the only precedent being what had been learned through the exploits of the SJDL and contact with other associations. Proposals were to be reviewed at an ADO Board meeting to be held in Las Vegas at the North American Open the following year.

There were two major concerns confronting the establishment of a youth program, amateur status and safety responsibilities. The "award of choice" for dart players was/is financial, and young players might have other activities that could be affected by cash awards earned while playing darts. The WDF and the manufacturers of lawn darts had shown concern over the impact of careless injuries to young players. Lawn Darts had been outlawed in the US due to safety issues, and no one wanted to see darts go the same route.

The only source of amateur status information that came to mind was the International Olympic Committee. A letter was sent to the President of the IOC, George Miller, asking for advice. He said that the IOC does not determine amateur status; each event has their own organization and set of rules. At the time, there were thirty-six different governing bodies. He sent the names of the contacts for each one. A form letter was sent out that inquired about how "dart" money might affect the amateur status within that particular sport. Many of the letters went to foreign countries. One by one, the responses came in: "No problem" in some cases, "don't even think about it" in others, and everything in between. It was obvious we had to declare neutrality.

After looking at the legalities and issues involved, two statements were generated to help protect the young players, local organizations, and the ADO:

- DISCLAIMER—AMATEUR STATUS: The host association and/ or the ADO assumes no responsibility for any adverse effects which Darts awards may have on the amateur status of any youth participant. Please check local regulations/restrictions.
- DARTS is an adult sport. It is dangerous for children to play without adult supervision.

After much iteration, a draft proposal was presented to the ADO Board in August 1985. There was still a lot of work to be done, and the ADO Board added a "Youth Director" position. A survey was created for ADO organizations known to have youth activities. Using information gathered from the survey and working with the ADO Board of Directors generated enough input to "tweak" the program to better meet the needs and capabilities of young players and the ADO.

In August 1986 the first National Youth Program was established and a "National Youth Manager" position was added to the ADO Board. Due to the obvious change in the ages of potential tournament participants, ADO organizations were strongly urged to place the amateur and safety statements on their tournament fliers. It was also recommended that any cash awards for youngsters be handed to a parent or person responsible for the young player. Hopefully, those funds would be used in trust. Work was begun on a program that would reward young players without influencing their amateur status in other sports.

It was during this same time that Tom Fleetwood, General Secretary of the ADO, was serving on the World Dart Federation Board of Directors. Communication with other WDF Board members had renewed interest in youth dart activities outside the United States. Just as the ADO was approving the new youth program; Tom received communication from the WDF stating that youth events were going to be added to the WDF agenda. Young champions from around the world would compete for youth titles during World Cup competition. The ADO program was designed to declare a "National Youth Champion," but had not been established long enough for the United States to crown a new champion under the new program guidelines. It was decided to take the highest-ranking youth player in the ADO point's standings and send him/her to the World Masters in England in December 1986. That first player was Greg Cruickshank from Southern Arizona.

The year 1987 was the first for the new ADO National Youth Program to crown its National Youth Champion. Only four Areas were able to send representatives; Area II, Pat Smith, Area III, B. J. Preston, Area IV, Ken Friend Jr., and Willie Hellman from Area VI. B.J. shot three 180s on his way to the first National Youth Champion crown. The round robin matches were close, and sportsmanship prevailed. As they stood on stage for their awards, the young players received a standing ovation from the myriad of players attending the North American Open.

ADO member organizations began writing and calling the ADO office for information about the youth program. A fifty-five-page ADO Youth Program Manual was developed to provide answers for those folks who wanted to start their own youth programs. The manual was based on the experiences of developing the Savannah Junior Dart League and the ADO program, and took a hard look at places to play, coaching, skill factors, etc. For those who wanted to get started quickly, there was a set of rules, Bylaws, and match sheets to build upon. The company I worked for at the time was generous enough to provide the printing of five hundred copies that were sent to over three hundred people who requested information. Copies were also distributed outside the U.S. to Canada, Japan, Australia, New Zealand, England, Italy, Norway, Spain, and the former Soviet Union.

There were many good suggestions for rewarding the efforts of young dart players. The ADO once again asked for a proposal based on a "continuing education" suggestion of Bob Bettis, who was an Area Manager at the time. Not a "scholarship" award in the classical sense, the program would help young people get started in post-secondary schools. The original program had two parts: The first provided funds for those who had earned their way to the National finals, and the second would allow the families of young players to apply for financial assistance. The fund would be supported through contributions from ADO member organizations, individuals, organizers, and sponsors. The first part of the program was immediately approved, but the decision was made to hold off on the second part of the program until the fund grew sufficiently to accommodate applicants.

The scholarship fund became a "Memorial Scholarship Fund" after K.C. Mullaney passed away during the North American Open in 1988. Shortly thereafter we lost Ed A'Hearn in a car accident. In many cases donations to the fund were/are made at a family's request as a memorial tribute to a fallen player, organizer, sponsor, or friend of the dart community. The goal was to establish a permanent memorial and to preserve the memories of those individuals and their contributions to the sport, as those that will use the fund go on to better lives.

Organizations continued to find ways to contribute to the fund and one, the Savannah Area Darting Association, became the main contributor to the fund for several years. It seemed youth activities and interest had come full circle, and the interest originally developed in Savannah had become infectious. The ADO established three Trustees to the fund;

Della Fleetwood, Kaye Axelgard Reeves, and myself. In typical Della grace and style, she is the one who does all the work. Kaye and I just get to kick her back into play once in a while. Della has personally handled the daunting task of distributing the scholarship funds and maintaining the communications necessary to keep everyone informed. As of this writing (November 2009) the ADO Memorial Scholarship Fund has helped fifty-plus young people get started in post secondary education! Della states that at any given time there are twenty-five to thirty young players who have earned eligibility for assistance through the fund.

A spin-off program has been developed for the children of Savannah Area Darting Association members based on part two of the original ADO proposal. The program provides typical startup assistance to those who have shown exceptional achievements both in and out of the classroom.

When asked to write this article, I was again honored and terrified. That seems a trait that goes with the territory. After I retired from the ADO in 1991 I continued to monitor the progress of the youth programs throughout the United States. The ADO Youth Managers have done a terrific job at expanding the program and making improvements to the system. But, I see disturbing ripples at the local levels. Although newer under-age laws have kept many young players from competing with the adults in league competition, some organizations have simply turned their back to young people instead of finding a way for them to remain active. Hopefully, this article will inspire others to work with young people and to re-kindle the desires for organized youth dart competition.

The overall quality of any project or program is measured by its success. Feedback has told us that the effort was worthwhile and there are so many feel-good and life-altering stories that have come from those children and adults who participated in, and helped to develop, youth dart activities in the United States. Youth programs have generated a host of high-quality players from all over the country. Some of the original members of the Savannah Junior Dart League have earned their own share of that success: Mike Rowell went on to become part of the four-person Georgia State Champions by taking out a 113 with a triple 1, triple 20, double bull in the final leg. Sean Morehouse has earned his way to several ADO National events, and was part of the 1994 Pacific Cup team. Sean also became ADO Representative on the SADA Board. Angel Cox played her way to many ADO National events and was elected President of the SADA adult League in 2003. Tiffany Rowell was an excellent Tournament Chairman for the SADA. Ken Friend Jr. represented Area IV in the very first National Youth Championships. Although not a member of the original SJDL, Staci Whitney recently earned the right to compete in the World Cup in Charlotte.

Many of the original SJDL players now play in the SADA and other leagues throughout the Southeast. I often find them talking about those Saturdays spent at Nick's Dance Studio and Cheers. There is but one regret; that most of these young people, who were so instrumental in changing the face of the Savannah and US dart community, never got a chance to compete in the ADO National Youth program. They did not set out to be leaders, but assumed the role through the quality of their intent and the integrity of their actions. Their legacy remains unchallenged, and no realistic value can ever be established for their never ending contributions to our sport. Southern Hospitality and the strong sense of family took control when these youngsters looked at Mom and Dad and said "I wanna play." And then came the phone call.

The concept of the ADO Youth Darts Program is still in effect today and dates back to this series of events back in 1985. It was conceived to provide a constructive and educational outlet for the enthusiasm and competitive spirit of America's youth. Players earn the right to compete at the national level through regional competitions held in early summer. The top eight finishers receive scholarship awards redeemable from the ADO Scholarship Fund. The National Youth Champion qualifies to compete in England at the WDF Winmau World Youth Championship and his or her name is engraved on a perpetual trophy.

In the fall of 1998, the Youth Program was expanded to include an eighteen-to twenty-year-old division. The Junior All-Stars, as these regional winners are called, earn a trip and the opportunity to participate in the East-West All-Star Challenge. Junior All-Stars receive a commemorative memento and a special award is presented to the highest achiever.

While the American Darts Organization seems to dominate the early history of darts in the United States, in later years, the development of the American Darters Association added yet another avenue for players to compete at their local, regional and national level.

The American Darters Association (ADA) is widely recognized as the leader in organized darts throughout the United States. The ADA has qualified trained personnel that own and operate their own dart areas throughout the country. Each player that signs up with the ADA becomes a member and receives a membership kit with a personalized card and membership number. You can check your schedule, stats, and personal achievements on the ADA website, which updates every thirty minutes, every day: www.adadarts.com

Late president and founder, Glenn Remick (1951–2009) had brought more than thirty years of experience in the sport of darts to the ADA. A celebrated player, in 1985, Glenn captained the United States World Cup team to a second place finish. He was the past president of the ADO (American Darts Organization) and helped write the governing rules for the NDA (National Darts Association). Since its beginning in 1991, the ADA has rapidly expanded nationwide in thirty states and now has a membership database of over 60,000 civilian and military members. The ADA has also expanded overseas with their ever-growing membership base to England, Spain, and Japan. CEO and acting President Gloria Remick with son and Vice President Karl Remick continue to keep the association strong. Currently, the ADA is the largest soft-tip and steel-tip league in the United States.

The ADA has worked in collaboration with all five branches of the United States Military to bring organized darts to thousands of service men and women worldwide.

In January of 2004 the YMCA of Greater St. Louis granted approval for the first YMCA Dart League to be held at the Tri-County YMCA, located in Wentzville, Missouri. The ADA approached YMCA's throughout the United States to provide teens and their families an opportunity to enjoy the game of darts in a safe, smoke-free, and alcohol-free YMCA environment.

Each year, around one hundred-plus members qualify for our Professional Darters Program. These qualifications come through weekly American Dart League play. The American Dart League is the number one benefit of the American Darters Association.

The ADA is currently in the process of pursuing senior leagues and independent youth leagues nationwide as well.

The ADA has a Regional and a National Championship each year throughout the country. Their Championship Series consists of:

Southern – Dallas TX

Mid Atlantic – Newport News VA

Mid West – Kansas City MO

Nationals – Chicago, Las Vegas, Orlando, St. Louis

Vice President Karl Remick would like to add a big thank you to all of the great members, representatives, partners and sponsors of the ADA. "Thanks for continuing the sport of darts!" he said.

One of the many faces of the future of darts—
Canadian player Steven Wilcox.

CHAPTER 12:
HISTORY OF US TOURNAMENTS

The game of darts has been played in the United States since the 1960s and has grown by leaps and bounds. Tournament play became more prevalent in the 1970s and grew to a tournament calendar that exceeds a total prize payout of more than $1 million. Some of those same tournaments that started in the 1970s and 1980s are still going strong today. This chapter is dedicated to those tournaments and their history as part of the growth of darts in America. At the time of publication, the titles for the longest running dart tournaments go to the Blueberry Hill Dart Tournament held at the world famous Blueberry Hill Bar & Restaurant in St. Louis, Missouri, which has been going for forty years, as well as the Oregon Open in Portland, Oregon, which is the longest known running event at forty-three years. There are many others that have also been around awhile. The Las Vegas Open has been around for thirty-four years, The Camellia Classic in Sacramento, California, has been going for thirty-six years, and The Syracuse Open has been going for thirty-four years. The Cleveland Extravaganza is thirty-five years strong and the Capital City Classic in Austin, Texas, has been going for thirty-three years. While there are many more that can be added to this list and deserve mention, I chose to highlight a few of the more prestigious and well-attended events in this chapter to show readers the progression of the game in America. The most obvious tournament to highlight first, while it did not run the longest and ended after thirty years, was well-known as the most prestigious singles title for a player to win in America.

The North American Open

The tournament that eclipsed all with being the most a significant title for an American to win from 1970 through 1999 was the singles title at the North American Open Dart Tournament. The first inaugural event held in Culver City, California, was hosted by the Southern California Darts Association (SCDA) and paid out a total prize purse of $2,000. More

than 250 players were in attendance from four states and one nation. The final year, the total prize payout was $45,000, 2,020 players were in attendance from forty-eight states and fourteen nations. The year of 1988 saw a maximum prize purse of $50,000 with 2,142 players in attendance from 46 states and 16 nations, which was the highest number for attendance in the entire thirty years of the event. This same event also saw the highest number of entrants into the men's singles event at 707 entries. In the thirty years of the event, only thirteen perfect 301 games have been thrown. Ray Fisher from Pennsylvania won the singles title in 1972 using the traditional American "widdy" wooden darts and then again in 1973 using brass darts. It was the premier event in North America and had the power to catapult a player from being a relative unknown, to instant stardom.

While these numbers may pale in comparison to the events held in England these days, this event was by far, the premier event in North America for thirty years. It was so big, even the top English players attended it for many years. People were excited to go there and have the chance of seeing and playing some of the best players in the world. I was sixteen when I went to my first NAODT in 1982. It was the most sensational event ever and everyone stayed to sit in the crowd and watch the staged finals on Sunday. The place was packed until it was all over. Everyone wanted to see who the next champion would be. Some were the ones you expected to see on that stage and some were not. That was what made the event all the more fun. You never knew who you were going to compete against and you never knew who was going to take home a title.

Stacy Bromberg (6)	Eric Bristow (4)	Kathy Maloney (4)	Maureen Flowers (3)
1995-301			
1996-301	1979-301	1985-301	1977-301
1997-301	1983-301	1986-301	1979-301
1998-301	1984-301	1988-301	1981-301
1998-cricket	1986-301	1993-301	
1999-301			

Roger Carter (2)	Ray Fisher (2)	Kathy Karpowich (2)	Gerry McCarthy (2)
1996-301	1972-301	1978-301	1971-301
1999-cricket	1973-301	1984-301	1972-301

Mandy Solomons (3)	Steve Brown (2)	John Kramer (2)
1989-301	1988-301	1981-301
1990-301	1989-301	1999-301
1992-301		

John Lowe (2)	Phil Taylor (2)	Lori Verrier (2)
1985-301	1990-301	1991-301
19987-301	1991-301	1999-cricket

There were many players that achieved multiple titles over the thirty years of this tournament. Some of the most notable winners were as follows:

The top ten title holders are Stacy Bromberg with a record fourteen titles, John Lowe with twelve titles, Lori Verrier with eleven titles, Kathy Maloney with nine titles, Mandy Solomons with eight titles, Eric Bristow and Bobby George both tied with seven titles, Bob Anderson, Paul Lim and Dennis Priestley tied with six titles, and Conrad Daniels, Keith Deller, Kathy Karpowich and Phil Taylor tied with five titles each.

1970: The first national dart tournament offering cash prizes ($2,000) was staged by the SCDA (at the time the country's largest dart league) at the Culver City (CA) Veteran's Auditorium. The event was attended by 252 players from four states. The singles event champions, Vince Lubbering and Robbi Dobbs, earned an appearance on the *Art Linkletter Show* in addition to their titles.

1971: Once again staged in Culver City, the prize purse doubled to $4,000. The event was attended by 319 players from five states and saw the first Canadian participation. The singles titles were won by Bob Thiede and young Gerry Dover (McCarthy).

1972: The event continued in Culver City, where it was attended by 384 Players from five states and Washington DC, as well as a few players from Canada who competed for $6,000 in the five events. Gerry Dover (McCarthy) repeated as Ladies' Champion and Ray Fischer won his first NAODT singles title, shooting 19s with wooden "widdy" darts.

1973: This was the last year the NAODT was staged at the Culver City Vet's Auditorium. The event was attended by 542 Players from ten states and Washington DC, as well as a few players from Canada who competed for $7,560. Ray Fischer repeated as Singles Champion, this time shooting 20s with brass darts. The number of playing boards increased to twenty-four.

1974: The tournament moved to the 20,000-sq. ft. convention center at the Disneyland hotel, with thirty-six playing boards, plus eight boards set aside for practice. The event was attended by 781 players from fourteen states plus Washington DC, as well as players from six nations (Canada, England, Mexico, Sweden, Wales, and the United States). All in attendance competed for the first ever $10,000-plus prize purse. The singles titles were won by Joe Baltadonis and Helen Scheerbaum. The first British contingent (twelve in all) was hosted (hotel, meals, tours, etc.) through the generosity of Bob Martel of Mothers Pub in Inglewood, CA.

1975: The tournament returned to the Disneyland Hotel Convention Center and featured a $15,000 total prize purse. Nicky Virachkul won his first NAODT title (the 301 Doubles with Joe Baltadonis). It was the Year of the Youth, with ten-year-old Darren Farley as a member of the champion five-person team, and seventeen-year-old Julie Nicoll, who captured the Ladies' Singles title.

1976: The total prize purse increased to $28,500 and utilized all four ballrooms situated on three decks of the Queen Mary. As matches were called, players were provided with maps to find their playing boards. Walkie-talkies were used to communicate open boards. The first Saturday night NAODT Dance was held in the Flamenco Room. The ever-popular James Gang shirt concession came on the scene. Unfortunately, the sound system went out before the start of the Friday night Mixed Doubles event. The event was called without a microphone and the staff used speakers belonging to a local player's teenage son for the rest of the weekend. Londoner Ricky Fusco won the singles title and he celebrated with a victory "belly" dance, which was a highlight of the weekend.

1977: The total prize purse increased to $30,000 during the second year aboard The Queen Mary. The event was attended by players from eight countries who witnessed Maureen Flowers take her first NAODT Ladies' Singles title. John Lowe won the first of his twelve NAODT Championships, the 301 men's doubles event with partner Tony Brown.

1978: The total prize purse increased to $35,500. Bobby George took the singles title and was the first NAODT Singles Champion to be invited to participate in the Winmau World Masters. At sixteen years old, Kathy Karpowich became the youngest NAODT Ladies' Singles Champion, a record that still stands today. John Lowe won three events this year: the mixed doubles, the 301 doubles, and the team event. The event was attended by 1,662 players representing thirty states and eleven nations.

1979: The tenth anniversary was celebrated aboard the Queen Mary with a total prize purse of $40,000. Eric Bristow won the first of his four Singles crowns and partnered with Leighton Rees to capture the 301 Doubles event. Maureen Flowers captured her second Ladies' Singles title. The event was attended by 1,781 players representing thirty-one states and nine nations.

1980: The prize purse remained at $40,000 and the tournament moved to Las Vegas's Hotel Sahara. L. David Irete filmed the finals for the first time. Len Heard defeated popular Canadian Fred Boyce in the Singles. The British contingent won all remaining events. The event was attended by 1,709 players representing thirty-five states and twelve nations.

1981: The prize purse increased to $50,000 and Coors became the first tournament sponsor. There were eighty-five playing boards set up for the event at the Sahara Hotel. Maureen Flowers took home her third Ladies' Singles Championship, while Southern California's John Kramer surprised and delighted the crowd by defeating Eric Bristow in the

Singles final. The event was attended by 1,797 players representing thirty-five states and twelve nations.

1982: The total prize purse remained at $50,000 and there were Americans in the winner's circle in all five events. Singles Champions Nicky Virachkul and Angie Burns were both invited to the Winmau World Masters. The late Kevin Hayes became the first player in NAODT history to achieve a Perfect 6-Dart 301 game, and he did it twice (back to back) in the Singles event. The event was attended by 1,669 players representing thirty-five states and twelve nations.

1983: Triple Crown Productions took over the operation and financial responsibility for the NAODT and added a Ladies' 301 Doubles event to the schedule. Watney's was the title sponsor. By the end of the first event, every available keg of Watney's beer in Las Vegas had been tapped. Frank Dickens drove back to Irvine, California (600 miles round trip), filled his station wagon with fifteen kegs of Watney's beer, and was back in time for the first event on Saturday morning. Eric Bristow won his second Singles title. Linda Batten won the Ladies' Doubles, paired with Keith Deller to win the Mixed Doubles, and Deller was also on the winning four-man team. The event was attended by 1,919 players representing forty states and sixteen nations.

1984: The NAODT was the first ADO Sanctioned event to be included in the new World Darts Federation Player Rankings. Eric Bristow became the first player to win three NAODT Singles title. At the ripe old age of twenty-two, Kathy Karpowich captured her second NAODT Ladies' crown. The event was attended by 1,806 players representing forty states and fourteen nations.

1985: Open and Ladies' Cricket Doubles were added to the tournament for the first time. Thanks to Triple 20 Productions, the NAODT finals were aired fifteen times on the nationwide FNN Cable TV program *SCORE*. John Lowe and Kathy Maloney each seized their first NAODT Singles crown. The event was attended by 1,824 players representing forty-two states and ten nations.

1986: Eric Bristow became the first player in NAODT history to win four Singles championships. Kathy Maloney repeated as Ladies' Champion, while Judy Campbell and her young partner Karen Lawman (Smith) successfully defended their Ladies' 301 Doubles title. The event was attended by 1,851 players representing forty-three states and twelve nations.

1987: Long-time actor, Ken Kercheval and his Old Capital Popcorn sponsored the eighteenth NAODT and players enjoyed fresh popcorn throughout the weekend. John Lowe won his second NAODT Singles crown and Kathy Karpowich received her first MVP award. The event was attended by 1,903 players representing forty-four states and sixteen nations.

1988: NODOR became the title sponsor. The tournament attracted more than 2,000 players for the first time in its history. Kathy Maloney captured her third NAODT Singles crown and Steve Brown took his first NAODT Singles championship. The event was attended by 2,142 players representing forty-six states and sixteen nations.

1989: The Hotel Sahara added a new tower of rooms just prior to the twentieth anniversary staging of the NAODT. Steve Brown was successful in his defense of the NAODT Singles title. Mandy Solomons took home her first NAODT Ladies' Singles trophy. The event was attended by 2,103 players representing forty-seven states and seventeen nations.

1990: Phil Taylor defeated MVP Ron Baxter in the Singles Final. Mandy Solomons repeated as Ladies' Singles Champion and won the Ladies' 301 Doubles (with Lil Coombes) and the Mixed Doubles (with

John Lowe). The event was attended by 2,023 players representing forty-six states and sixteen nations.

1991: Eighty new dartboard standards were set up for this year's event, which made it quite the sight as one approached the hall direct from the Sahara escalator. Sandy Reitan and Katy (Casillas) Hopkins became the first duo to win three NAODT Doubles titles. MVP Phil Taylor repeated as Singles Champion, needing only 29 darts in three legs to defeat Jerry Umberger, with a point-per-dart average of 31.14! The event was attended by 1,863 players representing forty-six states and twelve nations.

1992: For the first time in history, Americans did not make it to the Victory Circle. Alan Warriner was the Singles Champion. Mandy Solomons won her third NAODT Ladies' Singles crown and partnered with Belgian Vicky Prium to take both Ladies' Doubles titles, as well as the MVP award. The event was attended by 1,902 players representing forty-seven states and fifteen nations.

1993: Bob Anderson topped the Singles field. MVP Kathy Maloney became the first woman to win four NAODT Singles events and, in so doing, she tied John Lowe for the most NAODT titles (10), to date. The event was attended by 1,757 players representing forty-four states and fourteen nations.

1994: Sportcraft/Unicorn sponsored the Silver Anniversary staging of the NAODT. Mixed Triples replaced Mixed Doubles on the schedule. Newcomer Barbara Barnes shocked the darting world with her Ladies' Singles victory. The 1991 Ladies' Champion Lori Verrier partnered Stacy Bromberg to win both Ladies' Doubles events. The event was attended by 1,821 players representing forty-six states and fifteen nations.

1995: The tournament total prize purse decreased to $45,000; however, once again more than 2,000 players attended representing 47 states and 12 nations. Rudy Hernandez and Stacy Bromberg each won their first NAODT Singles title. Bromberg and Verrier repeated as the Ladies' 301 Doubles Champions. Bromberg then captured her first MVP award.

1996: Following the sale of the Hotel Sahara, the NAODT moved to the Tropicana Hotel, located at the opposite end of the Las Vegas strip. It was "survival of the fittest" in the overly large, metal-roofed hall. TCP rented carpet for the playing area, and players tolerated a bad sound system and poor bar service throughout the weekend. Roger Carter topped the Singles field for the first time. Bromberg repeated as Ladies' Singles Champion and won her third Ladies' 301 Doubles title with partner Lori Verrier. The prize purse continued at $45,000, and the event was attended by 2,007 players representing forty-eight states and fourteen nations.

1997: The Aladdin Hotel welcomed the NAODT event, willingly closing their twenty-four-hour bingo facility to accommodate the event. Winning both the Singles and 301 Doubles title, England's Peter Manley was named MVP. Stacy Bromberg continued her streak by winning her third Ladies' Singles and (partnered with Lori Verrier) her fourth Ladies' 301 Doubles title. The total prize purse continued at $45,000, and the event was attended by 1,882 players representing forty-eight states and fourteen nations.

1998: The tournament total prize payout continued at $45,000 and a new home was found at the Riviera Hotel. Men's/Ladies' Cricket Singles events were added to the tournament for the first time. Accudart/Winmau came aboard as title sponsors and guaranteed a special $50,000 cash prize for the first Perfect Cricket Singles Game. Stacy Bromberg wrote her own page in NAODT history: She won both Ladies' Singles and both Ladies' Doubles events. She became the first player to capture five Singles titles. She and Verrier had now won eight Ladies' Doubles events, which was more than any other Doubles duo. Bromberg had now won a total of thirteen NAODT Championships and now equaled Kathy Maloney's record by achieving her third MVP award. The event was attended by 1,956 players representing forty-eight states and fourteen nations.

1999: The Riviera Hotel welcomed the event to a brand new ballroom for the thirtieth NAODT, with its total prize purse of $45,000. The 1981 Champion John Kramer returned eighteen years later to defeat 1996 Champion Roger Carter in the Men's 301 Singles. Roger Carter defeated defending Champion Paul Lim for the Men's Cricket Singles crown and was named the 1999 NAODT Most Valuable Player. Australian Women's World Cup team Dot McLeod and Helen Chalson won both the Ladies' 301 and Ladies' Cricket Doubles titles. Canadians John Part and Gary Mawson repeated as Men's Cricket Doubles Champs. Finalists in both Ladies' Singles events were Stacy Bromberg and Lori Verrier. Verrier won the Ladies' Cricket Singles for her second NAODT Singles title. Bromberg won her fifth consecutive Ladies' 301 crown (her sixth NAODT Singles title) and now has a total of fourteen NAODT Championships. The event was attended by 2,020 players representing 48 states and 14 nations.

The year 1999 would be the last and final year for America's largest and most prestigious event. The title was sold to the Professional Darts Corporation (PDC), who hosted the PDC version of the North American Open in 2000; however, the event was not well-attended, was not continued after that year, and has yet to be re-established.

The Virginia Beach Dart Classic

One of the larger events in America today is the Virginia Beach Classic that is hosted by the Tidewater Area Darting Association. This association was founded in 1973 and fields teams from Virginia Beach, Norfolk, Chesapeake, Portsmouth, and Hampton, as well as attracting players from

Williamsburg, Virginia, to Elizabeth City, North Carolina. The league currently has a membership of about 350 dart players making up forty-three teams. TADA was one of the original members of the American Darts Organization when it was chartered in 1976. The mission of the Tidewater Area Darting Association is to bring together people of diverse heritage and background with the principles of open membership, fair

YEAR	Men's Cricket Singles	Men's 501 Singles	Ladies' Cricket Singles	Ladies' 501 Singles
1982	Rick Ney	Richard Long	None	Nancy Lilly
1984	Dave Anderson	None	None	None
1986	Rick Ney	Rick Reid	Kathy Karpowich	Kathy Karpowich
1992	Paul Lim	Paul Lim	Stacy Bromberg	Stacy Bromberg
1993	Jerry Umberger	Mick Sweeney	Kathy Maloney	Linda Sims
1994	Tony Payne	Danny Valletto	Shawne Sheluga	Frannie Frederick
1995	Jerry Umberger	Jerry Umberger	Stacy Bromberg	Bridgid Burke
1996	Peter Mills	Tim Frizzell	Stacy Bromberg	Stacy Bromberg

YEAR	Men's Cricket Singles	Men's 501 Singles	Ladies' Cricket Singles	Ladies' 501 Singles
1997	Jerry Umberger	Roger Carter	Julie Nicoll	Julie Nicoll
1998	Paul Lim	Paul Lim	Julie Nicoll	Stacy Bromberg
1999	Brad Wethington	Dieter Schutsch	Marilyn Popp	Marilyn Popp
2000	John Part	Roger Carter	Stacy Bromberg	Stacy Bromberg
2001	Jason Jarvis	Roger Carter	Stacy Bromberg	Stacy Bromberg
2002	John Part	Shane Meeks	Stacy Bromberg	Stacy Bromberg
2003	John Part	Ray Carver	Stacy Bromberg	Holly Part
2004	Bill Davis	Steve Brown	Stacy Bromberg	Stacy Bromberg
2005	John Kuczynski	Bill Davis	Stacy Bromberg	Stacy Bromberg
2006	John Kuczynski	Bill Davis	Stacy Bromberg	Stacy Bromberg
2007	Darin Young	Darin Young	Stacy Bromberg	Stacy Bromberg
2008	John Kuczynski	Bill Davis	Carolyn Mars	Marilyn Popp
2009	Shawn Brenneman	Brad Wethington	Paula Murphy	Robin Curry
2010	Nico DePaynos	Jerry VanLoan	Stacy Bromberg	Marilyn Popp
2011	Tom Sawyer	Stephen Panuncialman	Stacy Bromberg	Cindy Pardy Hayhurst
2012	Tom Sawyer	Brandon Rogers	Cindy Pardy Hayhurst	Sandy Hudson

play, and respectful competition while developing the skills and abilities of dart players in the Tidewater area.

The Virginia Beach Dart Classic tournament started as a local/ regional event in 1986 and has now completed its twenty-sixth year. The tournament quickly grew to become one of the premier darting events in the United States. The Virginia Beach Dart Classic is a sanctioned event for both the American Darts Organization and the World Darts

YEAR	Men's 301 Pro Singles	Ladies' 301 Pro Singles
2000	John Part	None
2001	Barry Russell	None
2002	Shane Meeks	None
2003	Dieter Schutsch	None
2004	Bill Bell	Tina DiGregorio
2005	Darin Young	Marilyn Popp
2006	Brad Wethington	Stacy Bromberg
2007	Brian Blake	Stacy Bromberg
2008	Brad Wethington	Marilyn Popp
2009	Joe Chaney	Robin Curry
2010	Bruce Davey	Stacy Bromberg
2011	Terry Hayhurst	Cali West
2012	None	Cali West

Federation and is a player's favorite on the yearly tournament calendar. The event also plays host to the largest youth tournament in the country. During the course of the event, the league has had the opportunity to raise almost $40,000 for the Special Olympics in Norfolk, Virginia, and has been twice awarded the Special Olympics Organization of the Year honors.

The Virginia Beach Singles Championship History:

In the year 2000, a Pro 301 Singles event was added to the tournament schedule and for the first four years, it was only a men's event. However, in 2004, a Ladies 301 Pro Singles was added to the tournament. In 2012, the Men's 301 Pro Singles was discontinued. An Open Pro Cricket event was also added to the tournament format. The winner of the Open Pro Cricket Singles in 2011 was Bob Sinnaeve and the winner for 2012 was Darin Young.

The Syracuse Open

In 1974, several photographers and graphic artists competed in matches in the afternoon at different studios. They then moved their competitions to a local pub and The Salt City Dart League was born. In 1978, the Tavern Division was created for five-person teams who competed out of four different local taverns. The Mission Statement of the Salt City Dart League is to promote interest in darting as a sporting and social activity: "to give and promote matches, entertainments, games lectures, and social affairs of all descriptions for the enjoyment

and instruction of the members; to provide darting matches among its own members and members of similarly constituted organizations for the benefit, enjoyment, instruction, and well-being of its members."

The Salt City Dart League currently has more than 400 members, with forty-eight teams playing out of thirty-six taverns. The league also has six board members, a tournament chairperson, a webmaster, and an equipment manager. The SCDL actively supports at least one benefit tournament a year and all the proceeds from the tournament go to the charity. In November 2012, the league was able to raise more than $2,600 for the Clear Path for Veterans.

The first Open tournament, simply called the SCDL Tournament, was held in 1978 and the prize money was based on the number of entries; however, the first year that the actual results were recorded into the league newsletter was 1985. The name then progressed to The SCDL Genny Light Open, and then eventually became the Syracuse Open. The results for a couple of years were lost in the shuffle of paperwork, but for the most part, you can take a look into the history of the event and its past winners. The tournament format began with a few events, which included a Men's and Ladies '01 Singles. In 1988, a Men's Cricket Singles event was added, and in 1997, a Ladies, Cricket Singles event was added, as well.

In 2013, the SCDL hosted the thirty-fifth annual Syracuse Open, which was attended by many world ranked players. The event has grown to offer a total prize payout of over $23,000.

YEAR	Men's Cricket Singles	Men's '01 Singles	Ladies' Cricket Singles	Ladies' '01 Singles
1985	no event	Geoff Murray	no event	Sue Hitchcock
1986	no event	Tim Kipp	no event	Stephanie Figi
1987	no event	Ron Baxter	no event	Gerda Madsen
1988	Jerry Umberger	Larry Butler	no event	Kathy Karpowich
1989	Rudy Hernandez	Rudy Hernandez	no event	Rani Gill
1990	Tom Martin	Dave Kelly	no event	Gail Thibault
1991	Phil Davis	John Part	no event	Rani Gill
1992	no data			
1993	Duane Hughson	Jim Widmayer	no event	Kathy Maloney
1994	John Part	Mick Sweeney	no event	Kathy Maloney
1995	Gary Mawson	Jerry Umberger	no event	Kathy Maloney

YEAR	Men's Cricket Singles	Men's '01 Singles	Ladies' Cricket Singles	Ladies' '01 Singles
1996	Mitch Payton	Jim Widmayer	no event	Jeanne Miller
1997	Jason Lucas	John Part	Kim Whaley	Rani Gill
1998	no data			
1999	Gary Mawson	Dan Olson	Rani Gill	Julie Nicoll
2000	Yves Chamberland	John Kuczynski	Kim Whaley	Kim Whaley
2001	Mick Manning	John Part	Kim Whaley	Carolyn Mars
2002	Tim Grossman	Tim O'Gorman	Kim Whaley	Kim Whaley
2003	Dan Olson	Jim Watkins	Tina Phillips	Tina Phillips
2004	Ray Carver	Ray Carver	Marilyn Popp	Carolyn Mars
2005	John Kuczynski	Andre Carmen	Marilyn Popp	Robin Curry
2006				
2007	John Part	John Kuczynski	Kim Whaley-Hilts	Robin Curry
2008	Larry Butler	Tim O'Gorman	Marilyn Popp	Nancy Huntoon
2009	Darin Young	Larry Butler	Robin Curry	Tracy Feiertag
2010	Larry Butler	Bob Sinnaeve	Kim Whaley-Hilts	Cali West
2011	Darin Young	Larry Butler	Debbie Driscoll	CJ Slater
2012	Larry Butler	Dan Olson	Robin Curry	Kathy Karpowich

CHAPTER 13:
HISTORY OF WORLD
TOURNAMENTS

Many tournaments all over the world have achieved the status of being known as world-class events and possess titles that every dart player wants to win. The list begins with prestigious events starting with the now defunct News of the World to the Winmau World Masters to the Embassy/Lakeside World Professional, along with the crossover to all the more well-known titles of the Professional Darts Corporation events. While it would be impossible to cover them all and to list all the winners, many of the older events carry a lot of history of the game and the names of some legendary players whose names will continue to be preserved in the annals of darting history.

News of the World

The News of the World dart tournament began in 1927 and was the first major darts competition set up by the staff and volunteers from the newspaper of the same name, *News of the World*. There were approximately 1,000 entries in the original 1927 event and by 1938–39, it expanded to six different regional events, the total number of entrants exceeded 280,000, and a record crowd of 14,534 spectators was on hand to see Marmaduke Brecon defeat Jim Pike. The tournament was organized on a regional level from 1927 through 1939 and it became the national championship in 1947 up until 1990. In 1996–1997, an attempt was made to revive the event, but it was then discontinued. The event was always noted for all their competitions being played at the 8 foot oche, rather than the regulation 7 feet 9 ¼ inches.

Although one player was unable to win the title three times, seven players managed to win the event two times: Tommy Gibbons (1951–52, 1957–58), Tom Reddington (1954–55, 1959–60), Tom Barrett (1963–64, 1964–65), Stefan Lord (1977–78, 1979–80), Eric Bristow (1982–83, 1983–84), Bobby George (1978–79, 1985–86), Mike Gregory (1986–87, 1987–88).

1947–48 Harry Leadbetter (Windle Labour Club, St Helens) beat Tommy Small (Sth Durham Steel & Iron SC, West Hartlepool) 2-1.

1948–49 Jackie Boyce (New Southgate SC) beat Stan Outten (Dr Johnson, Barkingside) 2-1.

1949–50 Dixie Newberry (Albert, Hitchin) beat Ronnie Ridley (King Edward Hotel, Newcastle-u-Tyne) 2-0.

1950–51 Harry Perryman (Home Office SC, Greenford) beat Laurie Runchman (Feathers, Felixstowe) 2-0.

1951–52 Tommy Gibbons (Ivanhoe WMC, Conisbrough) beat Jack Wallace (Low Seaton BL, Workington) 2-0.

1952–53 Jimmy Carr (Red Lion, Dipton) beat Ernest Greatbatch (Horse Vaults Hotel, Pontefract) 2-0.

1953–54 Oliver James (Ex-Servicemen's Club, Onllwyn) beat Johnny Bell (Sun, Waltham Abbey) 2-0.

1954–55 Tom Reddington (New Inn, Stonebroom) beat Johnny Bell (Sun, Waltham Abbey) 2-0.

1955–56 Trevor Peachey (Black Fox, Thurston) beat Les Campbell (Boot, Dinas) 2-0.

1956–57 Alwyn Mullins (Traveller's Rest, Tickhill) beat Len Baker (Corporation Hotel, Cardiff) 2-0.

1957–58 Tommy Gibbons (Ivanhoe WMC, Conisbrough) beat Eric Moss (Railway Tavern, Harleston) 2-0.

1958–59 Albert Welsh (Horden Hotel, Seaham) beat Frank Whitehead (White Rose Hotel, Rossington) 2-1.

1959–60 Tom Reddington (George Hotel, Alfreton) beat Dai Jones (Cambrian Hotel, Aberystwyth) 2-1.

1960–61 Alec Adamson (Prince of Wales, Hetton-le-Hole) beat Eddie Brown (Magpie, Stonham) 2-1.

1961–62 Eddie Brown (Magpie, Stonham) beat Dennis Follett (Cadeleigh Arms, Cadeleigh) 2-0.

1962–63 Robbie Rumney (Waterloo Hotel, Darlington) beat Bill Harding (Globe Hotel, Aberdare) 2-0.

1963–64 Tom Barrett (Odco SC, London) beat Ray Hatton (Flower of the Valley Hotel, Rochdale) 2-0.

1964–65 Tom Barrett (Odco SC, London) beat Norman Fielding (Station Inn, Swannington) 2-1.

1965–66 Wilf Ellis (Brookside WMC, Upton) beat Ron Langley (Arlington SC, Harlow) 2-1.

1966–67 Wally Seaton (Swan, Parson Drove) beat Brian Quarterman (Ivy Inn, North Littleton) 2-0.

1967–68 Bill Duddy (Rose & Thistle, Frimley Green) beat Gerry Feeney (Unicorn Club, Workington) 2-0.

1968–69 Barry Twomlow (Red Lion, Chesterfield) beat Paul Gosling (William IV, Truro) 2-0.

1969–70 Henry Barney (Pointers Inn, Newchurch, IoW) beat Alan Cooper (Plough, Filton) 2-0.

1970–71 Dennis Filkins (Barrow, Hepburn & Gale SC, Bermondsey) beat Derek White (Ship, Weymouth) 2-0.

1971–72 Brian Netherton (Welcome Home Inn, Par) beat Alan Evans (Ferndale Hotel, Rhondda) 2-0.

1972–73 Ivor Hodgkinson (Great Northern, Langley Mill) beat Ron Church (Royal Alfred, Shoreditch) 2-1.

1973–74 Peter Chapman (Bird in Hand, Henley) beat Paul Gosling (Portscatho Club, Truro) 2-1.

1974–75 Derek White (Belvedere Inn, Weymouth) beat Bill Duddy (Frimley Green WMC) 2-1.

1975–76 Bill Lennard (Cotton Tree Inn, Manchester) beat Leighton Rees (Ynysybwl USC, Pontypridd) 2-0.

1976–77 Mick Norris (King of Denmark, Ramsgate) beat Bob Crosland (Blackamoor Head, Pontefract) 2-0.

1977–78 Stefan Lord (Stockholm Super Darts Club) beat John Coward (White Hart BL, Sedbergh) 2-0.

1978–79 Bobby George (King George V, Ilford) beat Alan Glazier (George & Dragon, Wetherby) 2-0.

1979–80 Stefan Lord (Stockholm Super Darts Club) beat Dave Whitcombe (Naval Club, Chatham) 2-0.

1980–81 John Lowe (Willow Tree, Pilsley) beat Mick Norris (Earl St Vincent, Ramsgate) 2-0.

1981–82 Roy Morgan (Wheel o'Worfield, Worfield) beat Jim Hughes (Parcwern Country Club, Ammanford) 2-1.

1982–83 Eric Bristow (Foaming Quart, Norton Green) beat Ralph Flatt (Old Red House, Carlton Colville) 2-0.

1983–84 Eric Bristow (Milton Hayes BC, Stoke-on-Trent) beat Ian Robertson (Bell, Marston Moretaine) 2-0.

1984–85 Dave Lee (Ivor Arms, Pontllanfraith) beat Billy Dunbar (Woolwich Infant, London) 2-0.

1985–86 Bobby George (Old Maypole, Hainault) beat Rick Ney (US Darting Association) 2-0.

1986–87 Mike Gregory (Stones Cross Hotel, Midsomer Norton) beat Peter Evison (Halcyon/Spikes, Peterborough) 2-0.

1987–88 Mike Gregory (Stones Cross Hotel, Midsomer Norton) beat Kevin Spiolek (Cambridge Squash Club) 2-1.

1988–89 Dave Whitcombe (King's Head, Ipswich) beat Dennis Priestley (Horseshoe, Rotherham) 2-1.

1989–90 Paul Cook (Gorse Hill WMC, Swindon) beat Steve Hudson (Oakworth SC, Keighley) 2-0.

1996–97 Phil Taylor (Cricketer's Arms, Newcastle-under-Lyme) beat Ian White (Dockside Inn, Runcorn) 2-0.

Women

1989–90 Lynne Ormond (George, Alford) beat Jane Stubbs (Roebuck Hotel, Northwich)

1996–97 Linda Jones (Seven Stars, Chorley) beat Melanie Saunders (Railway Inn, Abergavenny) 2-0.

The World Masters

The World Masters is another of the longest running championship events in England that began in 1974 and continues to today. It is now considered the second biggest tournament, only eclipsed by the Embassy/Lakeside World Professional Darts Championship. From 1974 through 1981, there was only a men's event and a ladies' event was introduced in 1982. The most titles for this event were given to Eric Bristow and Trina Gulliver respectively, both with five titles each. Bob Anderson and Martin Adams have won three titles, and Dave Whitcombe, John Lowe, and Raymond van Barneveld have won the title twice. Michael van Gerwen was the youngest champion at 17 years and 174 days. Cliff Inglis won the inaugural event in 1974, with Alan Evans taking the title in 1975, John Lowe in 1976, Eric Bristow in 1977, Ronnie Davies in 1978, Eric Bristow again in 1979, John Lowe again in 1980, and Eric Bristow yet again in 1981. Sandy Reitan was the first American woman to win the title in 1991, and an American male has never won title.

Year	Men's World Masters	Women's World Masters
1982	Dave Whitcombe	Ann Marie Davies
1983	Eric Bristow	Sonja Ralphs
1984	Eric Bristow	Kathy Wones
1985	Dave Whitcombe	Lilian Barnett

Year	Men's World Masters	Women's World Masters
1986	Bob Anderson	Kathy Wones
1987	Bob Anderson	Ann Thomas
1988	Bob Anderson	Mandy Solomons
1989	Peter Evison	Mandy Solomons
1990	Phil Taylor	Rhian Speed
1991	Rod Harrington	Sandy Reitan
1992	Dennis Priestley	Leeanne Maddock
1993	Steve Beaton	Mandy Solomons
1994	Richie Burnett	Deta Hedman
1995	Erik Clarys	Sharon Colclough
1996	Colin Monk	Sharon Douglas
1997	Graham Hunt	Mandy Solomons
1998	Les Wallace	Karen Smith
1999	Andy Fordham	Francis Hoenselaar
2000	John Walton	Trina Gulliver
2001	Raymond van Barneveld	Anne Kirk
2002	Mark Dudbridge	Trina Gulliver
2003	Tony West	Trina Gulliver
2004	Mervyn King	Trina Gulliver
2005	Raymond van Barneveld	Trina Gulliver
2006	Michael van Gerwen	Francis Hoenselaar
2007	Robert Thornton	Karin Krappen
2008	Martin Adams	Francis Hoenselaar
2009	Martin Adams	Linda Ithurralde
2010	Martin Adams	Julie Gore
2011	Scott Waites	Lisa Ashton

BDO World Championships (Embassy/Lakeside)

The Embassy World Professional, also later known as the Lakeside World Darts Championship, have both been known as the BDO World Darts Championship and was the only world championship tournament until 1994, with the split between the BDO and the newly formed Professional Darts Corporation (PDC). Some of the greatest moments in darts have taken place at the BDO World Darts Championship. Those moments in darting history, such as American player Paul Lim hitting the tournament's only ever perfect 9-dart game, which he did in the second round against Jack McKenna from Ireland. Paul won a bonus of £50,000.00, which was more than the eventual champion received. Another more memorable moment in the tournament's history occurred in 1993, when Keith Deller, a twenty-two-year-old qualifier from Ipswich defeated the world's top three players, including Eric Bristow in the final to record one of the greatest upsets in the history of darts.

The most titles for this event have been won by Eric Bristow, with five titles. Raymond van Barneveld has won the title four times, Martin Adams has won it three times and Phil Taylor has won the title twice. The most appearances at the event title now belongs to Martin Adams with eighteen appearances, which surpassed the record of sixteen appearances set by both Eric Bristow and John Lowe, as the split in darts prevented both Eric and John from participating in any further events. The youngest champion Was Jelle Klaasen in 2006 at 21 years and 90 days old, and the youngest competitor was Michael van Gerwen in 2007 at the age of 17 years and 257 days. The oldest champion is Martin Adams in 2011, who won the title at the age of 54 years and 224 days.

There have been twenty different matches where a player has exceeded a 100 point average. The first player to achieve a 100 average was Keith Deller in the 1985 quarter final match against John Lowe, and he lost the match. Phil Taylor was the next player to achieve a 100 average in his semi-final match in 1990, and Raymond van Barneveld has reached a 100 average on six different occasions, his highest being 103.83 in the 2004 quarter final match against John Walton. The second highest average of 102.63 was achieved by Dennis Priestley in his 1993 first round match against Jocky Wilson. Mervyn King was next in line with a 101.55 average in his 2002 quarter final match against Raymond van Barneveld. Ted Hankey achieved an average of 101.55 in his 1998 first round match against Wayne Weenig and Marko Pusa achieved a 101.40 average in his 2001 second round match against Jez Porter.

The ladies first arrived at the World Championship at Lakeside in 2001. Since the inception, Trina Gulliver has appeared in eleven of the twelve finals and she has won nine of those titles, seven of them in a row until a new champion, Anastasia Dobromyslova, won the title in 2008. The year 2012 was the first that Trina was not in the final, as she lost the semi-final match to the eventual champion Anastasia Dobromyslova.

Men's

Year	Champion (average in final)	Score	Runner-Up (average in final)
1978	Leighton Rees (92.40)	(legs) 11–7	John Lowe (89.40)
1979	John Lowe (87.42)	(sets) 5–0	Leighton Rees (76.62)
1980	Eric Bristow (88.10)	5–3	Bobby George (86.49)
1981	Eric Bristow (86.10)	5–3	John Lowe (81.00)
1982	Jocky Wilson (88.10)	5–3	John Lowe (84.30)
1983	Keith Deller (90.00)	6–5	Eric Bristow (93.90)
1984	Eric Bristow (97.50)	7–1	Dave Whitcombe (90.60)
1985	Eric Bristow (97.50)	6–2	John Lowe (93.12)
1986	Eric Bristow (94.47)	6–0	Dave Whitcombe (90.45)
1987	John Lowe (90.63)	6–4	Eric Bristow (94.29)
1988	Bob Anderson (92.70)	6–4	John Lowe (92.07)
1989	Jocky Wilson (94.32)	6–4	Eric Bristow (90.66)
1990	Phil Taylor (97.47)	6–1	Eric Bristow (93.00)
1991	Dennis Priestley (92.57)	6–0	Eric Bristow (84.15)

Year	Champion (average in final)	Score	Runner-Up (average in final)
1992	Phil Taylor (97.59)	6–5	Mike Gregory (94.41)
1993	John Lowe (83.97)	6–3	Alan Warriner (82.32)
1994	John Part (82.44)	6–0	Bobby George (80.31)
1995	Richie Burnett (93.63)	6–3	Raymond van Barneveld (91.23)
1996	Steve Beaton (90.27)	6–3	Richie Burnett (88.05)
1997	Les Wallace (92.19)	6–3	Marshall James (92.01)
1998	Raymond van Barneveld (93.96)	6–5	Richie Burnett (97.14)
1999	Raymond van Barneveld (94.65)	6–5	Ronnie Baxter (94.65)
2000	Ted Hankey (92.40)	6–0	Ronnie Baxter (88.35)
2001	John Walton (95.55)	6–2	Ted Hankey (94.86)
2002	Tony David (93.57)	6–4	Mervyn King (89.67)
2003	Raymond van Barneveld (94.86)	6–3	Ritchie Davies (90.66)
2004	Andy Fordham (97.08)	6–3	Mervyn King (91.02)
2005	Raymond van Barneveld (96.78)	6–2	Martin Adams (91.35)
2006	Jelle Klaasen (90.42)	7–5	Raymond van Barneveld (93.06)
2007	Martin Adams (90.30)	7–6	Phill Nixon (87.09)
2008	Mark Webster (92.07)	7–5	Simon Whitlock (93.92)
2009	Ted Hankey (91.46)	7–6	Tony O'Shea (90.54)
2010	Martin Adams (95.01)	7–5	Dave Chisnall (93.42)
2011	Martin Adams (92.13)	7–5	Dean Winstanley (89.08)
2012	Christian Kist (90.00)	7–5	Tony O'Shea (87.78)

Women's

Year	Champion (average in final)	Sets	Runner-Up (average in final)
2001	Trina Gulliver (83.97)	2–1	Mandy Solomons (79.11)
2002	Trina Gulliver (84.36)	2–1	Francis Hoenselaar (82.95)
2003	Trina Gulliver (84.93)	2–0	Anne Kirk (70.20)
2004	Trina Gulliver (87.03)	2–0	Francis Hoenselaar (85.44)

Year	Champion (average in final)	Sets	Runner-Up (average in final)
2005	Trina Gulliver (79.68)	2–0	Francis Hoenselaar (73.89)
2006	Trina Gulliver (73.80)	2–0	Francis Hoenselaar (70.26)
2007	Trina Gulliver (80.61)	2–1	Francis Hoenselaar (79.23)
2008	Anastasia Dobromyslova (81.54)	2–0	Trina Gulliver (71.64)
2009	Francis Hoenselaar (77.39)	2–1	Trina Gulliver (75.19)
2010	Trina Gulliver (80.52)	2–0	Rhian Edwards (68.25)
2011	Trina Gulliver (73.95)	2–0	Rhian Edwards (73.86)
2012	Anastasia Dobromyslova (73.95)	2–1	Deta Hedman (74.13)

WDF World Cup

The World Dart Federation (WDF) World Cup is a biennial competition featuring team, doubles, and singles championships between teams formed by the supporting WDF nations. The tournament began in 1977 with only a men's competition, continued until 1983 when a women's competition was added, and a youth competition was added in 1999. The first American team member to win an event in the World Cup was Nicky Virachkul in 1979 with a men's singles gold medal. America's Sandy Retain captured the inaugural ladies singles gold medal in 1983. In 1985, the American team achieved phenomenal success with a 9-0 defeat of Team England in the team event, in which the American team then went on to win the gold medal in the team event, a bronze medal in the men's pairs, and a silver medal in the overall competition, which to date has been the highest finish ever achieved by an American team. Eva Grigsby captured the ladies, singles title in 1989, and in 1993, Kathy Maloney captured the title. Ray Carver, John Kuczynski, Bill Davis, and George Walls won the gold medal in the 2003 team event, and in 2009, Stacy Bromberg captured the ladies' singles title.

Year	Venue	Overall World Cup Winners	Men's Team Event
1977	London	Wales	Leighton Rees Alan Evans David Jones
1979	Las Vegas	England	Eric Bristow John Lowe Tony Brown Bill Lennard
1981	Nelson	England	Eric Bristow John Lowe Tony Brown Cliff Lazarenko
1983	Edinburgh	England	Eric Bristow John Lowe Keith Deller Dave Whitcombe
1985	Brisbane	England	Tony Payne Rick Ney John Kramer Dan Valletto
1987	Copenhagen	England	Eric Bristow John Lowe Cliff Lazarenko Bob Anderson
1989	Toronto	England	Bob Sinnaeve Rick Bisaro Tony Holyoake Albert Anstey

Men's Singles Champions	Men's Pairs Champions	Women's Singles Champions
Leighton Rees	Eric Bristow & John Lowe	
Nicky Virachkul	Eric Bristow & John Lowe	
John Lowe	Cliff Lazarenko & Tony Brown	
Eric Bristow	Eric Bristow & John Lowe	Sandy Reitan
Eric Bristow	Eric Bristow & John Lowe	Linda Batten
Eric Bristow	Eric Bristow & John Lowe	Valery Maytum
Eric Bristow	Eric Bristow & John Lowe	Eva Grigsby

Year	Venue	Overall World Cup Winners	Men's Team Event
1991	Zandvoort	England	Eric Bristow John Lowe Phil Taylor Alan Warriner
1993	Las Vegas	Wales	Steve Beaton Ronnie Baxter Kevin Kenny Dave Askew
1995	Basel	England	Steve Beaton Ronnie Baxter Martin Adams Andy Fordham
1997	Perth	Wales	Eric Burden Marshall James Sean Palfrey Martin Phillips
1999	Durban	England	Ronnie Baxter Martin Adams Andy Fordham Mervyn King
2001	Kuala Lumpur	England	Martin Adams Andy Fordham Mervyn King John Walton
2003	Epinal	England	Ray Carver John Kuczynski Bill Davis George Walls

Men's Singles Champions	Men's Pairs Champions	Women's Singles Champions
John Lowe	Keith Sullivan & Wayne Weening	Jill McDonald
Roland Scholten	John Part & Carl Mercer	Kathy Maloney
Martin Adams	Martin Adams & Andy Fordham	Mandy Solomons
Raymond van Barneveld	Sean Palfrey & Martin Phillips	Noeline Gear
Raymond van Barneveld	Ritchie Davies & Richie Herbert	Trina Gulliver
Martin Adams	Andy Fordham & John Walton	Francisca Hoenselaar
Raymond van Barneveld	Martin Adams & Mervyn King	Trina Gulliver

Year	Venue	Overall World Cup Winners	Men's Team Event
2005	Perth	Netherlands	Jarkko Komula Ulf Ceder Marko Pusa Kim Viljanen
2007	Rosmalen	Netherlands	Martin Adams Steve Farmer Tony O'Shea John Walton
2009	Charlotte	Netherlands	Joey ten Berge Willy van de Wiel Frans Harmsen Daniel Brouwer
2011	Castlebar	England	Scott Waites Tony O'Shea Martin Atkins Martin Adams

Men's Singles Champions	Men's Pairs Champions	Women's Singles Champions
Dick van Dijk	Raymond van Barneveld & Vincent van der Voort	Clare Bywaters
Mark Webster	Mario Robbe & Joey ten Berge	Jan Robbins
Tony O'Shea	Anthony Fleet & Geoff Kime	Stacy Bromberg
Scott Waites	Martin Adams & Tony O'Shea	Trina Gulliver

CHAPTER 14:
THE OLD TIMERS

Many of the new players today simply call them the old timers without any thought to what these players have achieved. They could easily be known as the legends of the Game. Of course, where would the game be today without those old timers, who stepped up to the oche and captured those titles? In the beginning, there were the players like Joe Baltodonis, Bob Theide, Conrad Daniels, Nicky Virachkul, Helen Scheerbaum, Dan Pucillo, and a contributor to this book, George Silberzahn.

Jump to the '80s and players like Jerry Umberger, Rick Ney, John Kramer, and Tony Payne made the headlines. At that time, Southern California was the hotbed of some of the best dart players in the country. Back in those days, you could walk into a bar, see a group of some of those top players, and if you wanted to play with them, you put your name at the bottom of the list and waited your turn to play the board winner. If you won, you continued to play until you lost, and when you lost, you kept score for the next match. This was the type of atmosphere where these players were groomed. They would have to defend the board against some of the finest players on the American stage if they wanted to continue playing for the night.

Of course, we cannot forget the ladies, where in the '80s, Sandy Reitan dominated the ladies' game for many years, along with Kathy Karpowich and Kathy Maloney. Then to the '90s with Stacy Bromberg and Lori Verrier, who probably have more doubles titles than any other ladies' team ever to play, but a close second to that title might be the team of Sandy Reitan and Katy Casillas.

Conrad Daniels, who made it to the top eight of the 1978 Winmau World Masters, also won the US Open and the North American Open in 1975 and the 1972 Indoor League in England. Nicky Virachkul, while being a citizen of Thailand, was a US resident for many years and competed as part of the ADO. Nicky won the World Cup singles title in 1979, and made the semi-finals of the 1978 Embassy World Darts Championship where he finished third after winning a playoff against Stefan Lord. He also reached the semi-finals of the Winmau World Masters in 1980 and reached the quarterfinals of the Embassy on 1981, 1982, and 1984. In 1982, he won the North America Open. Then there was Rick Ney, who made it to the finals of the News of the World in 1985–86. Tony Payne, who reached the finals of the 1985 WDF World Cup Men's singles event and the semi-finals of the 1985 Winmau World Masters, as well as winning the 1990 Lucky Lights Challenge of Champions.

These were the players that laid the grass roots of darts down for the players of today. They were the champs who were revered and idolized by many—and this was appropriate, considering their achievements. While so many of them achieved great success here in the United States, with a multitude of titles too numerous to mention, it was their finishes in international play, as well as the biggest tournaments that the United States had to offer, that really set them above the rest. These were also the times where many of the top players in the world also made the trek over to America to play. Every year, players of all levels could make the trip to Las Vegas for the North American Open for their chance to watch and possibly play against such notable players as Eric Bristow, John Lowe, Jocky Wilson, Cliff Lazarenko, Bob Anderson, Bobby George, Leighton Rees, Stefan Lord, Keith Deller, Mike Gregory, Barry Twomlow, and so many more. Players in the 1980s wanted to put their money in for the chance to play such a player and to test their mettle against the best of the best. These types of players were the driving force in the growth of the game back then.

Sadly, it does seem that a lot of this spirit has gone away from the game as these old timers move on to retirement or to the great dart tournament in the sky. The players of today have missed the opportunities to sit with these old timers and listen to the stories and hear their thoughts on what it takes to play at the levels they once enjoyed. We go to tournaments today and are relative strangers to all the new players who do not know their history. It's funny to hear the youngsters after the match bemoaning the fact that they just got beat by some no name old guy, while that old guy is enjoying the fact that he is turning in his winning ticket yet again with the knowledge of where he has been and what he has done; he has no need to tell the youngsters his name. If they do not know their history, it is their loss both at the board and a missed opportunity to meet a darts legend.

CHAPTER 15:
THE INTERVIEWS

I do not doubt that there are many players that people would like to read interviews from and there are a lot of interviews out there. My friend Charis in Germany started her own website to cover the darts scene on a regular basis and she conducts many interviews with the top players of the PDC. There are many other players and websites covering many other players. We all know things about Phil Taylor, Adrian Lewis, John Part, and other World Champions. My choices for the interview section were specific for a reason. Obviously, Stacy Bromberg is a most prominent player who has earned more titles than any other female player in the history of darts in America. She has also achieved and will remain the one and only PDC Ladies World Champion. She has a rich history of experience to share with the public. My second choice was Paul Lim. Paul has a rich history in darts that spans more than thirty years and includes crossing over to soft-tip darts to become a World Champion there, as well. Paul also has a lot of experience and is truly an ambassador to the game.

My other choices for interviews were Bob Sinnaeve, Julie Nicoll-Jennings, and Sandy (Reitan) Green. And most will say these are "not exactly household names in the world of darts these days." However, their experience and history in the game spans many years. Not only were they great players, but they were also often considered the "poster children" of darts in the eras in which they played. Bob was one of the most recognized names in Canada in both local and international play and a book about darts in North America would not be complete without including him in some way. Julie Nicoll-Jennings was part of what everyone considered "the first family of darts" in America and worked many years as an ambassador for the game. Sandy (Reitan) Green became one of the first female American players to win two world titles. Her history in American darts spans many years and her titles are too numerous to mention.

I also felt that the players that played those many years ago and still play today would be able to offer some opinion and insight into what differences they see in the game today as opposed to the yesteryears when the game seemed much more popular. We all wonder at the differences and what may have caused what many old-time players see as the decline of darts in North America compared to how alive the game was in the 1980s.

Stacy Bromberg

Stacy Bromberg has been and continues to be the most dominating female player in America today. Her path to success is littered with titles at all different levels of play. Since this is a book about darts, it only seemed natural to include a short biography and interview with a player that has achieved such greatness in the game.

Stacy Bromberg is America's best-known and accomplished female dart competitor, hav-

Photo courtesy of *Bull's-Eye News*. Subscriptions and archived issues are available at www.bullseyenews.com

Bromberg featured on the cover of *Bull's-Eye News*

ing won hundreds of titles in America as well as abroad. For the last twenty-five-plus years, her interest in darts has spanned from the youth level to the more experienced veteran players. She has not only gained fame for her darting victories, but has also worked tirelessly raising funds for children's charities through her Score For Charity program. Participants in this endeavor throughout the years have included the likes of Phil Taylor, John Part, and Paul Lim. Stacy currently lives in

Las Vegas, Nevada, and continues to compete as well as raise funds "for the children" as much as possible, time and schedule permitting.

I first met Stacy in 1998 at a national playoff for the World Masters that was held in St. Louis, Missouri. This year was my return to the game after being off for twelve years, so it was safe to say, she did not know me and I did not know too much about her. She was winning everything, I still received the magazines, and so I knew her name. As luck would have it, we were also drawn into the same bracket and she was my last match. At the time, I did not know what that the outcome would determine whether I made the cutoff into the final top eight playoff bracket. I am sure everyone there wrote me off considering my opponent, but I had surprise and some really good darts on my side and was able to get two of the three legs against her and make the final top eight. We later went to dinner with mutual friends and have been great friends since. Ironically, I have yet to beat her in a singles match since then, but with a friend like her, I am always a winner, so the darts don't always matter. Stacy to not only a great player, but also a fantastic person away from the dartboard. She has undergone so many trials and tribulations that if others had to face the same, they would probably just quit and crawl under a rock. Stacy has faced this adversity time and time again and yet continues to be the great player that she is. It is this reason that I felt she should have a chapter in this book. Not as my friend, but as a tribute to her success both on and off the oche.

Stacy "The Wish Granter" Bromberg was born on July 27, 1956, in Los Angeles.

Stacy started playing darts in 1987. By 1991, she rose through the ranks to become the #1 US ranked lady dart player. She achieved this status sixteen years now, with thirteen of those years being consecutive. Stacy has been a National Team member for twelve years, is a twelve-time ADO 501 National Champion, is a four-time ADO Cricket National Champion, and holds the distinction of being the only player to win six consecutive titles, the last six years the tournament was held, at the North American Open in Las Vegas. Stacy also made it to the finals of the 1995 Winmau World Masters and won the 2009 WDF World Cup Singles Championship.

Stacy also has the distinction of being listed in the *Sports Illustrated Millennium Issue*, in which they announced the top fifty sports persons of the 1900s for each state. Stacy was ranked #32 in the State of Nevada, putting her in the top 66 percent of individuals in Nevada for the century according to *Sports Illustrated*. (#1 was baseball's Greg Maddox followed by tennis great Andre Agassi.)

Stacy uses her own 26-gram signature dart for steel-tip play and an identical dart in 18 grams for soft-tip competition. Her sponsor Laserdarts/Horizon Darts markets both. She also uses her signature teardrop flight marketed by L Style Global with champagne caps and the L Shafts complete her shaft and flight set-up.

Stacy has her own Score for Charity fundraising program where she donates money to the Make-A-Wish Foundation, Southern Nevada, which is why she has the nickname The Wish Granter. To date, Stacy, with help from Phil Taylor, John Part, Paul Lim, and darters all over the world, has raised $111,000 for the children.

Who got you started playing darts?

In January 1987, I was at a friend's bar in the city in which I grew up (Culver City, California) and was watching Monday Night Football. As luck would have it, a high school friend was playing in a dart league there that night. Turned out they were short a player so I was asked to fill in. I  didn't even know how the game was played but agreed when my "teammates" said they'd tell me at which segment I should throw. It was a singles league and I was to play best of five legs, all 501. I ended up winning 3-1 and was then informed that I'd have to buy an annual membership in the SCDA (Southern California Darts Association) for my win to count in their league standings. The next day, I went to the local dart store and paid for my membership. While there, I was talked into buying an inexpensive set of darts in case I was asked to fill in again. And, thus, my darts career was started.

You have won so many titles, and experienced so many different things in darts, what would you say would be the best experience?
This is a tough question since I have had so many great experiences throughout the years while traveling to tournaments. The places I've visited, the people I've met, and the things I've done are priceless. Whenever I'd travel to a tournament in another country, I've always tried to take in some extracurricular activities. For instance, when I attended World Cup in Australia in 1997, I took time to scuba dive the Great Barrier Reef and visit the rain forests and Ayers Rock. When I traveled to South Africa in

1999, I added a visit to Robbin Island and the Cape of Good Hope to my schedule. China's first visit included climbing the Great Wall and visiting Tiananmen Square, the Forbidden City, and Temple Of Heaven. All told there are just too many memorable experiences to mention all of them.

As far as darting experiences go, if I had to select only one, I suppose it would have to be when I won he PDC Desert Classic Ladies Singles title in Las Vegas in 2003. The PDC always provides the toughest level of competition as well as the best payouts. Playing in Las Vegas has always been a special treat for me since I live there, but this event was especially good for me since my parents, who have only been able to see me compete a few times, were able to watch my final against Deta Hedman live on Sky TV from the comfort of their living room. That was special to me!

What would you consider the worst experience?

It's hard to think of a really bad experience in darts because I love the game. I think the expression goes something like, "A bad day/night of darts beats the heck out of a great day at work!" As in any competitive sport, it certainly has its "ups and downs" but I think my "worst" experience came to me in the form of a "disappointment." This happened in August 2011 when I was told that I was declared "ineligible" to return to the WDF World Cup to try to defend my 2009 Singles Title. At this point, I had somehow landed in the middle of a big "political" dispute between the WDF (World Darts Federation) and the PDC (Professional Darts Corporation). The whole experience was just so wrong that mere words cannot accurately depict the situation, but I will try to recount the basics.

In July 2010, I went to England to participate in the first (only, and last!) PDC Ladies' World Championship. It was advertised as being the largest payout in Ladies' darts (£10,000/$15,000 to the winner and a two-year PDC Tour Card), so I had to give it a try. The competition started a couple of month's prior when I went to Cleveland, Ohio, to compete in the US Qualifier. After winning that, I flew to Barnsley, England to play the competition until there were only two ladies left. The two ladies turned out to be England's Tricia Wright and myself. We were told we were to return to Blackpool, England in July to play our final match on stage at the PDC Worlds! For Women's Darts, this was truly a huge step! The whole experience was pretty overwhelming. Darts is produced at a whole different level in England. Over there, darts isn't just a "pub game" but a serious way to make a very good living. Not to mention the "notoriety" that goes along with the status in the United Kingdom. It was crazy. . . . I went to a pub in Wolverhampton once and people wanted to buy me drinks and have their picture taken with me. One gentleman said, "May I get a pic with you? The wife will never believe I met you!" Same thing happened in London and Belfast, Ireland. Really a great way to meet people but, at the same time, I came to understand that being in the spotlight requires you to let others into your "space." It was uncharted territory for me. But when I'd return to the United States, no one knew me so it was back to life as

Photo by Lawrence Lustig/PDC

Bromberg at the PDC Ladies' World Championship.

usual. I can't even begin to know what it must feel like to be Phil Taylor or Eric Bristow . . . they can't get away from the attention. But, I digress . . . back to my story of disappointment.

After winning the PDC Worlds and earning a PDC Tour Card for 2011 and 2012, something very coveted in the darting world, I felt I had to take a shot (no pun!) at playing some PDC events. I traveled over to England in February 2011 and played in two UK Open qualifiers and two Players' Championships. It was an incredible experience and I loved it. Sadly, traveling to England to compete was not going to be a frequent thing for me since it takes about twenty-four hours of taxi, plane, train, and another taxi to get from Las Vegas to the competitive venues in England, and it is quite expensive. So I did not return to England that year.

Later in 2011, I was scheduled to compete in the WDF World Cup to be held in Oct in Dublin, Ireland. I was really looking forward to defending my singles title I'd won at World Cup 2009 in Charlotte, North Carolina. Only three US ladies have ever won the World Cup singles so this was quite an accomplishment for me! But, sadly, defending my title was not to be. It seems that the WDF had passed a "new rule" saying that all World Cup competitors had to "play the majority of their darting events with the WDF" to be eligible for World Cup participation. I knew that there was a lot of "tension" between the WDF and PDC, but I never thought it'd be taken to the level it was. After the United States had submitted their roster, with my name on it, it had been accepted and published on the WDF website. Later, the WDF called my "eligibility" into question because a few of the male players had participated in a majority of PDC events and they were comparing their competitive record(s) to mine. The way it unfolded, the WDF decided to exclude me—the defending champion—because they said I had competed in four PDC and four WDF events and that was not "a majority." I argued that it was also not a "minority" and explained that I had competed in dozens of WDF events throughout the year via my ADO competitions on weekends in the States but they (the WDF) said they would only count their four International events. I stuck to my argument that I was neither in the majority nor minority according to their rule's interpretation and that, as defending champion, I should be allowed to play, but the WDF would have none of it. They did offer me the opportunity to go to England a week before the World Cup and play another WDF event, at my own expense of course, to "qualify" in but since I felt I should not be disqualified to begin with, I politely declined. I always believed I would compete in darts all over the world for all organizations, but the first organization to demand that I select them over another organization in which to compete would be the first organization for which I would not play! That's what happened here so I did not get the opportunity to try to be the first US lady to repeat as World Cup singles champion. And the saddest part of this whole story is that after I spent weeks trying to reason with the WDF and they wouldn't budge in their "interpretation" of their new rule, this same Board met at the 2011 World Cup in Ireland—the one in which they'd used their "majority/minority" rule to rule me "ineligible." At this meeting, the Board CHANGED this very rule to read that a player must play "65 percent of their events in the WDF." The fact that they had to reword the very rule they used against me was so very wrong that it left me feeling as if I may not want to participate for them anytime again soon. This situation shows how individual "policies" can hurt sports organizations on an international level for neither logical nor constructive purpose at all.

You are the reigning, and now will always be, the PDC Ladies World Champion. How did it feel to win this title?

"Incredible, amazing, and fantastic" would all be a good start to describing this experience but that would just be scratching the surface. Nobody in the world hosts a darting event on the level of the PDC. This was the break for which women's darts had been waiting! An incredible venue at the Winter Garden in Blackpool, England . . . the largest purse ever offered to the winner . . . and International TV coverage! In fact, it was even broadcast in 3-D for those who had 3-D televisions.

It was July 2010 when I returned to England to play the PDC World final and I was really looking forward to it. I'd put in more time than usual practicing and I felt pretty good going over. At this point, my toughest decision had already been made. I had selected my PDC "Walk On" song . . . Tom Petty's "American Girl." I've always liked this song, so I thought it fitting that from this point forward, I would always fondly think back on this World Championship whenever I hear it.

Photo by Lawrence Lustig/PDC

Prior to the World's, we were at the first UK competition in June in Barnsley, England, the event organizer, Tommy Cox, told us straight-away that this was NOT intended to be a "one and done" event. Naturally, all would ultimately depend on the audience's and the sponsors' reaction to the event and decisions for any further competitions for the ladies' events would be made accordingly.

Later, at the last minute, the scheduling for the ladies finals was changed. We were originally scheduled to play immediately prior to the men's final on the last Sunday of the tournament. For whatever reason, our final was changed to being played after the men's final. This minor move would have a huge impact on my own personal take of the future of the PDC Ladies' darts.

The reason this schedule change affected the audience's response was that it lost a lot of the live viewing audience in the venue since they came primarily to watch the Men's final and many were actually getting up and to leave as Trish and I were waiting for our "cue" to walk out to the stage. Had we played first, perhaps many spectators might have seen our match and realized that watching women's darts can be exciting too! But this lack of interest by the audience told me that there probably wasn't going to be another PDC Ladies' Worlds. So while I was on "Cloud Nine" as I prepared to walk out to the finals stage, in the back of my mind I was thinking, "These people leaving is definitely NOT a good sign for the future of ladies' darts."

As things turned out, I was right. We were not given a specific reason for the discontinuation of the Ladies' Worlds . . . just that it had "been scrapped due to lack of participation by the women." Truth be told, many top lady UK and European players were afraid of jeopardizing their standing with the British Darts Organization (BDO) and World Dart Federation, so they refused to even try to qualify into the PDC's event. Turns out that the lady players in the UK and Europe that did play had been given a "pass" by the BDO/WDF and suffered no repercussions.

But I made the best of it, played my heart out, and won in a very tightly contested match

Bromberg focusing on a winning throw.

Photo by Lawrence Lustig/PDC

winning 6-5 in a best of 11-leg format. And so it goes . . . one of the best darting experiences in which I was ever to compete, did in fact, turn out to be a "one and done" experience. But I am not sorry in the least for playing in it. The stage, the venue, the professionalism with which the PDC presents their tour events was one of my best darting experiences. I was even honored with a chorus of "Walking In A Bromberg Wonderland" by the audience, a song usually reserved for the one and only Phil Taylor. And finally, the fans that attend these events are the best! Their enthusiasm overflows during the match. It was definitely an experience I will never forget and I will always be grateful to the PDC for allowing me the one-time opportunity to be a part of this darts history. I suppose I'll always be the PDC Ladies' World Champion . . . at least until there is another one held. But I wouldn't hold my breath for that to happen.

Is there a title that has eluded you? If so, what would that title be?
For the most part, I am content with my tournament performance over the past twenty-five years. I have won many events, both on a national level and an international level. I would have loved try to defend my World Cup singles title but that was not to be. So, in the alternative, I'd like to win an Open PDC event but I believe that door is now closed for me. I have won a few Men's/Open events in the United States, but that is just not at the same level of play that is in the PDC.

The way things seem be going I now am turning more of my attention to soft-tip (electronic) darts. This is huge in Asia and, I believe, will be an even greater force in US darts in the future. I would like to, someday, win a DARTSLIVE stage event since these are also "Open" events where the men and women compete against each other in singles matches. To me, therein lies the real challenge!

What do you feel is the biggest differences in tournaments or the darting experiences of yesterday compared today?

The biggest difference(s) between tournaments of "yesteryear" and "today," in my opinion, are both social and financial.

Socially, years ago, many people went to tournaments to touch base with friends not seen frequently and/or to simply see friends in a somewhat social setting. This has changed with the "Internet Boom" to a great degree. Now people simply "Twitter" or "Facebook" each other to keep in touch on a minute-by-minute basis. Times change so methods of communication change.

An even greater change has resulted through a "financial" means in several ways. Costs, such as airfares and hotels, have skyrocketed making travel for the "recreational" tournament player nearly impossible. Even to drive to a tournament has become more costly in that fuel prices have also surged! Combine these facts with the reality that, since late 2007, when the US recession set in, many corporate sponsors cannot continue to financially support tournaments. This, as well as the limited finances of most dart players makes traveling to tournaments on a regular basis very difficult today.

I, personally, am most baffled by airfare costs. A round trip airfare from Las Vegas to the US east coast may cost as much as $600, while a round trip ticket from Las Vegas to Shanghai may be found for less than $900! So, in the modern era, travel becomes a huge issue when considering which tournaments to attend.

Paul Lim

Paul Lim Leong Hwa was born on January 25th, 1954 and his darting nickname is "The Singapore Slinger." Paul is a former military policeman and chef. He served his National Service in the Singapore army between the ages of eighteen and twenty-one. He came to Britain for a course in cookery, studying at Battersea and Westminster Colleges in London and became a chef at the Chelsea Hotel in Knightsbridge. It was while he was in England studying that he was introduced to the game of darts. A few of the chefs were sharing an apartment, and they would go down to the local pub for a drink or two, and since he was not much of a drinker, he would throw some darts while they were there.

Paul Lim

Paul has been playing darts since 1976 and credits his actual start in the game to when he used to play in a pub called the Robin Hood, near Gunnersbury Station in London, Chiswick. It was not a league, but just a weekly knockout tournament. Players would buy in for 50 pence and the winner would get a bottle of whiskey, which gave him a lot to have in stock for Christmas and New Years.

Paul Lim, nicknamed the Singapore Slinger, will forever be remembered for being the first player to hit a perfect nine-dart finish during the Embassy World Professional Darts Championship in 1990. It remained the only televised nine-dart game to have been achieved in either version of the world championships until 2009. The bonus prize of £52,000 was more than eventual tournament winner Phil Taylor claimed for becoming world champion. Paul is more well-known nowadays as the best soft-tip player in the world, even having a dart game programmed with his voice called "out on a Lim."

Paul has been married to his wife Janet for years and they have two sons, Christopher and Michael, who are both actively involved in the soft-tip darts game as promoters and players. Paul is currently making his temporary home in Hong Kong (China), as a consultant and promoter for the newly-formed DARTSLIVE International. Paul's role with the company is to promote and expand worldwide the technology of DARTSLIVE's game and system. While playing the role as consultant, he is also able to do exhibition and teaching and participate in tournaments where and when available. Currently, though based in Hong Kong (China), he travels frequently to new territories worldwide.

Paul uses his own darts set-up for steel-tip and soft-tip, Paul Lim Signature Darts from DMC, along with L-Style tear drop Paul Lim flights and Carbon shafts.

We asked Paul a few questions about some highlights of his career and what it felt like for him to be a part of those moments.

What do you feel was the highest achievement of your darting career?
The nine-dart perfect game in the Embassy Professional. That record will forever be there for me. (No more Embassy professional tournament.)

Is there a title out there you wish you had won?
A PDC World Championship

How do you get yourself ready or prepared for competition?
A lot of people might disagree, but I think you have to get yourself

Paul Lim and his wife, Janet

psyched up to compete. It is important for me to really get involved in the match.

Do spectators affect your play or bother you?

I like spectators! I think that makes the difference between players. Spectators can really boost your level of play, whether they are rooting for or against you. It is an unconscious reaction, but they definitely make a difference and I like having them there.

Is having a specific dart important to you, or can you throw as well with any dart?

Well, I can throw with almost any dart, but when you ask a professional sports person to perform at their best, they will do so when they use their own specific tools of the trade. To throw well consistently, a player must throw their specific dart.

You have traveled the world as a darts player and have played competitors from all parts of the world. What are some of the differences between the players of different countries?

There is a real difference in attitude from one country to another. Most dart players from other countries have a more casual attitude. They are not so serious. I have been in one country and the players there were not anywhere near as serious as the players in the United States. The players in the States really do want to win, whereas, in this other country, winning was as important, but the players were much less serious. I think, as other countries get more involved in international competition, their player's attitudes will change to a more serious nature.

You are now listed in the Guinness Book of World records for your nine-dart game. Can you describe to everyone reading what that experience was like?

Lim taking aim.

Photo courtesy of ©DARTSLIVE Co. Ltd.

It still gives me goosebumps when I think of it or watch it. It is at that moment I felt everything seemed to go the right way and in slow motion . . . a sensational feeling of accomplishment.

You are actively involved in darts in a new way. Can you tell us more about your role with DARTSLIVE and what you hope to achieve with it?
I have been in the soft-tip industry for quite a few years. I was with a dart manufacturer named Medalist and worked for them on promotions and marketing internationally for quite a few years. I was very involved in Asia, as the company was based out of Thailand. And my popularity grew fast in the Asian countries. By then, I was not playing much steel-tip darts, as I was more involved with soft-tip darts as a job. But as of two years ago in 2010, I was offered a position as Consultant to Steve Ngu,

the CEO of DARTSLIVE INT. The offer was more than satisfactory, because I am able to play darts again competitively, while I am working as a consultant and doing promotions for DARTSLIVE. Since then, I have won many competitions. So it has been a busy year and a half winning most of the tournaments I go to. It is really because of the opportunities given to me by

Photo courtesy of *Bull's-Eye News*. Subscriptions and archived issues are available at www.bullseyenews.com

Lim on the cover of *Bull's-Eye News*.

DARTSLIVE'S CEO Steve Ngu, and for encouraging me and supporting me.

**You recently won the first DARTSLIVE World event. Can you share
how that experience felt with the readers here?**

Not comparing it with steel-tip darts, this World Grand Final is in many
ways as prestigious as any steel-tip major Championship. The popularity of the soft-tip game has grown so much in the last five years, and
the World Grand Final was the biggest as it comes and it was live on U

Photo courtesy of ©DARTSLIVE Co. Ltd

Stream. So many people watched it. I am glad that after all these years of
dedication and involvement in promoting the sport, I can still at this age,
after thirty-six years of playing the game, still compete and be able to win
with the same devotion, desire, and love for the sport of darts. So there is
still plenty of hope out there for those who play in the same decade as me
. . . come on.

Recently, DARTSLIVE and the Professional Darts Corporation (PDC) have entered into a strategic relationship to unite the steel-tip and soft-tip darting industry. How do think this will help the progression of darts in the world?

This merge will definitely help the progression of darts in the world. First of all, there is no doubt at all in figures, the number of new players that has started to actually play darts is through the soft-tip industry for various reasons. Technology, simplicity, and awareness. In Asia especially, the growth of soft-tip new players has been increasing in such a fast rate that eventually it overflows onto the steel-tip sector. It definitely benefited the steel-tip association with more members and more league plays. And we all know that in any organization or association, members in numbers are the key, which shows the success of such. Thus on the other hand, the PDC needs bigger numbers to watch, participate and that leads to more sponsorship for televised programs. Obviously, there is a difference of the game itself . . . but there is no difference to the players playing the game. A soft-tip player can walk up to a steel-tip board and throw his or her darts, play a game of 501 or Cricket, and so does a steel-tip player doing the same. There is a difference in concept, but no difference in theory. Towards the end, it is all about DART Players. All about the numbers, watching, playing, buying accessories, spreading the game of darts, and growing the popularity of this game or sport. Therefore, I am certain that this merger will enhance the popularity, awareness to public, and finally the addition of more new members to our sport.

As a result of this partnership, you have now been given the opportunity to compete at the next PDC World Championships. Given that earlier in the interview before this partnership took place, you indicated that your

one regret was not winning a PDC World Championship. How does it feel to once again be given another opportunity to achieve this goal? As you and all know since working for a soft-tip company, trying to make a living, I have somehow stopped competing in the steel-tip circuit, whether in United States or PDC. I have always been in contact with the PDC news, of what is happening and who has been winning what, and who are the new up and coming young stars, and so forth. I still practice and throw steel-tip almost everyday, as wherever I moved to, the first thing was to hang a steel-tip board up. I love this game. During the last two years, I am very fortunate to have more opportunities in playing soft-tip tournaments and practice. I have to thank DARTSLIVE INTERNATIONAL CEO Mr. Steve Ngu for encouraging me and giving me all the support. At the back of my mind, all the time, is hope I have the opportunity to play on the big stage again, the PDC World Championship. I had a chance two years ago, trying to qualify through the two tournaments PDC sanctioned in United States and Canada. I did really well on the US tournament, and I bought my ticket for the Canadian one. At that time I was working for Medalist and due to work load, I wasn't able to go to the Canada tournament, and after which, I was told I missed the cut by a measly 5 pounds . . . thus giving Gary Mawson the spot. Well, now WHAT A SURPRISE! I am actually feeling like a kid given a new toy. I am all excited, been watching the matches on the Grand Slam of Darts . . . analyzing, absorbing the atmosphere and the big stage. I know it is not going to be easy . . . been there (long ago) and all I know is I have the capability, the experience, and the love of this game . . . but most of all, I have the heart. I just am so blessed with this opportunity and I just want to do my best. Could be my last chance . . . but who cares? I AM GOING TO THE DANCE ON THE BIG STAGE.

Lim at the IDF World Cup in Shanghai, China

Paul recently competed in Shanghai, China and once again had the opportunity to represent his home country of Singapore in the event and had this to say about the experience:

It's a great feeling to be carrying the flag of the country you represent, and playing a sport that you love and with the friends you have known for years. It has been such a long time. Playing in the IDF World Cup in Shanghai, China with Harith Lim, Kelvin Yap, and Shin was my honor. In Shanghai, there were twenty-three countries represented. But unfortunately, only eighteen countries were able to take part in the Team Cup event due to some countries not having enough team members. I believe, in time to come, this event will grow to be one of the biggest World Cup events with many more countries participating. Regardless of all differences, I hope players will be able to represent their country without any restriction, because it is the ultimate, to represent your country. I want to congratulate Russia for winning the Cup in 2012. I want to also congratulate Hong Kong (China) for getting the silver and Canada for the bronze. Great darts, great representation, great competition and great sportsman-ship. We all should be proud to be part of the IDF. Being able to meet players from all over the world, sharing the same interest and loving the same game, it is an honor and our privilege. For Singapore, all I can say is we tried our best. We lost to Slovenia in the knockout round. There will always be another time, till we all meet again and let our arrows fly. Good Darts.

Wins:

- World Masters: Last sixteen in 1981, 1985, 1987, and 1988
- World Championship: Last sixteen in 2001
- World Matchplay: Quarter finals in 1995
- World Grand Prix: Last sixteen in 1998
- Desert Classic: Last thirty-two in 2004
- Australian Grand Masters Champion: 1983
- five-time Singapore Open Champion
- five-time Malaysian Open Champion
- three-time Asia-Pacific Cup Singles Champion, 1980, 1984, 1986
- Eight-time Medalist (Soft-Tip) Grand Master Singles Champion
- First player to achieve a nine-dart finish at a World Championships, 1990
- The World Grand Final 2011. Hong Kong (China)
- DMC CLASSIC KOBE JAPAN 2011, 2012
- IDF SHANGHAI PRO SINGLES 2011
- MACAU OPEN PRO SINGLES 2011

- USA OPEN WORLD PAIRS 2012
- SINGAPORE CHAMPI-ONSHIP 2012

Julie Nicoll-Jennings

While darts had been popular well before the 1970s, it did not seem to solidify into the growth spurt it would experience until the mid '70s with the creation of the American Darts Organization, the governing body for darts in America that is still in existence today. Back then, there was West Coast darts and East Coast darts and it was pretty infrequent when players from both sides of the United States would get together to play at a larger event in different locations across the country.

Julie Nicoll-Jennings on the cover of *Bull's-Eye News*.

Julie Nicoll-Jennings was born in Springfield, Massachusetts, in 1958. Her husband of twelve years and she reside in the town of Wilmington, Ohio, a small farming community with a lot of country charm. Her two daughters, Jessica and Jennifer, also reside in Wilmington with their husbands and her four grandchildren, Myla, Sophie, Zoe, and Lilly.

When she is not playing darts, her daughter Jessica and she have a small home décor business that specializes in all sorts of handmade items, as well as paintings, sculptures, and nineteenth-century penny rugs.

As Julie remembers, "I started playing darts at the age of fourteen with my entire family, Bill Sr., Ellie, Bill Jr., Greg, and Timmy. My family was

considered the "First Family of Darts" and my brothers and I were also the first youth players in the United States. To our benefit, at that time, there were no youth events and we ended up playing against the adult players, which brought our game level up considerably."

You won the ladies singles of what at the time was the biggest tournament in the United States. How did that feel?

One of the biggest tournament wins for me was in 1975 when I won the North American Open Ladies Singles 301 at the Disneyland Hotel in Anaheim, California. There were 190 ladies who played that year and I cannot begin to explain how that felt for me at the age of seventeen to have accomplished such an amazing title. What people forget is that we didn't have a large amount of events at tournaments compared to the number of events we currently have. I won $500 for first place and I remember my father saying . . . "Here you go Jul, take this $ 100 and spend it however you want." I went and spent $50 on a new pair of jeans (which at that time was a lot of money!) and then took the rest of the money and gave it back to my dad to cover our expenses.

It didn't really sink in that I had won such a prestigious tournament, until a couple of months later when our local paper did an article about my win. My friends were so proud of me and the school had me bring in my trophy and display it in the school trophy case, as well as put a picture in the school yearbook that year. The very best thing about it all was that the school Phys Ed department added darts to the school's curriculum.

You played for a number of years competitively, what was your most enjoyable experience?

The best moment of my career was watching my daughter Jessica, a third-generation American dart player, play in the youth finals of the $100,000 Golden Harvest Tournament in Saskatchewan, Canada. The amount of emotions I was feeling was overwhelming and I can only imagine what my father felt when he watched me win the North American.

If there was one title out there that you wanted to win, what was it? Why?

I would have to say the US Open, the reason would go back to January of 1976, at that time the US Open was sponsored by Black & White Scotch and I was not of legal age to promote alcohol in the United States if I were to win. My father felt that it was necessary to contact the president of this company and fight for the opportunity to compete even though I was only seventeen years old and had won the last three major tournaments in a row, they felt that my chances of winning were very high and they were not willing to take that chance.

What dart are you currently using and what did you use when you started?

I use a custom 95 percent tungsten barrel; the weight is 32 grams with no knurl and no grooves. Currently I use a "Rob Spears" long thin point, in previous years I have used a fixed point, hammerhead and graphite point. I have used this barrel since 1973 and am very comfortable with this barrel and will continue to play with this style until I throw a perfect dart every time. I think that every time you change your equipment, you lose confidence in your darts and that is extra worry that you do not need to contend with.

Is there anything else that you would like to add, that you feel is important for people to know?

I was not just a dart player, I worked for six different dart companies throughout my career and my primary job with each company was

sales, marketing, and promotion and product development. We displayed our full product line at The Sporting Goods Manufacturing Association Trade Show every year; it is the largest sporting goods trade show in the world. My job was to demonstrate and educate how to play the sport of darts. Many times I had to make decisions whether to attend the trade show or compete in a major dart tournament, I chose to educate

A promotional shot from Julie's early career

and promote the sport of darts instead of furthering my competitive career in darts.

My career had not gone uninterrupted over the last four decades, starting with the touring I did with my family for darts as well as television and radio shows. Then there is my family and my work career, as well. I have and always will have a tremendous amount of passion for the sport of darts as well as the people I have met along my journey. If I were to say anything to the up and coming darters of America it would be play as much as you can and always play better darts players than yourself, learn you're out shots and strategies.

What do you feel is the biggest differences in tournaments or the darting experiences of yesterday?

One of the biggest changes is that more people understand the sport compared to the 1970s. I believe we need to thank the electronic machine age for the growth spurt we had through the '80s and '90s. The electronic machine did what the steel-tip dartboard could not do, by bringing the people to the machine with its lights and sounds. It educated the people by explaining the game and assisting with the mathematics. The original steel-tip dart board had round wires and because of the round wires there was not as much room in the doubles and triples scoring area as today's banded dart boards that have a thin band to replace the round wires, which prevents interference in hitting the target and less bounce outs. Another large factor is the distance from the board in the '70s was 8 feet whereas today it is 7' 9¼", due to the formation of the World Dart Federation, it made the throwing distance throughout the world the same. Due to the improvement of equipment and the amount of growth in our sport, the number of better players has increased. In the '70s we had to educate and promote by word of mouth to gain membership in the sport.

Nowadays you can find a dart tournament on any given weekend, throughout the '70s we were lucky to have one every few months. In the '70s, there were fewer events and the payouts were larger due to this reason. Now we have MORE events and that prize money is the same, but spread out over the number of events. So, when you win a singles, you are in fact only winning a third of what you would have won in the '70s. Now you need to win three events to make the same amount you would have made in one event in the '70s. The level of appearance in the dart player has also changed; in the '70s, basically anything worn was fine, in the '90s, it went to a more business casual in order to attract television-viewing time. Now some tournaments have instituted a dress code and if it is not followed you are not permitted to play.

Wins:
- St Pat's Open - San Diego, California
- Cincinnati Spring Fling - Cincinnati, Ohio
- Queen City Open - Cincinnati, Ohio
- Blueberry Hill - St. Louis, Missouri
- Virginia Beach Classic - Virginia Beach, Virginia
- Virginia Beach Muscular Dystrophy Tournament - Virginia Beach, Virginia
- Ray Chesney Pennsylvania Open - Philadelphia, Pennsylvania
- Inductee into the National Dart Hall of Fame

- USA Dart Classic - Stanford, Connecticut

Sandy (Reitan) Green

Sandy Green

Sandy was born in Duluth, Minnesota, and now resides in Anaheim, California, with her husband, Andy. Sandy began playing darts in 1979 and credits her start in darts to Stan Haske, Carl Pedersen, and Pacer Darts. Sandy retired from competitive darts in 1993. When Sandy was competing full time, she used her 26-gram signature darts from Unicorn.

Sandy's career in darts has spanned for more than thirty years. We asked her of all of those years of competing, what would she say was the most important title that she ever won? "There are two, the World Cup, because of it being the first Ladies' World Cup event and also because the English pretty much ruled the dart world at the time, so it felt pretty special. The Winmau World Masters was also very special, as it is one of the premier tournaments for women."

Green on the cover of *Bull's-Eye News.*

Photo courtesy of *Bull's-Eye News.* Subscriptions and archived issues are available at www.bullseyenews.com

In 1984, Sandy was ranked at the World Dart Federation's #1 ranked female player in the world. When asked how she felt about it, she said she felt super, but still felt like herself. She didn't feel that the title had changed her any, but she did feel very fortunate.

Photo courtesy of *Bull's-Eye News*. Subscriptions and archived issues are available at www.bullseyenews.com)

What many people also didn't know about Sandy was that she was the official spokesperson for the Lucky Strike Dart Series in the 1980s and appeared on several news and talk shows prior to Lucky Strike Series events in various cities. One such appearance was for the morning show, *Regis & Kathy Lee.*

What is the one title that meant the most to you both professionally and personally?

"The World Darts Grand Prix in Japan. It was an Invitational event with the top 16 men and top 8 women in the world invited to play against the top 16 Japanese men and the top 8 Japanese women. I was presented with a beautiful kimono during the award ceremony. There was a banquet that evening and my very special Japanese friends Eri and Aoi were kind enough to dress me in my kimono, I even ended up on stage as part of the entertainment, beating the drums! I felt pretty much like a princess in a fairytale ending of a most wonderful experience in Japan."

For many years, you were probably the most popular ladies player in America, as well as being one of the best female players to ever play the game. Can you tell us what made you decide to pursue being a touring

player at a level that most people would consider a professional?

"It actually wasn't something I decided to pursue. I really enjoyed playing for fun on weekends at Pacer Darts. I joined a league with Stan and Tuffy (Carl) and then started playing local tournaments and started winning and that turned into more playing and more travelling."

Can you tell us what it was like to travel weekend after weekend from tournament to tournament to compete?

"It was a challenge at times, but also very rewarding. After a long weekend of play and hours travelling, Andy and I still had full time jobs and two young kids at home. One of the many benefits is the friends we've made and being able to catch up with them from time to time."

What advice would you offer to other lady players that would like to become professional players?

"I think the best advice that I could offer would be is to always keep a positive attitude. It seems that there are a lot of female players out there that just throw their darts without even thinking about it."

Can you tell us what the tournaments were like in those days?

"I believe there was much more camaraderie between players back then than now. We were friendlier and more supportive of each other; it seems much more cutthroat when I watch players now."

How do you rate the top US players against the world?

"England is where more of the top shooters are, and in general, they take darts much more seriously in England than darters here in the United States. One of the problems the United States has is that most of the top men shooters have to work as well as play darts. For women, the seriousness is much more evident in England than the United States. The women still work at other jobs, as most do in the United States, and they are fortunate to get away to play in tournaments. The women's darts is very much different from the men's darts in England, too. There is little money in women's darts in England. I think the US top players definitely have the potential to make a mark in the world standing; it's just a matter of time. There are many more opportunities today for players to earn world-ranking points than ever before."

What do you feel is needed for the growth of the game in America today?

"Sponsorship, there seem to be more dart companies getting involved, which is great for the players. I still believe one of darts biggest challenges is a viewer not understanding the scoring, that it isn't all about shooting at the bull. That can be a challenge in keeping their interest."

Wins:

- 1991 World Masters Ladies Singles Champion
- 1983 World Cup Ladies Singles Champion

Bob Sinnaeve

- 5-time ADO #1 Ranked Ladies Player
- 1984 WDF Women's World #1 Ranked Ladies Player

Bob Sinnaeve

Robert "Bob" Sinnaeve was born on October 10, 1949, in Tillsonburg Ontario and now resides in Langton, Ontario, with his wife Judy, and has three children: Lisa, Michelle, and Adam, who are all in their thirties, as well as three grandchildren: Samantha, Cameron, and Keira.

Bob began playing darts in 1973 as an alternative to bowling, as he felt the darts circuit would give him more time to spend with his wife Little did he know, the opposite would happen with all the travel. He first appeared at the World Masters in 1979 and made his World Professional Darts Championship debut in 1981. Sinnaeve appeared at the World Championship on eleven occasions and his last appearance at the World Championship came in 1992. Sinnaeve once managed to reach number four in the world rankings, and his best performance in a major tournament was reaching the final of the Winmau World Masters in 1986—an event in which he competed each year between 1979 and 1991. Internationally, he was part of the Canadian WDF World Cup winning team of 1989—the only time they have taken the team event title. Sinnaeve finished as runner-up in the 1986 Butlins Grand Masters losing to Mike Gregory, the 1987 World Cup Singles, and the 1988 MFI World Matchplay, victim to Eric Bristow

Bob Sinnaeve defeated Paul Lim in the OS 501 finals. Together Bob and Paul won the OD Cricket event.

both times. He was also runner-up to John Lowe in the Canadian Open in 1986. He reached the semi-finals of this event in 1990 and further semi-final places in the 1987 Denmark Open and 1988 North American Open.

He received recognition as one of Canada's greatest ever players, winning a record five national titles (1979, 1983, 1986, 1987, and 1991)—a record that stood until John Part equalled it in 2007. He also won the Ontario Singles five times (1978, 1980, 1983, 1984, and 1987) and four All-Canada Cup singles titles (1985, 1986, 1987, and 1988). Sinnaeve was Canada's number one ranked player between 1981 and 1992.

He retired from competitive darts in 1992 and was inducted into the Canadian Darts Hall of Fame in 2002.

Recently, Bob has returned to the game playing many events in America and has met with much success. Bob currently uses 26-gram Laserdart Phantom, which is a dart he designed almost thirty years ago, but is in process of waiting for his Signature Darts from Monster Barrel Designs. His set-up is completed with his Signature Champagne teardrop shaped L-Style flights and L-Style Laro shafts.

In 2012 Bob received a Lifetime Membership into the National Darts Federation of Canada. He was also honored at Thunder Bay on June 14, 2012 with a Distinguished Service Award for his contribution to the sport of darts in Canada; he is only the fourth person to receive this in the thirty-five-year history of the NDFC.

Because Bob has been a consistent participant for many years in Canada and in America, as well, we took the time to ask Bob a few questions about darts and what some of his accomplishments meant to him.

Bob does not give credit to any particular win as his most significant title, and found the question difficult to answer, as he felt that he achieved great personal satisfaction by reaching the finals of many international events, which he feels is quite an accomplishment in itself because he played darts part time while running a business. He does state thought that obviously winning would have been a lot sweeter.

Bob says that his five Canadian titles mean the most to him personally. Each one had meant something at different points in his life, and he feels that winning in your own home country is the hardest title to achieve. He credits the first Canadian National title as the most overwhelming, knowing that he would be representing his country overseas at an international event where the best players in the world would be gathered to play. Bob says that he was the guy

Photo by David Holmes

that no one remembered in high school, who was from a small village and was very unassuming.

Bob says that he took great pride in wearing his Canadian shirt while representing his country in international events, as it was an opportunity that very few people are able to experience. There was a lot of sacrifice involved in competing at this level, as there was no money earned while income was being lost while away competing; however, Bob says that regardless of this, representing Canada is something that he will never regret.

Bob has had the opportunity to compete in many events in Canada and in America, so we asked him what he felt was the biggest difference between the events in the two countries?

The biggest difference is the format that is used. In Canada, we have only maybe four events for a weekend and use the round robin format extensively usually playing best of five. The transition of the events in the Unites States from the 1980s until now has changed with the prize structure, the number of events, which I feel is too many, and the short, knockout format with a minimum amount of games played, which really does not create players who can compete internationally in the longer formatted events.

You played a lot of national and international events in and around the 1980s. How do you feel that darts compares from then to now in Canada?

In fairness, I stepped away from darts from 1992 until late 2008, but did still follow the progress. Darts in Canada has declined in many areas, but some of the provinces still have a strong following. I do believe the longer format and round robins give a truer picture of the top players because consistency will usually win out. We have produced some strong players on the international scene because of it."

How do you feel that darts compares from then to now in America?
The biggest change is the prize structure and number of events resulting in the reduction in the number of players attending tournaments. There seems to be fewer top competitors created because of the costs associated. Sponsorship for darts is just starting to come back with the arrival of overseas companies injecting a much needed revival of interest in the sport.

How do you feel that darts compares from then to internationally?
This is where the biggest change has happened with promoters coming in and presenting it in a professional and entertaining manner. It is run as a business and has generated great public following in England and Europe. It has also created stars.

What do you feel is needed for the growth of the game in Canada and in America?
I recently formed the North America Professional Darts Alliance or NAPDA. It is hoped that by working with the existing organizations in Canada and America we can set up a structure to provide a professional tour for the interested top players to compete thereby creating players in North America that can compete on the world stage. We work

with existing tournaments to have a singles event offering better prize money and longer formats, something many players are asking for.

You recently received a Lifetime Membership into the National Darts Federation of Canada for your success in darts, and no doubt as an ambassador to the game. How did you feel about this experience?

It is always an honor to be recognized by your peers and country. It amazes me how many people still remember me and have congratulated me on my accomplishments over the years. I have heard many times especially recently how I have influenced players that watched me play "when they were young" and I am honored to think I in some way have helped them. I get numerous requests for practice routines and ways to improve their games, which is something I really enjoy talking about. I guess I will always have darts in my blood."

CHAPTER 16:
ADVICE FROM THE PROS

Because we started playing this game so many years ago, we have seen so many changes in the game and have so many fond memories of the people and players from yesterday and today. We have seen players come go, but what always remains is the camaraderie between the players regardless of how long they have been playing or if they are beginners. Everyone always has a story to share or a tale to tell. Some can be everyday players with new experiences and some can be legends of the game that are sharing stories. But one main thing that they have in common is that they are always ready with words of advice to help other players become better players. So with that, I wanted to find out what some of the most important things that top players would like to share with newer players today, so I took the time to ask some of the top players in the North America to provide the best advice they would want to give a new player. They covered many aspects of the game in their responses, however, the main goal was to help new players learn how to get better and to help existing players take that next step in their game. Here are some of the responses:

Photo by David Holmes

Stacy Bromberg

"Don't take yourself too seriously and enjoy the game and experiences that come along with it. Life is short . . . live for the day That's MY advice, along with when the last dart ends a game, whether it is your dart or your opponent's, accept it and let it go! This is easer said than done, but if you learn something from every match you lose, then it is not a complete loss. Use it to benefit yourself in the future."

Photo by David Holmes

Darin Young

"My advice to playing well and improving your game would be a couple of things. First, when practicing, have goals. This will prevent you from not concentrating 100 percent. If you do not try your best, you gain nothing from your practice session. It can be a negative effect where you may pick up a bad habit and cause poor play. Also, try to play the best players possible, there is no sense in 'sandbagging' to stay in a lower division. Always push yourself to improve and strive to reach high goals that you set for yourself. Self-satisfaction leads to confidence, which leads to overall success!"

Photo by David Holmes

Cali West

"One thing to remember about the game of darts is that everyone was a beginner at one time. Everyone has had tough losses to deal with and even the great players have lost a lot of times, before they started winning. Don't be discouraged by a loss. Instead, learn from it. That will make you a better player. I have always analyzed my losses, and from that, set up practice routines around the weakness I feel caused my loss. Sometimes it would be as simple as practicing my doubles. Other times, it would be working on a specific range of out shots. You may even find it's a weakness that has to be addressed by playing other people, not by solitary practice. Being able to be your own coach and critic will help you identify and tackle those weaknesses and make you a tougher opponent. Keep in mind that even when you practice every night, you may not always get the immediate results you are looking for. Again, don't be discouraged. It takes months, even years to make huge strides in your game. Just because you practice for an hour a night for three weeks, doesn't mean you will be throwing for a first place trophy in week four! However, it may mean getting a round or two further at the next tournament. This game can be very rewarding if you can dedicate yourself to practicing, as well as traveling. But I will warn you this is an addicting sport! It seemed to me, whether I did really well or really bad at a tournament, almost before I even got out the door of the hall, I would be thinking to myself . . . 'Where's the next one?'"

Photo by David Holmes

Chris White

Chris began playing darts with his family, and when he was around six years old, his family would have their own in-house league where they would meet with their friends once a week to play. By the time he was eight years old, Chris was playing quite a bit. When Chris was ten years old, he started playing in the local youth darts league in Ontario.

Chris believes that dart players are made, not born, and that you have a little bit of natural talent, but after that, it's all just hard work. When you are just starting out; first, you want to make sure that you have decent form, and after that, it is how much are you willing to work at it? You really have to dedicate yourself and put in that time. Play as many great players as you can, play better players than you and play as much as you can. Play as many local tournaments as you can and keep moving your way up to the national level. But definitely lock yourself in the basement or garage, wherever your board is and put in, as much time as you can, three to five hours a day is definitely needed to achieve any level of success.

When it comes to what darts to choose, Chris suggests that you go with whatever works best for you. It is a trial and error process to find a set-up that feels comfortable, but once you do, stick to it and don't give up on it until you have given the set-up enough time for you to know whether it is working for you or not.

Jeff Smith

"When a new player has been introduced into the game, he/she can easily be intimidated by many things. There is much to learn from start to finish. Math, technique, dart etiquette, strategy, and most of all confidence. When I started as a youth player, I wasn't allowed to compete until I proved myself with my breakdowns on my finishing (my grandfather's rule). Turns out it was one of the best lessons he could have taught me, as I went on to win the Provincial every year after. So how did I accomplish this so early?

I chalked matches for the better players every chance I could, and asked a lot of questions. The next lesson I learned was sportsmanship. When I graduated the NDFC Youth Program, I went on to play Adult Nationals my first year. And was lucky enough to finish joint third with a paid trip to the World Masters. I was on top of the world and didn't think I should be beat. Well was I wrong! It was very difficult to accept when I started losing first and second rounds every event. Then I was approached about it. I clearly needed an attitude adjustment in the way I played. So after some very important words from a friend, the way I approached the game took a very positive spin. It's very easy to make friends in darts, but it's much more important to keep them. If you want to improve you will need to set goals (start small). If you are happy with playing casually and taking a game now and then . . . awesome. Now if you have a competitive side, and want to see how far you can go, you will need to put the time in to do so. I spent hours and hours practicing, but that is only a part of learning to improve. Practice needs competition! Competition will let you know where you stand in your game. With that, competition brings new elements and goals to conquer. Set new goals and repeat. With just a few key elements you will soon see improvements in your game. But the best attraction I have learned along the way, are the many friendships I've made. There are so many great people playing darts, and every tournament I play now becomes a reunion."

Photo by David Holmes

Robin Curry

"I have been playing darts for many years, but it seems like only yesterday that I got my first set as a Christmas present from my brother Ron. I started to practice and began to play in some local tournaments.

"Eventually I started traveling and I haven't stopped yet. My darts have taken me to the likes of Perth, Australia, and just recently Belize in Central America. If you like to travel and meet new people this sport is for you.

"My practice routine involves primarily going around the board going for doubles finishing with the bull and then reversing the order and doing it again. Doubles are key to your game if you can hit the final double before the other player you will win 100 percent of your games (01 games of course). If I find there has been an aspect of my game that has let me down recently. . . . I will then practice that. Practicing with friends who are at your level or even a bit more advanced is in my opinion the best way to develop more consistency and to prepare you for those pressure shots. A practice game I have recently started doing is starting with fifty-one and keep finishing every number as high as you can go with three darts. It is great practice even for the more advanced player just to go thru the motions it will help develop your muscle memory. When muscle movements are repeated over a length of time, a long-term muscle memory is created for that task, eventually allowing it to be performed without conscious effort. Focus and concentration also play a very big role in your success. Mental preparedness will come with time and experience. It has recently been brought to my attention I mentally visualize a lot more than I ever realized. Mentally visualizing your shot, the dart going in where you want is almost as effective as physically doing it. Some say you have to believe . . . for me it is TRUST. Trusting that I have done everything I could to prepare for a match allows me to relax and focus on the task at hand."

A Ken MacNeil image

Ken MacNeil

"I started playing darts at a very young age; I was around ten when I won my first darts tournament, from that day on I was hooked on darts. My mother and father were both good players and had played in lots of leagues and had lots of trophies and awards in my house when I was a child. I mostly got into playing darts because of my Aunt Carol. She was probably one of the best female players I've ever seen even to this day. Carol and I would play darts all hours of the day and night, and when I was old enough we played tournaments together and won a lot of prizes through the years. I owe all my finishing power and knowledge of combinations to my mother though; she taught me all my combination finishes when I was about fifteen years old. I would practice them every chance I had the time. I have accomplished every goal I set for myself in the game except one, and I still have three years to reach that goal and believe me I will succeed. I could write a book of my own on what I've sacrificed and went through to get to where I am and the things I've achieved have all come with a price, from sleeping on park benches and parking lots to traveling with almost no money just to gain ranking points at national tournaments. I used to practice eight to ten hours a night after working a nine-hour day scaffolding. That means getting around three hours of sleep a night every day for a year, which is the first time I won the Canadian title of number one ranked player. I've had opportunities of a lifetime taken away from me because of politics and at times felt like giving up the game altogether, but I chose to stick with it and work harder and just keep plugging away. I plan on being around in this game for a long time to come and believe me people are going to know my name soon enough because I will not stop till I reach my goals. I'm a firm believer in everything happens for a reason and if it's meant to be it'll be. I have come so close to achieving great things only to fall short by the wayside, but inside of whining and complaining about it, I just get off my backside and work harder then before. I know what it takes to succeed and success doesn't come easily; you have to really work for it and be mentally strong to reach those goals. Okay now for advice to new players or even experienced players: I believe to really succeed in this game you need experience, experience can't be bought, it is something you have to gain by traveling outside of your comfort zone (your basement, local leagues). Players can practice as many hours and reach great averages in the basement all they want, if they don't go out to tournaments and put this practice into motion against other players they'll never know how to handle the mental part of the game which is pressure and pace of different players.

"I've always told players that I was mentoring that there are three basic components to darts in my opinion. They are as follows:

1) Basic Mechanics 25 percent

2) Mathematical Combinations (Percentage Out shots) 10 percent

3) Mental (Handling Pressure and other non physical situations) 65 percent

"As you can see the highest percentage of your game as a player is the mental part of the game, because without being strong mentally you'll have a very hard time succeeding and being a winner. Mechanics and Math can be practiced and honed in the basement alone, but to become strong mentally you must play against other players on a regular basis and learn to lose games which gives you the motivation to get better and come back and succeed at a level of your choosing. I would also like to say don't ever let anybody tell you that you can't do something or achieve certain goals, only you have the power to prove them right or wrong, if you believe in your abilities and work hard at achieving your goals the rest will fall into place, it may not happen right away but whatever you do, do not give up because as soon as you give up you stop trying and give all the people that told you that you won't succeed the satisfaction of being correct. I don't let anybody tell me I can't do something, remember one of the best feelings in the world is achieving something in life that others have said you could not achieve. In closing to all you new players, believe in yourself, ask a lot of questions, watch a lot of players and watch what they all do similar, and most important thing of all I believe is to play as many competitions as you can whether it be a local shoot at the pub or a major national ranking tournament and of course practice, practice, practice and when you think you've practiced enough, practice some more because remember when you are not practicing, someone else in the world is."

Paul Lim

"Throwing darts is not a difficult thing to learn and do. But it is definitely tough to be good at. There are various points you need to look at if you are a beginner and want to learn the game or if you are an intermediate player and want to get better AND finally if you are a good player and want to compete. But please bear in mind all these steps (of want to be) strongly base on the foundation of your basic fundamental of throwing darts.

1) Be comfortable in all sense (i.e. the grip, the stance, the balance, and the throw) you have to feel comfortable.

2) Cut down, as many movements of your body as possible, do not use your body to help throw the darts.

3) Learn the basic fundamental of a simple throw, using your upper hand, the throw with the wrist break and follow through with the palm facing down at the finish point. The follow through is the most important.

4) Practice the follow through routine as much as you can, so that the throw becomes a memory (muscle memory). This will build consistency.

5) Understand the line of throw and the flight path of the dart to the target on the dartboard.

6) Do not find excuses of having no time to practice. All you need is fifteen to thirty minutes of throwing and you can do it at home, so there are no excuses.

7) When playing a match, throw the same way like you do during practice whenever and whoever you are playing against.

8) Watch how your dart lands on the dartboard, because you can tell if you are releasing your darts properly or consistently from the way it sticks in the dartboard.

9) Do not try to be to careful throwing because in doing so you will throw differently. Just look at the target, set up and throw. The more you think and analyze your throw, the more damage there is. More simply, do not think too much.

10) And last , enjoy the game. Have fun regardless. This is supposed to be fun from the start, so have FUN . . . and enjoy the game."

Photo by David Holmes

Cindy Hayhurst

"I have been playing darts for about fourteen or fifteen years, I have always been around darts. Both of my parents from Newfoundland played darts and so did my grandpa. It was actually my parents who got me into the game. I was at the community center with parents, and my friend Ashley and I were playing pool and my dad asked me to come over to where he was playing and said, 'Cindy why don't you try playing darts?' I said, 'Well I'm not sure if I'm good at it.' So I picked up my dad's darts and threw them. My first three darts were 20, 20, 20, and my dad smiled at me and said, 'You can play on my team any day.' So from there I played on their team and joined the youth league.

"Some advice I would live to give to new player and old: The biggest problem I find is jealousy from other people, coaches, family, and people who say they're your friends. The best thing to do is walk away (easier said than done). Just keep your head on straight, stay positive, surround yourself with positive people, and practice . . . you cannot forget to practice."

Jerry Umberger

"I have played darts for a very long time at many levels. The first bit of advice that comes to mind is for everyone to show good sportsmanship. Be considerate; shake hands before play and after, even if you lose. I also suggest to all players to learn the out-shot combinations. It will benefit their game in the long run, as they will not have to stress about what to throw to win the game.

"I always advise players to have specific practice routines such as practicing all the doubles. Another technique for practice that I like to share with other players is to take four darts, and throw the first dart. This is your target dart. You must then throw your remaining three darts at the first, target dart. Make sure each round; you throw your first, target dart to different locations around the board. Ex. First target dart at the bulls-eye, then the second, target dart at double 20, and the third at the triple 18, and so on. Remember the only way to get a 180 is to have a tight group.

"And finally, I recommend to all players to have a good quality of dart. It is important to be happy and comfortable with the equipment that you are using."

Photo by David Holmes

Bob Sinnaeve

"I started in 1973, and my advice is to learn to have fun first and then set realistic goals for you as a player in order to progress. If a player becomes too ambitious without gaining the experience, it will discourage a player from improving."

Robbie Phillips

"I've been playing since before I can remember. When I was eleven my dad told me I wasn't good enough to play doubles with him and his friends. That really fired me up and on my twelfth birthday all I wanted was my own darts and dartboard. It's been an incredible journey ever since.

"I'm sure you've heard the phrase, 'There's no right or wrong way to throw a dart.' While this may be true, there are definitely better techniques than others. This is your foundation and may limit your potential. My advice would be to watch and talk to the best players you know. Watch dart videos and take mental notes; what are they all doing in common? I was fortunate enough to receive VHS tapes of past British tournaments thanks to Wade Wilcox. This enabled me to do this before the likes of online videos. Once you're comfortable with your technique, it's all about steady practice until you no longer think about your stroke. This is where patience comes in. 'Practice: Don't expect to be better tomorrow, know you'll be better in the future.' You can't get your expectations too high. One step at a time.

"I've received some great advice over the years from my mentors and colleagues. One of my favorites came when I was 16. I was playing mixed doubles with a lady that had been playing for many years. She sensed my nervousness and told me, 'Just hit a solid 60. Whatever you do with your other two darts is up to you.' It got a smile out of me and really helped settle me down. We weren't in a world final, just a first round at a small tournament. Think of what you can do, not of what to avoid.

"Confidence is huge in this game and it can change wildly with momentum. Many things can affect your confidence as well. Keep your body language upbeat. The last thing you want is to give your opponent a boost.

"Learn your numbers! I don't want to hear the excuse you're bad at math. A lot of dart math is really just memorization. You don't need to know all of the ways to take out 108; you just need to know the one that works for you.

"Lastly and the most important, sportsmanship. We all love this game so treat it with respect. Darts would be little fun without opponents. They're trying just as hard as you are and it's not luck that they hit the double 7 to beat you. Shake their hand. You'll live to play a new game.

"The future of this game depends on us. We can't just expect people to find it we have to share it. The kids of today will be the stars of tomorrow. There's nothing better than watching a kid hit his first bulls-eye. 'Coaching in the local youth league is a highlight in my darts career. One of the kids, Kyle Gaulthier, went on to win the Youth National Title and I was there to witness it. It doesn't get much better than that!'

"Enjoy your journey!"

Photo by David Holmes

Sandy Hudson

This bit of advice is a bit unusual in its delivery, but has a wealth of knowledge just the same. While Sandy is one of the best female players in the country, she does not seem to analyze her game or how she interacts with new players and youth players. So we changed things up a little bit and received her perspective and her advice through the eyes of someone close to her: her husband Chuck.

"I never cease to be amazed by my wife, in life and especially playing the sport of darts. One might expect that a player of her caliber would have a regular practice routine to keep their stroke sharp, but think again. Sandy Hudson is a talented player on a national and international level, yet she hardly ever practices even before big events. Now she plays league darts and gets a good workout there, playing the best local players, but when it comes to practice, she just doesn't like it, it doesn't motivate her the way competition tends to do.

"The one game she does play with me when she can find the time is simply called 121. We enjoy playing this at home and in the dart bars before or after matches. Beginning at 121 you have three rounds (3-9 darts) to get down to a double and hit it. When you do, you advance to the next higher number 122, 123, and so on. If you do not double out you start again at 121. The one exception is a 3 dart out, which means you cannot fall below this number. (Example: 3 dart out at 127 means you start here when you miss your outs.)

"It's a simple but effective practice that allows you to learn combinations and outs. You begin to understand the best options for your game and you get plenty of darts to refine your skills. Like they always say, Keep It Simple Sandy, or something like that. This is a great individual practice game and works well with up to four players. You can keep score in your head, which heightens the mental workout of this, her only, practice game.

"This is the game she teaches the youth dart players to stay loose at tournaments. Sandy has always loved children and she has a long history of supporting youth darts in America. In her career she has been fortunate to compete with and against some of the best darters that have ever played the sport in this country, men and women. She loves the competition and has teamed with some true legends, but the most fun she has in darts is with the kids. No lie.

"She not only teaches them dart skills, but life skills, as well. She explains the game, makes them think about what they need to do and keeps them focused between rounds if they start losing interest. She treats them with respect and makes darts fun for them. She has been involved with many youth players through the years at the local and tournament level and it would be unfair to single out any one or few because she bonds with each of them differently.

"If you get her to rummage through her dart bag, she will produce pictures that dart kids have drawn for her, many dating back years and some from this year. She takes them with her wherever she travels. Some of the children that touched her life have grown, some have passed, some have put the game aside and some still have a fire burning to improve. Some have been national champions and some have been beginners. She has autographed her plaques and given them to her youth partners through the years. She was especially touched when a boy that was a partner won his first singles event. He was happy to autograph the plaque and give it to her, it still sits on the bookshelf today.

"She gives her time to these children freely, often making for a longer, more exhausting day. But it is her favorite thing about darts and ironically, she is teaching them to practice, because 'practice makes perfect' or at least that's what she always heard."

David Fatum

"The first thing every player should do if you're new or looking to make changes is start with the stroke. It needs to be a long, full stroke. So many players I watch only throw a dart half way. What I mean is this; if your fingers are not pointing at the floor after you've thrown the dart you are just not getting a full throw. When you 'short stroke' your throw will never be all it can be as it does not have a follow through. In every other sport the follow through is everything and it is the same here in darts. In basketball the wrist has to break, baseball your arm needs to go all the way around you could not do these events well if you stopped as soon as you let go could you? With all of us having video on our phones, now have someone video yours to see where you are. Throw a handful of darts not just three while making this change, as you need to have a solid, dependable stroke before your hand and eye can ever communicate leading you to hit what you look at.

"The second piece is 'Do not let others limit you' or do not set your goals on the players you see around you. So many times I hear people say 'I want to beat Player x.' Why would you ever look to a short goal? The world of darts is so much more then what you see in the pub. I can tell you the world of professional darts is SO TOUGH now that going into a game and throw 6.8mpr going first does not mean you will win the game at all. Focus on the process of throwing well and the winning takes care of itself. The last piece people need to remember that it is just a game . . . to most people. For most that play darts, it will NEVER CHANGE YOUR LIFE! If you get focused on thinking it will I can guarantee it will cost you things in your life. I have done a lot in the game of darts but I can sit here and tell you way more things I missed out on or gave up to do what I have done. I have seen the world and made a bunch of cash but looking back . . . I wish I had gone fishing more. So even though we should all strive to play better and do the work it takes just do not get all caught up in the DREAM that you are going to be the next great one. Enjoy darts for what it is . . . a game that allows you to meet others and have a good time with friends."

Steve Brown

"Most people who play darts do so for the love of the game; that's why they started playing. Even at the very top level—particularly at the top level, in fact—the players truly love the game. That is the most important single factor in a player's success. At times during your career, you will struggle, and you will suffer slumps, but the easiest way to overcome these problems is with confidence. So, just try to remember the reason you started—for fun.

"The other thing to do is to watch the top players—closely. Study their mechanics, their stances, even their body language, and facial expressions. Watch for indications of confidence as well as weaknesses. However, do not try to model yourself on a particular player, more a combination of players. We are all physically different, and it is impossible to totally replicate another individual's mechanics, but you will see many recurring themes and habits. Adopt these themes and habits in a way that is natural to you.

"It may seem strange to think about these things so early in your darts career, but learning the right way when you start out—rather than having to constantly make major changes as you strive to improve—will make the process of development so much easier.

"From there, the best thing is to just get on a board and throw. However, just be aware that there are different practice modes. Sometimes you just want to loosen up, and also work on things like pace and rhythm. Then, there are practice sessions where you want to work on your mechanics, and tweaking things like your grip.

"Finally, there is the serious practice session where you drive yourself to get better. Many players say they get bored when they practice alone, but if that is the way you genuinely feel, you will never get anywhere in darts. It's not about quantity of practice, but quality.

"Throwing aimlessly will do nothing. Use different routines and games, even developing new ones, but make sure you keep your figures. That way, you are giving yourself goals, but realistic goals. As you improve and reach your goals, you will be able to raise the bar and set new ones. You will learn to be competitive.

"Having said that, no amount of practice will prepare you for the cut-and-thrust of real competition. If you do intend playing tournaments at some point, then the only way to prepare yourself is to get out and compete! It may seem scary, but never wait until you "think" that you are ready; you will never be ready. You will be tense, and you will get nervous, but competition is the way to overcome these issues. It's not that you can stop them from affecting you (they are perfectly normal human emotions), but you will learn to control them, and to use them to your advantage. Remember this: You can get good overnight, but you cannot get experience overnight."

Photo by David Holmes

Gordon Dixon

"There are two major things to remember when playing darts in my mind. One has to do with mechanics and the other with the mental game.

"The first, BY FAR is developing a good follow through. This is the one consistent thing I see most if not all top-level players do. It will be the biggest factor in how quickly you can progress in this game. If you don't have a good follow through every dart is thrown separately. What I mean is each time you let go of the dart it is a crap shoot on your release point, and therefore, on where your dart ultimately lands. With a good follow through your focus can be on the weight of the dart to make sure you hit or at least come close to your target. If you fall short of a full follow through, you are not doomed. I do however believe the amount of practice hours it will take to consistently compete will be greatly increased.

"The second is curtailing your emotion as much as possible. As I say this you probably are retorting to yourself 'those guys on TV don't.'

TV is a very specific place for pomp and circumstance. Players are told to be more boisterous on stage for the sake of the TV cameras. Believe me they are not saluting after a 180 or jumping up and down after each double hit at a floor tournament. They also aren't getting escorted to the board by a hottie either. There are already a lot of variables in this game to try to keep in check, so keeping the ones you have control of to a minimum is paramount. The less energy spent on celebrating or commiserating can only propel you forward. I am not saying that there isn't a place for either of those things. I have just seen in my own game and from afar the players that do the best; one can't really tell what they hit from their reaction. There is an external piece to this as well. Ask yourself these questions. Why expose to your opponent if you are playing well or not? If you are playing well why motivate him/her to beat you by cheering each time? If you are struggling, why make them any more comfortable with their situation by hanging your head or complaining?

"Good Luck and Happy Darting."

Scott Kirchner

"I have played the game of darts for twenty-three years. I am mainly a soft-tip player now, but I have been all over the world playing in both soft-tip and steel-tip at the highest levels. My advice to players of all levels may be a little different than most of the top level players. 'Keep the fun in the game.' When you first start playing darts it is because it is fun. As we move through the process of improving our games we need to keep that in mind. I have seen many players come and go in this game over the years and almost to a person the ones that have left the game have said they lost the passion. I think for most of those people would say that they no longer have fun while playing. You will get all kinds of advice on practice routines and other things that WILL help you improve your dart game. What I ask is, keep in mind why you started. As long as you can keep the game fun you will always want to continue to play and compete."

John Kramer

"After almost forty years of playing, the advice I would give to someone starting out is to find a dart you can pick up and throw without trying to find where to hold it. This should be a natural process. After this, you can find the shaft and flight combination to make the dart fly just the way you want. When throwing, try standing sideways to the board, then while extending your hand and forearm toward the board in a throwing motion, you release the dart. Where the dart lands will improve with more practice. The less movement you have in your mechanics, the more consistent your throw will be. Try to get out and watch the better players to see what they have in common, and try what you see in your own throwing style to see what works for you.

"The best advice I can give I will steal from the great champion and my old friend Bobby George: 'Look where you are throwing, then throw where you are looking.'"

Randy Van Deursen

"Over the years I get a lot of people asking this question. There are two things that I believe will help players become the best they can be. The first

step is to find a player that has the same passion for the sport as you do, who is also very close to your level of skill at the game and make that person your practice partner. If you play against someone who is significantly better than you are and you subsequently get beat all the time, it may eventually deter you from playing and you could wind up quitting all together. On the other hand, if you practice against someone that is considerably below your skill level you may run the risk of picking up some bad habits or you could find yourself becoming a lazy player simply because you are not being challenged and you don't have to try as hard. By finding a practice partner with the same level of skill as your own you will both grow together? If at some point one becomes a little better it will force the other player to practice that much harder in an effort to get better than the other player. This back and forth battle between you and your practice partner will help you both climb the ladder to greatness. The second thing I tell people is to go out to different locations (if possible) to get the experience of playing against other people. There is a tendency for a lot of people to just go to their local bar and play the same people, never venturing out of their little dart world to see what else is out there. This could hinder a player from really reaching their full potential. To really get to the top of the game a player needs to get out and experience what it is like to play other players from all over the globe. These will not only help the player find out where they stand in the game, but they could also pick up some valuable new ideas on strategies to help their game. There is a whole big dart community out there with thousands and thousands of players. So get out there and experience it to truly become the best dart player you can be and by doing so you will develop some great friendships along the way that will last a lifetime."

Benny Dersch

"I think the best advice I can give to anyone wanting to be good at this sport is patience . . . And of course PRACTICE . . . PRACTICE . . . PRACTICE!!! I was a born natural athlete so when I started throwing darts it was terribly frustrating! Frustrating to the point I could not handle the losing all the time! I had to figure out how to get better . . . I tried and tried, but just wasn't there for some reason. For me it took a lot of years of struggle to find the correct stance, correct grip, just what felt comfortable to me. . . . I was always forcing it. . . . Here's the thing about darts, very few have that EL NATURAL ability, most of us have to work and work hard . . . So no matter what you do stay PATIENT with it. . . . If you want it bad enough you will achieve! One last thing, PRACTICE, PRACTICE, PRACTICE!"

Shea Reynolds

Photo by David Holmes

"My advice for newer players would be pretty simple. Be YOU! Don't try to be Phil Taylor, John Part, or Darin Young, set realistic goals for yourself, whether it is to be the top shot in your local league, winning the State Title or making the Top 10 in the national rankings. Then you should be very diligent about your practice sessions, it does not always have to be a specific practice routine you use or the amount of one-on-one games you play. Just practice as you would play in a match! And last but not least, keep a positive attitude, I am reminded often by a very close friend to think . . . 'it's not IF I win, it's when I win!'"

Marilyn Popp

"Darts have been a part of my life for over twenty-five years. I have accomplished much in the time: the travel to different countries and international play, the many friends all over the world are all the things I will never forget.

"I started as a practice partner for my husband Marshall and it took off from there. The better I became the more men I had to play. I've always said that women do not have the egos that men have so if I beat them, I would always tone down my enthusiasm.

"The one most important thing I've learned is how to win and lose gracefully. You can act appropriately for years, but the one time you lose it in front of people is the one those people will remember.

"Another thing I've learned is there is always someone out there better than you. You can have a good run for years, you are up on top and all of sudden there's a bulls-eye on your back. Everyone is out to beat you, they don't want to be embarrassed losing to you. So they up their game. I once lost to someone who had been playing for only three months.

"I was never one who practiced a lot. I found it boring. Some people I've spoken too practice two to five hours a day. If you practice that much and you are still mediocre, you must realize that's as good as you're going to get. I'm not saying you shouldn't practice, but it is what it is.

"Please remember that darts is a game, that's all it is. The friends you meet and play with and against are for more important.

"I have frequently double-booked partners for tournament but never on purpose. Please don't dump people for better partners. It will always come back and bite you in the a—.

"I'm toning down the competitive part of my career in 2013. Attending twenty-plus tournaments a year takes it's toll. I will be playing tournaments close to home for fun. I will be leaving that part of the game to wonderful women competitors whom I've come to respect and love. If you meet them at the dartboard please afford them the respect they deserve."

Photo by David Holmes

Scott Wollaston

"The first thing that I like to tell a player is to do whatever it takes to maintain your focus. There can be a lot of outside distractions during your match that will try to take your attention away from the task at hand. If you lose that focus, you have decreased your chances of hitting that critical winning dart for the match. Do what you can to work on your concentration at all times, so when you are in a difficult situation such as loud music playing, or people talking to loud, you will not be bothered.

"I feel that the most important aspect that every player needs to remember is to be a great sport whether you win or lose. Nobody likes to lose, but as a player, you worked hard to get there and so did your opponent, and someone has to be there. Some days it might be you and some days it might be someone else. Always remember to be a great sport and win graciously and lose graciously.

"Finally, I don't feel that there is anything to the sport if we do not support the younger generation and encourage them to step and take over for all of us when we retire. If we do nothing to encourage the next generation of players, the sport will die a slow and painful death."

Photo by David Holmes

Brenda Roush

"Learn to play against the board, and to meet your personal goals. I've had many a day that I played well and lost, or played horribly and won. The emotional highs and lows of winning and losing will always are there. But, learn to chart your own progress not by the games that you win, but by the percentage of times you hit your target, the number of darts it takes to finish a game, and the number of darts it takes to hit a double. And speaking of personal goals, what are yours? Make sure you have some clear short-term goals, along with long-term goals of what you plan to achieve in darts.

"Learn smart strategy as soon as you can. Often players play for years before learning finishes for 01 games and smart cricket strategy. By then you have developed bad habits and it is much tougher to have to stop and think about your shot than it is when you are first beginning. If you have a natural talent you can get away with poor strategy for a long time, but that won't be true when you get to the top of your game. And when you are competing at the higher levels it is a huge advantage to be completely confident in what you need to shoot with each dart.

"Learn a set of outs for 501 as soon as you can. The longer you continue to have someone else tell you what to shoot, the longer it will take for you to reach your potential in the game. When I started playing, Chuck Spackman was my partner. He took the approach of never telling me what to shoot when I was at the line. He taught me basic strategy and then gave me the space and time to figure things out for myself. After a game, if he had a different suggestion, he would share it. By the end six months of shooting, my basic out strategies were pretty solid.

"Learn one set of finishes first. It might be from an out chart, a book, or a player you respect. There are many finishes where different players shoot different combinations. Most outs between 61 and 70 fall into this category. Pick the outs that you are going to shoot and keep shooting that whole set until you have learned them and you easily remember them. Then, you can look at testing out different strategies, and pick your favorites.

"Find someone to play against on a regular basis that is the best competitive level for you. For me, that has generally been someone that is about two steps above my ability. For other people it might be someone right at the same level. There was a point when I intentionally played practice games against players much less skilled than I was. That wasn't because I got a sick pleasure out of beating them, but rather that I had found I had a tendency to "play soft" against weaker players, often leaving a door open for them to win. I needed to learn to play my best all of the time, and get through the mental challenges that softened my game.

"Never take anyone for granted. Particularly as a woman, I felt frustration with players that I saw as less knowledgeable than I was, giving me advice. I felt that men, and sometimes women, often underestimated me because I am a female. So, maybe they were taking me for granted, and I now realize, I was taking them for granted.

"Now I assume that other people I meet are approaching me with good intentions. When they offer advice, it is meant to be helpful and I am appreciative of that intent. Sometimes it can be the start of a great friendship or partnership. And, it generally creates less internal stress.

"More than anything else, stay connected to what excites you about darts. It might be the competition, winning money, making new friends, travel or a range of other things. I still go back most every year to the Blueberry Hill Open. It was the first tournament I ever played in, at the bar where I threw my first dart. Each time I walk in that door I remember all over how much darts means to me."

Photo by David Holmes

Paula Murphy

"My advice to new players would first be to find equipment that works for them. There are different weights, flights, shafts, and points. There are three different flights that you'll notice most of the top players use. The standard, teardrop, and speed flights. As for shafts you have the fixed and spinning shafts. I prefer the spinning shaft as I usually have tight groups and that helps for fewer deflections. Experiment with the different flights and shafts till you find what works for you. Once you find a setup that's comfortable to you stick with it.

"Practice is always important if you want to improve your game. Find a place where there is no distraction. Maybe put on some music to help you get in a rhythm. Start out with a pattern, it doesn't matter what you throw at. After you throw the first dart try to throw the other two at the first. Once you develop your pattern you can move it around. The amount of time you practice depends on you. You can practice from half an hour to three or four hours. Always remember, a good short practice is better than a long bad practice. One way I used to practice was to have my husband videotape me, that way I could see for myself what areas I needed to work on. If you don't have a video recorder, have someone watch you. They can see any problems you might be unaware of.

"Having a good mental attitude is key to playing a good game. Positive thinking will prevail, as this is a game that is 80 percent mental, 10 percent strategy, and 10 percent skill. If you tell yourself you can't hit something you won't. On the flip side, if you're positive and tell yourself I'm going to hit this, you're more than likely going to nail it. I had several girls I used to help with their game. One girl had a problem with 16s. She said she couldn't hit them and I said she could. I said the reason she did not hit them was she kept saying she couldn't so she didn't. I told her to think positive, tell herself that she loved the 16s. Next thing you know she couldn't miss them. So don't get mad if you're having problems hitting a number. Just remember to think positive, focus and concentrate. Sportsmanship. Enough can't be said for sportsmanship. Even if you're playing your best game and you get beat never be ungracious in your loss. Respect the other player and he will respect you. This is a game that starts with a handshake and ends with a handshake. So in summary, you need a good dart setup, a time and place to practice, good mental attitude and sportsmanship. If you can get these four things to connect you'll be on the right road to win. GAME ON!"

WORLD RECORD ATTEMPTS

There are world records listed in the Guinness World Record books for darts. Many times players have attempted to break records or set their own records, however, they have failed to achieve the status of world record holder. I thought it would be fun to share a few of the most current ones listed.

The first World Championship nine-dart finish is in the record book. The first nine-dart finish in any darts World Championship match was made by Paul Lim (USA) in his Embassy World Professional Darts Championship match against Jack McKenna (Ireland) at Lakeside, Frimley Green, UK on January 9, 1990.

The most darts to be thrown within the inner and outer bull's-eyes in one minute is seven and was achieved by Anastasia Dobromyslova (Russia) on the set of Guinness World Records Smashed at Pinewood Studios, UK, on March 31, 2009. Anastasia shares this record with Winston Cadogan (Barbados), who achieved the same number on the set of Morning Barbados, St. Michael, Barbados for Guinness World Records Day on November 9, 2006. Anastasia equaled her own record a second time on the set of Zheng Da Zong Yi in Beijing, China, on May 22, 2010.

The record for the highest darts score in two minutes achieved by two players when only counting bulls-eyes and 25s is 475 (15x25 and 2x50). Josette Kerdraon and Yannick Geay (both France) achieved the record on the set of L'Ete De Tous Les Records, Benodet, France on August 5, 2004.

The most darts bulls-eyes in ten hours by a team was 1,505 by Jon Watson, Bill Foot, Matty Wilson, Del Fox, Gary Ellis, Bryan Pidgeon, Sean Kerry, and Bob Anderson (all UK) at the Winnersh British Legion Club in Winnersh, UK, on January 9, 2011. Anderson, the 1988 British Darts Organization world champion, assisted the seven teammates in raising approximately £10,000 ($16,066) for Cancer Research UK and The Royal British Legion. A maximum of eight team members are allowed for this record and all standard darts rules (height/distance of board, three throws per turn) must be followed.

DARTING FOR THE CAUSE, MORE THAN A GAME

iDart Benefit

Despite all the differences in the players all over the world, we all share some common ground. We all love the game and love to compete. And we are all like one big family that bands together for a good cause or to help our fellow players in need. This togetherness was brought to light in a very large way in March of 2011, when an earthquake struck Japan, resulting in a tsunami of epic proportions that struck the Sendai District of Northern Japan. Ironically, there also happened to be a big tournament on that day in Sendai, so a lot of players were affected by it. Miho Kadokawa drove with two other friends, Miho Iwanaga and Takeshita Maiko, and her husband, Tsuyoshi Kadokawa, to Sendai to play in the Perfect Event (which at the time, it was the largest soft tip dart tour in Japan and it is organized by the Phoenix Company). The venue was located a little more inland, but the group of them figured they had some time before the event, so they stopped at a convenience store to grab something to eat, and it was then that they felt the earthquake. They were talking about it, how big it was, but never at any time did they think about a potential tsunami.

While driving to the venue, they realized that they did not buy any food and they were getting hungry. Although they could have gone to any other convenience store, they decided to go back to the one they had gone to earlier, which was close to the ocean. Miho Kadokawa was the only one to get out of the car to go into the store to grab some food for everybody. While in the car, the three others saw some waves and even saw cars being taken away, but it seemed far away to them, so they did not pay much attention to it. In a matter of seconds, the water also took their car away and they could not retrieve Miho K from the store. The car was taken away by the water, banging its way through the neighborhood. Miraculously they found themselves stuck in a big warehouse/factory type of building. While the water level rose, they were able to get on top of the roof of a bigger truck to stay above the water. Miho Iwanaga was able to send a few text messages and emails to their sponsor, Jinta of L-Style, and her other sponsor, Cross Design, to let them know where they were trapped and needed to be rescued.

Meanwhile, they thought Miho K. was safe for awhile because she was in the convenience store, but a car came smashing the front windows of the store, causing the water to gush in and the level inside the store rose quickly. Miho's arm was dislocated when the car came in the store. She is not sure if it was the car hitting her or something else that caused her shoulder to be dislocated. While the water rose, some people could not hang on and were washed away out of the store. With her dislocated arm, Miho climbed on top of the counter desk and, luckily, a man next to her hung on to her tight so she would not be swept away by the water. The water rose quickly, and soon, they were both floating and touching the ceiling. When the water almost rose all the way to the ceiling and Miho was about to give up, the guy kept telling her: "You can make it, don't give up, just don't give up". Just like in a movie, and because it is a convenience store (where they always sell drinks, and therefore, have straws), one straw just happened to float by. The guy grabbed it and gave it to Miho. Miho had her entire head under water, but was able to breathe through that straw while the guy was breathing with his mouth almost kissing the ceiling and still hanging on to Miho. And just as they thought it was over, the water started receding. Then another wave came in and they struggled again, but at the end, she made it. She was the only female to make it in the entire store, thanks to the guy who hung on to her. The next miracle is that amongst the survivors, there was one lady who was a professional massage therapist, and she was able to give a good massage to Miho's frozen legs and keep a minimum blood flow. Without that, although she had survived, Miho would have lost both her legs. Not only did she reunite with her husband and friends, but also with Jinta, who was able to find them (he was the only crazy guy to drive to the devastated area to find his way through the destroyed villages) and take them to safety right away. Mr. Satoh at DartsHive received them at his home and gave them food, a warm bath, and a bed to sleep in. After a few months of rehabilitation (during which she could not move both her legs), Miho was up and wanting to play darts more then ever before!

Sendai was the hometown of Mr. Satoh and DartsHive, which is the biggest online shop in Japan that also used to have many bars, shops, and their major warehouse in Sendai. Sadly, many of their bars and their warehouse were damaged or washed away.

The entire iDart Benefit raised a total of $15,000 and the first portion of the donations, which totaled $5,000, was given to Miho Kadokawa to help her, as she was unable to work and had accumulated many medical bills. She was very happy to receive the donation.

JohnnyK's Toys-4-Tots

Another annual event seems to gather the masses together every time without fail to achieve higher goals every year. This event is the annual Toys-4-Tots fundraising event held by John Kucszynski. John resides in Zion Grove, Pennsylvania, and has taken this event year after year to higher levels. In 2011, he achieved the highest goal of record with a total of $20,000 in toy purchases donated. His story is featured every year on the local news and in the local newspapers. His fundraising efforts start online around September 1 and continue up until his benefit tournament on December 1. In 2008, he collected $1500, 2009's collection grew to $10,000, 2010's collection ended at $15,000, and 2011's collection ended at $21,000. In 2012, the collection total reached $26,500, his highest total to date.

Darts for Kids

The next event is destined to become an annual event supported by many dart players across the United States: the Darts for Kids event created by Bob Hudzik and Tammy Bourland from Gillespie, Illinois. Bob states that he had just signed his new sponsorship contract with a dart company out of Japan, and his fiancé asked him if since he had done this, would he be willing to "give back" to the people and area that had been supporting him for years to reach his goals. Bob was completely on board, but the condition was that they were to help children. He says they were able to find the kids pretty easily; Bob worked with the dad of one of the girls and the other little girl was the niece of some fellow players in their local leagues. The area where he lives is, as he states, smack dab in the middle between St. Louis, Missouri, and Springfield, Illinois, and the area includes neighboring counties, Macoupin and Montgomery. One child is chosen from this area and the other child can be from anywhere. The goal is to try to help out the "Dart Family" if they have a child in need. Bob states that they have grown so much in one year that they have a board to make this decision and part of the board members are in Kansas City, Missouri. 2012 was the first year of the benefit and they were able to raise about $10,000. There were about two hundred people in attendance for the event, along with silent auctions, raffles, etc. Bob indicates that they have already started preparing for next year. You can find more information about the Darts for Kids fundraising event at www.dartsforkids.com.

Chris Helms Benefit

Most recently, one of our darting family members had a terrible accident that many of us thought would end in tragedy. Chris Helms from San Antonio, Texas, has not only been playing darts a very long time, but he has also been involved for many years as an area manager for the American Darts Organization (ADO) and was recently elected to the position of president of the ADO. While at work at a construction site, he slipped from his second-story location and fell to the ground. Emergency responders were called and Chris was airlifted to the local trauma center for care. It was noted that the major concern was that he had cracked his skull from ear to ear and doctors worked as fast as they could to relieve the swelling. Chris was placed in a medically-induced coma for many days until the swelling subsided. It was a true miracle, and to this day, Chris is recovering well. Fundraising efforts were put into place to assist the family with the medical costs incurred and, as of January 2013, the donations are still being sent as Chris continues his journey to recovery.

Darts for the Troops

This is one close to my heart and, when a long time friend asked me to help, I jumped in with both feet and never looked back. My friend, Wayne, lives in New Hampshire and back in 2011, there was a large group of reservists being deployed to the Middle East. One of them was his good friend and darting buddy, Ken. Ken was in charge of one of the units that were headed out. Once they arrived in the Middle East, he contacted Wayne about the possibility of getting some darts and supplies sent over for the guys to be able to play in the recreation area. Wayne talked to me about helping, I put a page on my website, and together we ended up sending a total of 140 sets of darts, 2,200 sets of new flights, 750 sets of new shafts, 5 brand new dart boards, and 3 slightly used dart boards. There were also large amounts of miscellaneous dart stuff and supplies sent, as well. Ken eventually got back to us after receiving everything and told us they were able to give each person a set of their own darts and they would hold blind draw dart tournaments every Saturday night to keep the morale up.

It was such a great effort by everyone who donated. And we are happy to say that Ken and many of his troops returned to the United States safe and sound. I had the opportunity to meet Ken in April of 2012 and all I could do was give him a huge hug. I didn't have any words right away. It was a very emotional and overwhelming experience to be so personally involved with these guys that sacrifice so much, talking to them often and praying they stayed safe, all so that people like me can sit here and enjoy the freedoms we sometimes take for granted. In the end though, I cannot wait until the next Darts for the Troops event starts!

So Much More . . .

There are many other fundraising and charity efforts across the country that take place, but get little to no promotion or exposure publicly to get the respect and accolades that they deserve, but they are no less deserving than those that do get the accolades and exposure.

One such story took place at a tournament in the southern United States this past year. One of the vendors/suppliers, who had a store set up, had a great experience with one of the locals that they wanted to share. A youngster walked up to their booth with a handful on one dollar bills, and asked, "Are there any darts I can get with $18?" Within ten minutes, the youngster had darts, extra flights, extra shafts, a dart case, and a Phil Taylor poster. At another event, this same vendor also provided each youngster a $25 gift certificate to purchase his or her own equipment. They even instituted creating diploma-style certificates to give to all the participants.

But they also want everyone to know that they don't only give back to dart events; they also give back to other events that either are or have affected the dart community. They have donated loads of shirts and other things for fundraisers for medical costs or charities. These events are things that they may not be able to attend due to their schedule, but they are still compelled to participate in some way.

There are so many other vendors/suppliers that participate in the same way and do whatever they can to support their local events and their players, as well as taking extra steps to make sure any youth events are fully supported with funds, equipment and personnel to help run the event. I purposefully left the name of the company out because the story is the same throughout the country. It would take half a book to list them all, along with all their efforts, but I did want to take the time to make a mention of them and all that they do to support the sport of darts.

There are so many more examples of how players today will band together to help their friends in need and these are just a few of the shining examples of the power of this group of people. It is a game, or sport, that truly knows no bounds when it comes to coming together for a common goal. All it takes in one message to spread like wildfire online to alert the masses, who then step up to help a friend in need.

Darts player Dominik Pundt

LEAGUE AND ASSOCIATION
INFORMATION LIST

Alaska

Alaska Dart Association
Anchorage Darts Association
Cook Inlet Darting Association
Golden Heart Dart Association
Homer Dart League
Juneau Dart Association
Kenai Men's Dart Association
Mat-su Dart Association
Nome Dart Association
Peninsula Dart Association
Upper Susitna Dart Association
Valdez Dart Association

Alabama

Birmingham Independent Dart
Association
Capital City Dart Association
Magic City Dart Association
Rocket City Dart Association

Arizona

Arizona Dart League
Arizona Federation of Dart
Associations
Central Arizona Darts League
Colorado River Dart Association
Huachuca City Dart League
London Bridge Dart Association
Prescott Darting Association
Sierra Vista Dart Association
Southern Arizona Darting
Association

Arkansas

Central Ozarks Dart Association
Ft. Smith Darts Association
Little Rock Dart Association
NW Arkansas Dart Association
Razorback Dart Association
The Fayetteville Classic Dart
Association

California

Antelope Valley Dart Association
Bay Area Darts
Central California Dart
Association
Chico Area Darts Association
Darts San Francisco
Delta Dart Association
Foothill Dart Association
GSDDA (Greater San Diego
Darting Association)
Humboldt Dart Association
Inland Valley Dart Association
Manny Pacquaio Darts
Association
Marin County Dart Association
Monterey Bay Dart League
Moonspinners Darts Club
North Bay Darts Association
Northern California Darts
Association
Pacific Darts Association
Peninsula Darts Organization
Redwood Empire Dart
Association
Royal Hawaiian All-Star Darting
Team

Sacramento Valley Dart
Association
San Francisco Dart Association
San Gabriel Valley Dart
Association
Santa Clara Valley Dart
Association (SCVDA)
South Bay Darting Association
Southern California Darts
Association
The Dart Shop
The Stockton Dart Association
Valley Dart League
Valley Dart League
Ventura County Darts
Association
Ventura Darts Association
Yuba-Sutter Dart League

Colorado

Colorado Springs Dart League,
Inc.
Northern Colorado Dart
Association
Rocky Mountain Dart
Association, Inc.

Connecticut

Central Connecticut Dart
Association
Eastern Connecticut Darts
Association
Middlesex County Dart
Association
New Haven Dart League
Norwalk British Darts League

Southeastern Connecticut Dart
League
Thames Valley Dart League

Delaware

Diamond State Dart League
First State Dart League

Florida

Alachua County Dart Association
Bradenton Area Dart Association
Brandon Area Darts Association
Broward County Darting
Association
Central Florida Darts Association
Conch Republic Dart Association
Dart Proprietor's Association
Florida Dart Association
Fort Pierce Dart League
Gulf Coast Darting Affiliation
Highlands County Dart
Association
Jacksonville Beach Dart League
Lakeland Area Dart Association
Martin County Dart Association
Manatee County League
Miami Dade Dart Association
NE Florida Darting Association
Palm Beach Co. Dart Association
Panhandle Darting Association
Pasco County Dart Association
Sarasota Darting Association
Southernmost Dart League
S.C.D.A. Space Coast Darting
Association

South West Florida Dart
  Association
Tallahassee Area Dart Association
Tampa Bay Dart Association
VIDO Steel League

Georgia

Atlanta-Decatur Dart Association
Classic City Dart League
Metro Atlanta Darts Association
Middle Georgia Dart Association
Savannah Area Darting
  Association
Savannah River Dart Association
Warner Robins Dart Association

Hawaii

Aloha Dart Association

Idaho

Boise Dart Association
Idaho Falls Darts Association
Pocatello Dart Association
South Idaho Dart Association
South Idaho Dart Association

Illinois

Central Illiana Dart Association
Northern Illinois Dart
  Association
South Illinois Dart Association
Southern Illinois Dart
  Association
Southside Dart League
West Suburban Dart Association

Windy City Darters Tournament
  Players Association
Windy City Darters

Indiana

Bedford Dart League
C & C Dart League
Circle City Dart Association
Fort Wayne Dart Association
Indianapolis Darters Association
SE Indiana Darting Association
Southern Indiana Dart
  Association
Three Rivers Dart Association
Tri-City Darts Association
Wabash Valley Dart League

Iowa

Cedar Rapids Kids in Darts
Des Moines Dart Association
The Hawkeye Dart Throwers
  Organization

Kansas

Dart Rebels of Wichita
Frogs Darts Association
Kansas City Dart Association
Lawrence Dart Association
Lawrence Darts Association
RAM Dart Association
Topeka Dart Association
Wichita Dart Association
Wichita Dart Frogs

Kentucky

Blue Grass Darting Association
Darters of Northern Kentucky
Greater Louisville Darting
Association
Heartland Dart Association
River Cities Darting Association

Louisiana

Baton Rouge Dart Association
Fun Dart League
Greater Calcasieu Dart
Association
Greater Hammond Darts
Association
Greater New Orleans Dart
Association
Greater Slidell Darts Association
New Orleans Dart Association
South Louisiana Darts
Association
Shreveport-Bossier Dart
Association
Southeast Louisiana Dart
Association
St. Bernard Dart League

Maine

Central Maine Dart League
Downeast Darts Association
Maine Dart Association
Western Maine Darts Association

Maryland

Baltimore Area Darting
Association

Central Maryland Darting
Association
Coors Charles County Dart
Association
Howard County Darts
Association
Mid-Atlantic Tournament Players
Southern Maryland Dart League
Tri-County Dart Association
Washington Area Darts
Association
Western Maryland Dart
Association

Massachusetts

Berkshire County Dart League
Bristol County Dart League
Cape Cod Dart League
Central Mass. Darts Organization
Greater Lowell Dart League
Martha's Vineyard Dart League
Mid Cape Masters Dart League
Mill City Dart League
Milltown League
Minute Man Dart League
Montachusett Dart Association
Patriot Dart League
South Shore Dart Association
TTS Darts
Western Massachusetts Darting
Association

Michigan

Bay Area Darters Association
Capitol Area Darting Association
Detroit Darts Association

Detroit Open Dart League
(D.O.D.L)
Grand Rapids Dart League
Great Lakes Darts League
Greater Flint Dart Association
Huron Valley Darts Association
(H.V.D.A.)
Lapeer County Dart League
Metro East Dart Association
Michigan Darts Organization,
Inc.
Mid-Michigan Darters Club
North Michigan Darts
Association
North Oakland Darting
Association
Outlaw Dart League
Paul Bunyon Darting Association
Saginaw Valley Darting
Association
Wolverine Dart Association

Minnesota

Bull's-Eye Marketing, Inc.
Twin City Dart Association

Mississippi

Greater Jackson Darts
Association
Gulf Coast Super League
Hub City Cart Association
Mississippi Gulf Coast Dart
Association
Mississippi Sound Dart League
Mississippi Valley Dart
Organization

Vicksburg Darts Association

Missouri

Blueberry Hill Darts Association
Central Missouri Dart
Association
Central MO Dart Association
Columbia Dart Association
Kansas City Dart Association
Mississippi Valley Darting
Organization
Ozark Mountain Dart League
RAM Dart Association
St. Charles Darts League
Tri-State Darting Association

Montana

Yellowstone Dart Association

Nebraska

Central Nebraska Dart
Association
East Nebraska Dart Association
Lincoln Dart Association, Inc.

Nevada

Bud Light Dart League of
Southern Nevada
NE Nevada Darts Association
Southern Nevada Dart
Association

New Hampshire

Lakes Region Darts League
Seacoast Dart Association
Portsmouth Darts Shooters

New Jersey

Association of Bergen County
Dartists
Atlantic County Dart Association
Bergen County Dart League
Hoboken Dart Players
Association
Hudson County Dart Association
North Jersey Dart Federation
Tri-County Darting Association
USA Dart Club

New Mexico

Cannon Dart Association
New Mexico Dart Association
Pecos Valley Dart Association

New York

1st Capital City Dart League
Ben-Ridge Dart League
Buffalo Area Dart League
Central New York Dart League
Chemung Valley Dart Association
Genesee Valley Darts Association
Gotham City Dart League
Gr Suffolk Dart League
Hilton-Hamlin Outlaw Dart
League
LB Enterprises, Inc.
New York Darts Organization
Niagara Frontier Dart Association
Queensborough Darts
Association
Salt City Dart League
Salt City Dart League (Syracuse)
Schuyler County Dart League

Southern Dutchess Dart League
Southern Tier Dart League
Stillwater Dart League
The Parting Glass Dart League
Tri-City Dart Association (NY)
Viking Pro Darts
Westchester/Putnam Dart
League

North Carolina

Azalea Coast Dart Association
Bull City Dart League
Capital Area Dart Club
Carolina Darts Association
Crystal Coast Dart Association
Crystal Coast Darts Association
Dogwood Dart Association
Down East Dart Association
Foothills Dart Organization
Jacksonville Dart Association
Onslow County Dart Association
Piedmont Dart Association
Piedmont Dart Association
Queen City Darting Association
Queen City Youth Darting
Association
Raleigh Dart League, Inc.
Triangle Dart League
Western Carolina Darts
Association

North Dakota

BisMan Steel Dart Association
Minot Airbase Dart Organization

Ohio

Akron Canton Dart Club
Central Ohio Darters
Class City Dart Association
Cleveland Darter Club
Columbus Darters Association
Columbus Pro League
Darters of Cincinnati, Inc.
Dayton Darting Association
East Side Dart League
Greater Akron Darters
Lake Erie Darts Association
Little Miami Dart Association
Mahoning Valley Dart
    Association
Mid-Ohio Dart League
New World Dart Series
North Coast English Dart
    League
Southern Ohio Darting
    Association
Steel Valley Dart Association
Youngstown Dart Association

Oklahoma

Lawton Fort Sill Dart Association
Oklahoma City Dart Association
Tulsa Dart Association

Oregon

Mid-Willamette Valley League
Portland Area Dart Association
SW Washington Dart League

Pennsylvania

The Bud Light Dart League
    of Philadelphia, Bucks and
    Montgomery Counties
Lakeland Area Dart Association
Pittsburgh Dart Association
Quaker City Darts Association
Quaker City English Dart
    League
Three Rivers Darts Club

Rhode Island

East Bay Dart League
Rhode Island Darter's Association
Rhode Island Darts League
Wickford Dart Association

South Carolina

Aiken Singles Series Dart League
Greenville Shrine Darts League
Flowertown Dart League
Palmetto Darts Association, Inc.
Savannah River Darts Association
South Carolina Upstate Dart
    League
Thoroughbred Darts Association
Low Country Fun Dart League
South Strand Darts Association

South Dakota

Aberdeen Area Dart Association
Black Hills Dart Association
Rushmore Darts Association
Sioux Empire Dart Association
South Dakota Dart Association
Dakota Prairie Darts Association

Oahe Steeltip Dart League

Tennessee

Greater Chattanooga Darting
    Association
Greater Johnson City Dart
    Association
Greater Knoxville Darting
    Association
Greater Nashville Darting
    Association
Greater Tri-Cities Darting
    Association
Memphis Area Dart Association
Queen City Dart Association
River City Darts League
Stones River Dart Association
The Chattanooga Dart Club, Inc.
Tullahoma Dart Association

Texas

Abilene Dart Association
Alamo Dart Association
Amarillo Darts Association
Amarillo Garage Darts
    Association
Austin Heat
Bastrop, Elgin, Smithville, Texas
    (BEST) Dart Association
Bexar County Darters
Big Country Dart Association
Capital Area Darts Association
Capital City Darts Association
Centex Darts Association
Central Texas Dart Association
Concho Valley Dart Association
Corpus Christi Dart Association

Dallas Darts Association
Dallas District Darts
Ft. Worth Darts Association
Galveston Area Dart Association
Golden Triangle Darts
    Association
Harris County Darts Association
    (Formerly Houston Darts
    Association)
Heart of Texas Dart Association
Lone Star State Singles League
Lubbock Darts Association
Metroplex Darts Association
National Dart League. Inc.
North Texas Dart Association
Permian Basin Dart Association
Red River Dart Association
Rio Dart Association
River City Darts Association
Rose City Dart Association
San Antonio Metro Dart
    Association
San Antonio Women's Dart
    League
San Marcos Darts Association
South Texas Unified Pro
    Independent Darts
Spring Creek Darts Association
Texarkana Dart Association
Texas Tournament Darts
    Association
Tex-Mex Darts
Tri-City Dart Association
Tropical Darts Association
Tyler Dart Association
VFW #9174 Dart Club
Waco Darts Association

Utah

Chambers Dart Association
Utah Dart Association
Wasatch Dart Association

Vermont

Burlington Men's Dart
Association
South Vermont Darts Club

Virginia

American Dart League of
    Virginia
Blacksburg Area Darters
Central Virginia Dart Association
Central Virginia Dart Association
    Pro League
Greater Tri-Cities Darting
    Association
Prince Williams Dart Association
Shenandoah Valley Darts
    Association
Tidewater Area Darting
    Association
Washington Area Darts
    Association

Washington

Bremerton Area Dart Association
Emerald City Darting
    Organization
NE Washington Dart Association
North Whidbey Dart Association
Peninsula Dart Association
Seattle Area Dart Association

Snohomish County Dart
    Association
Tournament Darts International
Tri-Cities Darting Association
Washington Area Darts
    Association
Washington, District of Columbia

West Virginia

Clarksburg Area Darts
Mountaineer Dart Association
Winchester Dart League

Wisconsin

Greater Milwaukee Darters
Oshkosh Darting Association
Wisconsin's Independent Dart
    Leagues

Wyoming

Natrona County Darting
    Association
Platte River Darting Association
Natrona Country Darting
    Association

RECOMMENDED READING

It seemed appropriate that while writing a book about darts, that a section about books about darts should be included. I recently found a web page online where someone had listed all the books about darts that they owned and the list was just a few short of 100. Many of them were books on how to play, different games, some history, and some were player biographies. However, it sure seemed like a lot of books devoted to this subject and his collection was impressive considering that a majority of them were no doubt out of print by this time. A large amount of the books were from the seventies, eighties and nineties, however, some dated back to the 1930s, and with the oldest one being published in 1935. While I do not know if this was the first book every published, it was the oldest book on this list.

First and foremost on the list for anyone's library has to be *The Official Bar Guide to Darts* by darts historian Dr. Patrick Chaplin. Followers of his work will know that he has previously co-authored books with three-time World Darts Champion John Lowe (2005 and 2009) and eight-time Women's World Champion, Trina Gulliver (2008) and had the book based on his PhD (*Darts in England 1900-1939: A social history*).

I have asked some of the authors to contribute to this section because I firmly believe that these people have gone above and beyond to make an impact on the game and to do something for the game and its players. These authors have so much to contribute to the growth of a player and their story should be shared again and again for the good of the game. For more information on obtaining any of these books, they are all listed on the books page of my website.

David Kirby

David Kirby is the author of the *Definitive Darts Coaching Manual* published in January 2012. His latest offering, a book titled *Darting Essays a*

Coaching Critique was just released in January 2013. David has experience as a martial arts and athletics coach and had used these concepts to embed within the structure of his coaching books. David is a successful ultra runner and now spends more time running and playing for a UK based darts super league team. His first two books are suited to both the soft and steel tip games. There are three more planned in this current coaching series. In April 2013, Jamie (Jabba) Caven's first book on his life to date has been published. Jamie is a professional player on the PDC circuit and world ranked. David assisted Jamie as his ghostwriter.

Book 1: The Definitive Darts Coaching Manual

Coaching: This manual can be used in two ways. You may wish to self-coach and appraise your own game. I have made many references to the fact that if you are going to work alone, then an open mind is very necessary. I would suggest firstly a light read through the whole manual. Perhaps highlighting in the margin areas of note so to come back to at a later point.

Once read through, then you can work on particular areas of interest. To make these sessions efficient, you will need to read and think through what you are trying to achieve. You may disagree or have an alternative method. This will not be incorrect, but at least think through the points made to see if there are any areas when you could adopt for the improvement of your own game. The second scenario is where you may be acting as a coach for a colleague. To start with you will need the co-operation of the student. Peer advice as seen at the oche works for the odd statement, and perhaps for young players. For instance, a kindly word for an inexperienced campaigner about *'leaving it sweet'* when playing pairs may help to develop their game strategy. To make the coach/student relationship work, co-operation from both parties should be assumed.

Book 2: Darting Essays – A Coaching Critique

The Professional Game: There is so much you can write on this subject and it is a constantly changing field. We can explore some of the generalities to give an essence especially to those aspiring to this standard. In no particular order here are some of the things that you should consider. You may find it useful to either employ an agent or at least have someone who helps you on a day-to-day basis. You may be lucky and have a friend or relative who can assist.

With a professional agent a business arrangement will need to be agreed from the start. You should be able to glean some information and guidance from current professional players before talking to a potential agent. A key point is the agreement. It has to be right for the agent and it has to be right for you! You may wish to phase your approach keeping your day-job whilst developing your professional darts standing. This can be built into the agreement to suit both parties. It may also be worth seeking professional advice from an accountant or solicitor before signing on the dotted line.

Book 3: They Way Eye See The Game-The Jamie Caven Story

A biography around Jamie Caven's darting career to date and a look at the issues he has had to overcome, on his journey into the professional game of darts. It covers Jamie's career from his first ever league game at the age of 13 where he averaged 85, through to his World junior title at 17 and including his many wins on the professional tour.

All this has been achieved from a backdrop of diabetes and blindness in one of his eyes. This is truly a remarkable story centered on a wonderful individual and should serve to inspire all of us involved in the world of darts.

George Silberzahn

The website www.howtodarts.com was created in response to the *PDC World Series of Darts* that was held in Boston with $1,000,000 first place prize money if an American won. I wanted to give any person interested in learning more about darts a place to learn about darts, not just how to play the game/sport. It is designed to be browsed through and to help a person learn and understand what darts is. There are interviews with individual players & League Directors, and a tournament designed for recreational players (all with the theme of how to play, where to play, who plays). There are my books, many memorabilia items that span my fifty plus years in the game, and an introduction to Flight School, an online tutorial on how to play and improve as well as comments from players about their experience with Flight School and their increased enjoyment that came from being a Flight Schooler.

My latest book, *DARTS: Beginning to End* (B2E - my nick name), covers all aspects of the sport/game: Who can enjoy the game - from when they first pick up a dart to when their skills/enthusiasm diminish and all the issues that occur across that time (regardless of their physical challenges) with comments from players who have dealt with the issues. There is a DIY Flight School chapter and all the drills and techniques needed to become as good as a person can, or wishes, to be. There are interviews with highly ranked people from North America designed to give insight into the life of a 'pro,' how and why they got that way and what it takes to be a Dart Pro beyond perfected control of the flight path of their darts. There are interviews with some hopefuls for Pro status as well. Some interviews with people who organize and run some of the largest, most successful American style dart tournaments. B2E simply covers DARTS, from beginning to end.

Flight School is the definitive tutorial for increasing a person's enjoyment of the game/sport through the proposition that Darts is primarily intuitive. I take the approach of perfecting 'how you do it' rather than instructing 'how it needs to be done.' There are hundreds of Flight Schoolers worldwide, from beginner to pro to those who needed Dart Emergency Room level of help (Stroke 911), who have expressed satisfaction with Flight School techniques, suggestions and drills.

Paul Seigel (aka "Dartoid")

Paul Seigel (aka "Dartoid") is the most prolific – and most insane – darts journalist in the world. His column (450 issues to date), "Dartoid's World," in print since 1995, appears monthly in darts publications worldwide. His four books have sold no copies and won no awards, pretty much paralleling his unheralded career at the oche. Paul lives in Tampa, Florida, with his wife, Marylou, and their two best friends – a golden retriever, Marky, and a rescue dog from Romania named Romy (who may actually be a werewolf). Both dogs have beaten Dartoid at 501. Website: www. dartoidsworld.com

Book 1: It's a Funny Game, Darts. Life.

You have got to love a book that has references in its early pages to Ernest Hemingway, Sir Arthur Conan Doyle, Primo Carnera and the immortal Joe Louis. As someone who has for nearly thirty years tried to elucidate my passion for tungsten projection by reference to modern literature, pop music, the Bible and the classics, I salute Dartoid and heavily recommend this book to aficionados, backpackers and Joe General Public. Dartoid's zany passion for our sport is matched by his happy gift of recreating vividly the exotic ambiences it is played in. I have myself trod the very oches in the Patpong district of Bangkok that he portrays and visited the Schooner Bar in Hong Kong (China), with its exceedingly odd nibbles - yes, they do taste like Yellow Zonkers! Whether your 'heart of darkness' is set on Boston or Beijing, this book is a veritable tungsten tosser's guide to the world. As a true Brit, I have to admit I shed salt tears of shame on the proofs as I read Jerry Walters' poetic account of the 1974 defeat of the haughty English by a scratch Team USA, followed by the victory of Ray Fischer over my pal, the late great Alan Evans. This is merely one of (almost one hundred) well-told, often self-mocking yarns. One of my other favourites is Dartoid's account of a cork-fevered night at Fordes Bar in Cork, Ireland, and the following mornings 'plopping of Alka Seltzers'. Eat your heart out W.B. Yeats. Just as bullfighting got its Hemingway and baseball its Malamud and Roth, now darts has got its Yankee Boswell. This book will be the first thing I pack when once again I pick up my microphone and go a-commentating. *The late Sid Waddell, Sky TV Darts Commentator*

Book 2: The Year 2008 in Darts

More than anyone, Dartoid has found a way to capture the spirit of the ever-evolving sport of darts – from its roots amidst the smoke and camaraderie of the pub to the spotlight of the professional stage where darts is a business and the very best can earn hundreds of thousands of dollars a year. 2008 – The Year in Darts is a good read, a solid history, and certain to bring many smiles along the way. *The Old Dart Coach, Howie Reed*

Book 3: The Outrageous and Completely Untrue History of the Sport of Darts

This is Dartoid's most recent and tiniest work of darts fiction and we should indeed be grateful for the latter. I can solemnly attest that it is, in my very humble opinion, quite the most historically inaccurate and stupid thing that anyone has ever put to paper. Despite his advance apologies to his God, and many others, I am certain that they are insufficient to prevent him from being cast into Hades when the Grim Reaper eventually comes to call. Having said that, IT IS FUN!!! *Patrick Chaplin, Ph.D.*

Book 4: The Diary of an Unhealthy Dart Throwing Slug

Dartoid and I have been friends since the early days of the old North American Open. I have watched him compete and count myself among the many who enjoy reading his column. But more than any of his columns this little book struck a cord with me. While I doubt that the ideas, or any others for that matter, will help Dartoid's game, many of them are principles I now practice. They are presented in Dartoid's unique humorous easy-to-read style and are certain to improve your health and the way you feel and throw. *Jerry Umberger.*

And currently in various stages of completion but coming soon to a bookshelf near you: *Double Outs I've Loved and Lost, The Best of Dartoid, Volume II*, a yet to be titled adventure about a bike ride from Dublin to Moscow where for 32 days and 2,000 miles the Dartoid character drinks his way through a blur of darts bars, two historical pieces - one about the five Las Vegas Desert Classics and the other about the PDC's World Series of Darts, and a serious novel set in Asia about trade in endangered species (but with a strong darts theme) titled *Shooter.* Stay tuned!

Bobby George

Robert Francis George was born on December 16, 1945, in Manor Park, London. Bobby started playing darts later in life compared to most, at the age of 30, and won the first tournament he entered in. George was well known as one of darts more flamboyant personalities, making his way to the stage decked out in gold jewelry, while wearing a crown and cloak and carrying a candelabrum, all done to the tune of "We Are the Champions".

Bobby made his first appearance at the WDF World Masters less than a year after he started playing and has won many tournaments all over the world, including the News of the World Championship in 1979 and 1986. For Bobby's NOTW win in 1979, he was the only player to never lose a leg during the entire course of the event, the only player to ever do so. Bobby also won the Butlin's Grand Masters in 1979 and 1980; the Nations Cup Triples competition in 1980, while teamed up with Tony Brown and John Lowe, and appeared in two World Championship finals.

Since 1998, he has also worked for the BBC during their coverage of various darts tournaments. Bobby stopped playing regular tournaments in 1986 and became the first full time exhibition player, where his outgoing and colorful persona and has enabled him to achieve much success.

Bobby now lives with his wife and manager Marie, and their sons Robert and Richard at George Hall, an 18-bedroom self-built mansion he jokingly refers to as "the house that Bobby built."

Book 1: Bobby Dazzler: My Story

After a tough childhood helping his imposing dad in the garden and looking after his pigeons, Bobby George left school barely able to read or write. A life in the building trade-digging the Victoria Line and laying granite floors-or minding Essex pub doors in the post-Krays era seemed to beckon.

That is until, after a day's fishing off southern Ireland in the summer of 1976, a game of pub darts got off the ground. By the end of the night, Bobby had taken on and beaten the whole pub. He was a natural. And he has never looked back: threw years later he won the News of the World Championship.

Bobby George burst onto the darts scene just as the popularity of the game went through the roof and it began its golden era. Slimmer and better looking than most darts players, Bobby, with his glittery shirts and flashy jewelry, brought showbiz to darts. Here he relives the gripping tension of the News of the World and Embassy finals. He looks back over the ups and downs of life with characters such as Eric Bristow, Jocky Wilson, John 'Stoneface' Lowe and Keith Deller; and also the agony of the 1994 Embassy final, which he played in a steel corset after breaking his back.

From rags to bling, from the world if Essex pubs in the 1970s to behind the scenes with the BBC at Frimley Green; from films and videos to *Celebrity Fit Club, Bobby Dazzler: My Story* is the vividly entertaining tale of one of the country's best loved and charismatic showmen.

John Lowe

John Lowe was born on July 21, 1945, in New Tupton, Derbyshire, England, and now makes his home town in Chesterfield, Derbyshire, England with his wife, Karen.

John throws with his 21gram Unicorn World Champion Golden signature darts and threw the first televised nine-dart game on October 13, 1984 during the World Matchplay tournament 1984, which earned him £102,000, and he went on to win the tournament. John is also one of only five players to have won the World Championship 3 times, and has done it in three different decades.

John has won World Championships in 1979, 1987, and 1993, and World Masters titles in 1976 and 1980, while competing in the British Darts Organization. John also won the News of the World Championship in 1981, the British Open in 1977 and 1988, and the WDF World Cup singles title in 1981 and 1991, among many other titles.

Due to his demeanor, John earned the nickname Old Stoneface, which is also the title of his autobiography, which was published in 2005. In May 2009, John's latest book, *The Art of Darts*, was published, in which he offered his personal insights into the game to all levels of players.

John Lowe has spent over 45 years playing the sport of darts, during which time he has accumulated over 1000 titles World Wide, he has been Champion of the World three times, in three separate decades: the '70s, '80s, and '90s. He captained England for 7 years, during which time they did not lose a match, and in 1984 John became the first player in the history of the sport to achieve the perfect game of 501 in 9 darts on Television, winning $160,000. John is the author of four books: *The Lowe Profile, Darts John Lowe Way, Old Stoneface, My Autobiography,* and the top selling coaching manual: *The Art of Darts.* In October 2012, John made the very first coaching application for iPhone and iPad, an adaptation of his book *The Art of Darts,* and released under the same name, the app is almost 40 minutes of in depth instruction, how to choose your darts, the grip, the stance, the throwing arm, the release, fine tune your game, and much more, John does not play on the professional circuit anymore, but continues to play exhibitions, and appear in promotions.

Book 1: The Art of Darts

The Art of Darts is three-time World Champion John Lowe's darts master class that caters for every level of player, from the obsessed amateur to the fledgling professional, and reveals the secrets of his three decades of experience at the pinnacle of the sport. Every conceivable aspect of the game is covered, from choosing the right grip, darts and practice routines that suit you, constructing out shots and perfecting your stance at the oche, to tips on how to cope with the pressure of a sold-out noisy arena in your first professional match. Whether you want to improve your game wholesale or simply fine tune some misbehaving aspects, *The Art of Darts* is essential to every darts player, fan or enthusiast and is well set to becoming the first classic darts text.

John's autobiography *Old Stoneface* and *The Art of Darts* are available from www.legendsofdarts.com. John is always willing to sign all copies, and provide that personal message. The Art of Darts application is also available in the iPhone, iPad, and iTunes application store.

Patrick Chaplin (aka 'Dr. Darts')

Dr. Patrick Chaplin has been researching and writing about darts for more than 25 years and is generally regarded as the authority on darts history. He has been playing darts (in his fashion) for longer than he cares to remember.

Winner of a few pub-level darts trophies Patrick began delving into darts history in the mid-1980s when, in a local pub his best friend asked, "What's the true history of darts then Pat?" Patrick said he would let him know in a fortnight.

That was back in the summer of 1985….

Author of several books on darts, including collaborations with Bobby George, Trina Gulliver and John Lowe, Patrick is the only person on the planet to have obtained a PhD in the social history of darts (2006), a fact that led to him being dubbed 'Dr. Darts' by the tabloid press a soubriquet that suits him fine. He also writes occasional articles and reviews for the darts press including *Darts World* and *Bull's-Eye News*.

He also has an authoritative website www.patrickchaplin.com and produces his monthly Dr. Darts' Newsletter which has hundreds of subscribers from around the globe. (To subscribe, simply send e-mail to Patrick at info@patrickchaplin.com.)

In recognition of his achieving his PhD, Patrick was made an Honorary Visiting Research Fellow in History by Anglia Ruskin University, Cambridge.

Patrick lives in Essex, England, with his wife Maureen.

COLLABORATIONS

Book 1: Old Stoneface: The Autobiography of Britain's Greatest Darts Player

John Lowe (Three-time World Professional Darts Champion). In a career spanning more than three decades John and his fellow professionals transformed the traditional English pub game of darts into a successful, professional sport with legions of fans and big money prizes. John has become a legend in his own lifetime. Filled with tales from all the major matches and tournaments, along with his sometimes-controversial thoughts on his big name opponents, the man who took up darts 'by accident' shares his fascinating and exciting life with his readers.

Book 2: Golden Girl: The Autobiography of the Greatest Ever Ladies' Darts Player

Trina Gulliver: (Nine-time Ladies' World Professional Darts Champion) Trina is the most successful ladies' darts player ever. Up to 2012 she has won the Lakeside World Ladies' Darts Championship an amazing nine times. In her autobiography Trina, who is fiercely passionate about her sport, tells how with grit and determination she was able to realize her dream. Heart-warming and inspirational, this book should be read by not only darts lovers but anyone interested in a story of success against the odds.

Book 3: Scoring for Show, Doubles for Dough – Booby George's Darts Lingo

Bobby George (Twice winner of the News of the World Individual Darts Championship and twice runner up in the Embassy World Championships)

Have you ever watched a darts match on TV and wondered what on earth the players and commentators are talking about? In this book, darts professional Bobby George 'The King of Bling' and 'Dr. Darts' provide an extensive list of darts language heard on TV and in bars across the world and explain each one in an informative and hilarious way.

SOLE AUTHOR

Book 4: Darts in England 1900-39: A social history

This is Patrick's key work of darts history based on his PhD. Drawing on an eclectic range of primary and secondary sources Patrick examines the development of darts in the context of English society in the early twentieth century. He reveals how darts was transformed during the interwar years to become one of the most popular recreations in England, not just amongst working class men and, to a lesser extent, working class women but even among the middle and upper classes. He also dispels a number of myths relating to the sport and shows how the foundations of the modern game of darts were firmly laid in England during those years.

Book 5: The Official Bar Guide to Darts

In this book commissioned particularly for the North American market, Patrick examines every aspect of darting, from the origins of the sport to the necessary equipment, from the rules of play to how to improve your game. Whether you are a beginner or a seasoned member of a league, this is the must-have guide to a long-standing and beloved tradition.

Chris Carey, author of *The American Darts Organization Book of Darts*, says, "Patrick is a real authority on darts...this book is an essential addition to any darts library and will certainly be a useful and trusted resource for dart players of all skill levels."

Book 6: 180! Fascinating Darts Facts

In *180! Fascinating Darts Facts* Patrick Chaplin (aka 'Dr. Darts') delves deep into his mind-boggling archive and, with not a brain-numbing list of statistics in sight, presents a plethora of darts trivia never before gathered together in book form.

"Why did darts never make it to the 2012 Olympics?", "Why are darts matches usually played as from 501 and not 500?", "Who scored the first perfect nine-dart game?" and "Were early dartboards *really* made out of pig-bristle?" The answers to these and many other darts questions, which have been troubling darts fans for ages (or not as the case may be) can be found in this book.

From the big guns of yesteryear to the stars of the modern game and from the origins of darts to fans drinking a darts venue dry, it's all here in *180! Fascinating Darts Facts*.

Colin Saunders

The Complete Records of the Embassy and Lakeside World Professional Darts Championships 1978 to 2012

This record is a two volume hard back set A4 in size and contains over 850 pages. The volumes can be purchased individually or as a set.

An *INTRODUCTION*

I started the project of documenting the Embassy World Darts Championship just over ten years ago, and at the time started with a lot of enthusiasm and a very naïve belief that it would probably take about 3 years. It took me just over 4 years to get all the information for the history and to set up a system to ensure I would get information from the continuing years, and I have to say I never lost any of the enthusiasm I started with.

The years went by and a book that looked like 300 pages grew into 500 then 600 I followed by this by thinking this is going to be heavy and then went from one volume to two volumes and the number of pages grew and grew. There are many things I have not been able to put in these first two volumes, and in fact I think another book with player's interviews (a lot of which I have already done but did not have room to include them) and effects the championships have had on players all over the world but this maybe for another time.

Over the ten years I have gone from the highs of reading old score sheets (I found these to be the most interesting) and reports, to falling asleep at the computer typing in the records, to a feeling of, I do not what to be doing this! As I tried to proof read 100's of pages of numbers I had already type in, but the best moment of all was the great satisfaction I felt when I picked up the first proof copies.

I may still have got it wrong but that is for you to decide, but with the effort I have put in I have to say I do not think I could have done any more, so I hope you enjoy the history of the greatest darts event for the last 35 years, an event that has done more for Darts Worldwide than any other. Colin's website is www.dartbydartbooks.com.

Dan William Peek

Dan William Peek is a writer, banjo player and marketing consultant. He lives with his wife Joy in Columbia, Missouri, five minutes from their grandchildren, Grace and Spencer. Dan has written a number of articles, essays and reviews on a variety of subjects and was for several years a contributing writer for *Bull's-Eye News*. In addition to *To The Point: The Story of Darts in America*, he is the author of *Live! At the Ozark Opry* (the History Press). Dan is co-founder and Executive Director of Grandparents and Others on Watch, Inc., a non-profit child advocacy organization.

Book 1: To The Point: The Story of Darts in America

Darts Mythology-There is a story of wide currency that sets forth the claim that darts came to America on the Mayflower. No one offers any provenance for this tale. Derek Brown (1981) in his reasonably definitive book, Darts, states that there is no proof of the commonly told tales of darts' medieval origin nor of its transplantation to the New World on the Mayflower.

Brown, a darts journalist and long-time editor of the darts page of the *London Daily Mail*, writes that if the pilgrims did occupy a portion of their trans-Atlantic time throwing whittled-down arrows at wine casks, it is nowhere recorded. That activity, he notes, would have been an archery game called "Butts." He cites an American, Edmund Carl Hady, "an expert on darts who lives in Pennsylvania" as a source of the Mayflower story.

In any event, Brown observes, throwing any sharp object while perched on the planks of a ship like the Mayflower on the high seas would most likely have resulted in a punctured pilgrim or two, and a resolve to toss no more darts until safely on shore.

Brown's argument is bolstered considerably by an article about darts, which appeared, somewhat improbably, on the front page of the *Wall Street Journal* on August 15, 1974.

"Dartings origin is obscure. Though it is assumed that English darts began in Britain – where it is the most popular participation sport after fishing – nobody knows when and how. Tales that are almost surely apocryphal credit its invention to midget kings who couldn't handle a bow and so threw their arrows instead.

"The *Encyclopedia Brittanica* asserts that passengers on the Mayflower whiled away their idle hours playing darts. But Lawrence Geller, director of the Pilgrim Society – a historical group that isn't especially eager to link the Mayflower crowd with a saloon pastime – says, 'in all I've read (about the pilgrims) I've never seen anything about darts.'"

GLOSSARY OF TERMINOLOGY

Arrows-an alternate term for darts.

Average-the score calculated for three darts thrown, which is the total of all three divided by 3.

Barrel-the heavier metal portion of the dart set-up that you grip to throw the dart.

Bed-a section of a number on the board, generally refers to a single, double, or triple.

Bounce out-describes the dart that bounces off the wire and does not stick in the board.

Breakfast-refers to a score of 26 (single 5, single 20, single 1). The term comes from the typical price of a bed-and-breakfast in times gone by: 2 shillings and sixpence, or "two and six." (*See also* chips).

Bulls-eye (or bull)-the center circle targets of the dartboard.

Bust-over scoring, resulting in a lost turn.

Chips (or fish and chips)-also refers to a score of 26 (single 5, single 20, single 1).

Cork-the center of the dartboard; the bulls-eye. The term comes from the cork in the end of a keg where it is tapped. The ends of kegs were used for targets in the game's early days.

Cover shot-shooting an alternate triple when a previously thrown dart is blocking the triple 20.

Cricket-alternate game from 01 that involves hitting 3 of each number, 15-20 and bulls-eyes.

Diddle for the middle-a throw of a single dart to determine who throws first in the game by means of being closer to the bullseye.

Double-the narrow outer ring of the board. The double section counts for two times the number hit.

Double-bull-on dartboards configured with a bulls-eye consisting of two concentric circles, double-bull refers to the inner circle, which is commonly red and worth 50 points.

Double in-when a double is needed to start the game, generally used for 301 only.

Double top-the double 20.

Double trouble-not being able to hit the double needed to win the game.

Feathers-refers to flights, since early flights were made from feathers.

Flights-the "wings" at the end of a dart that help it fly straight and land point first.

Game on-called by the referee to advise all players that the match has now started.

Game shot-called by the referee to signify that the match winning double has been hit.

Leg-one game of a match. Most professional matches are made of a number of sets, each of which is split into a certain number of legs.

Lipstick-usually refers to triple 20, as this portion of the board is commonly red in color and resembles an upper lip, but may refer to any red double or triple.

Mad house-the double -1. The lowest score that can win a game by hitting a double.

Marker-refers to a scorekeeper for a match.

Maximum-a score of 180.

Maximum check-out-a score of 170 to end a game (triple-20, triple-20, inner bull).

Mugs away-loser of the previous game goes first in the next game.

Nine darter-when a player completes a game of 501 in the minimum required nine-darts. Also known as a perfect game.

Oche-the line on which a player stands to throw.

One-hundred-and-eighty!-called by the referee to announce that a player has scored a maximum.

Perfect game-a nine-dart game for leg of 501.

Perfect score-the maximum score of 180.

Perfect finish-maximum check-out of 170.

PPD-average "points per dart" thrown.

Robin Hood-throwing a dart into the shaft or flight of another dart that is already in the board, which will stick, sometimes splitting the flight.

Round of nine-throwing three triples that close (before being closed by opponent) or point in one turn in cricket.

Set-a scoring method used in many tournaments.

Shaft-the part of a dart behind the barrel when the flights are mounted.

Shanghai-refers to hitting a single, double, and triple of the same number in the same turn.

Shut out-when you lose a game without ever scoring in it.

Single-bull-on dartboards configured with a bulls-eye consisting of two concentric circles, single-bull refers to the outer circle, which is commonly green and worth 25 points. The inner circle is commonly red and worth 50 points.

Skunked-when you lose a 301 game without ever scoring in it because you did not hit the initial double to start scoring.

Slop-darts that score, but did not hit the target they were intended for.

Splash-taking two or more darts in hand at once and throwing them at the board at the same time.

Spray and pray-a humorous term for darts thrown aimlessly.

Straight in-a game that requires no special shot to begin scoring.

Straight out-a game that requires no special shot to finish a game. (e.g., Hitting a single number to win the game rather than having to hit a double.)

Three in a bed-three darts in the same number, regardless if it is a single, double, or triple.

Throw line-another term for oche.

Toe line-another term for oche.

Ton 80-three darts in the triple 20, which scores 180 points: only in 01 games.

Ton-a score of 100 in any of the games of 01.

Tops-double 20.

Triple (or treble)-the thin inner ring of the board that counts for three times the number hit.

APPENDIX A:
THE STUDY OF PRACTICE
ROUTINES AND THEIR
EFFECTIVENESS

Levels of practice can vary from player to player when you determine that you are playing for fun or in a casual atmosphere, as opposed to deliberate practice for professional players. 1985 World Cup Ladies Singles Champion and long time player, Linda (Batten) Duffy pursued her PhD, where she investigated the psychological aspects of throwing practice and used pro dart players in her studies. While her studies were published in some academic journals, they have never been published in a book about darts until now. Linda has graciously agreed to share her findings with us here.

> **The study focused on how dart performance is affected by various practice methods amongst professional men and women players.**

Abstract

A modified version of Ericsson, Krampe, and Tesch-Romer's (1993) semi structured interview schedule was employed to examine the relationship between gender, level of professional standing, and facets of practice amongst men and women professional and amateur dart players. Players accumulated number of practice hours were classified at four periods during their sporting history, namely; at years 3, 5, 10 and 15 in relation to engaging in playing league darts, playing for fun, playing in competitions, engaging in solitary deliberate practice, and deliberate practice with a partner. The samples were twelve professional male dart players, mean age 41.7 years, twelve amateur level male dart players, mean age 41 years, six professional female dart players, mean age 36.6 years, and six amateur female level dart players, mean age 42 years. All participants were right-handed throwers. The main criteria for both male and female professional level players was to have attained international level of performance, at least one singles win at World level and five singles wins at International Open Championship level, and to be ranked in the top 16 of the World rankings for at least 75 percent of their playing career. The criterion for both male and female amateur was to have no attainment of international level of performance and to have played county darts for the duration of at least 15 years.

The results showed superior dart performance being related to the accumulated number of hours engaged in various types of deliberate practice, independent of gender, or vary according to player's ratings of level of enjoyment, concentration, or physical effort involved in practice. Implications of these findings are discussed.

Introduction

There is now a growing body of research examining factors such as implicit and explicit memory and its contribution to achieving professional level of expertise in various sporting activities. Whilst cognitive skills may be considered to be a significant factor in certain sports, such as soccer, they are comparatively less important to other sports, for example playing darts. Indeed, in a sport like darts the key contributing variable may be argued to be the quality and quantity of time spent on practice and competitive performance rather than purely cognitive skills such as memory. The aim of the present study is to examine the extent to which Ericsson, Krampe, and Tesch-Romer's, (1993) "Theory of Deliberate Practice" may account for dart performance amongst professional and amateur men and women players. The theory of deliberate practice, as referred to by Ericsson et al (1993), Ericsson and Charness (1994), Ericsson (1996), and Ericsson and Lehmann (1996) was originally derived from two studies with violinists and pianists of varying levels of skill. Their approach was to employ semi-structured interviews incorporating an activity chart designed to record taxonomy of weekly activities and to estimate how many hours per week each individual would engage in each of the activities throughout their careers.

In particular, one could have a break down of facets of practice as follows: practice with friends for fun, participation in official settings, practice for purposes of improving your performance (alone), and practice for purposes of improving performance with an instructor or partner. Ericsson et al's (1993) used information derived from the semi-structured interviews and activity charts from the musicians and found evidence suggesting that the accumulated number of hours spent in activities designed purely to improve performance (deliberate practice) were a function of skill level for musicians. Ericsson et al's (1993) claim that experts, when compared to novices, do in fact engage in vast amounts of deliberate practice has now been tested in several sporting activities requiring motor skills (e.g. soccer and field hockey, karate, wrestling, figure skating, and on long distance Canadian runners).

The present study extends the examination of the relationship between facets of practice and professional performance among British dart players (see following pages for a description of the sport of darts). The question pursued is whether there is a difference between professional and amateurs in their accumulated number of hours engaged in various facets of practice. Moreover, to examine if there is a difference between darts player's ratings for practice as a function of their skill level. In particular, the study examines the possibility that higher enjoyment ratings of practice by professionals might explain why they engage in more deliberate practice than less skilled players.

Also incorporated in the present study is the issue of possible differences due to gender on dart performance. There is now universal agreement that in tasks incorporating motor skills and, in particular dart throwing, there is a significant male superiority, although there are fewer consensuses as to why such differences exist. Some researchers maintain that biological/genetic factors are influential predictors of throwing skills between males and females. Others argue that environmental factors are the more crucial contributors to gender differences in throwing. The interesting position, however, is that gender differences in dart throwing have been demonstrated for both and world professional dart players.

Indeed, in a recent study Duffy, Baluch, and Ericsson found that, when investigating performance between genders, the magnitude of differences in accuracy of target throwing is the same for both naïve and professional dart players. In other words, the extent 7 of differences (in millimeters) to which a naïve female dart player deviates from her male counter part in accuracy of dart throwing is the same as the extent to which a professional female dart player deviates from the target compared to her male counter part. This suggests that whilst there has been significant improvement in accuracy of dart throwing for women as a result of professional dart playing, there nevertheless remains a gap between the genders, which is comparable to the differences seen for naïve participants. Furthermore, it was found that male professional players of lower levels of ranking scored significantly higher than women dart players of a higher ranking, even though physical factors namely; height and arm length were controlled for. In the present study, facets of dart practice and its relationship between genders will also be examined in an attempt to shed more light on gender differences in target/dart throwing.

Features of Dart Playing

Darts is a non-contact target sport with universal playing rules. Championship matches are played over a pre-designated number of legs; each leg starts at 501 points and must be finished on a double segment.

Each player throws in turn and deducts each score thrown until they have completed 501. The aim is to complete each leg before your opponent, i.e., by hitting the winning double first. In addition to recording wins and losses, level of performance can be measured using the single dart average, which is calculated by dividing the original number of points required to complete a leg by the number of darts used by a player to complete the leg. For example, if a player takes fifteen darts to complete a leg of 501 (501/15) the single dart average equals 33.40. Alternatively, if a player takes sixteen darts to complete a leg of 501, their single dart average would be 31.31, which is less than 33.40. Due to the nature of the scoring system one can reliably assume that superior players will record a higher single dart average. Based on dart finishing averages and number of losses and wins, dart players have been ranked in their professional standing and level of skill as intermediate, county level (amateur) and international (professional). Each dart player has an updated single dart average that is a reflection of their current standing. In the present study, single dart averages have been used as a measure of player's performance (see also British Darts Organization Year Book 2002). Research questions: First, to examine the ratings given by players on various aspects of practice. In line with previous studies extending Ericsson et al's (1993) claim, one would expect that dart players ratings for enjoyable aspects of practice to be different from aspects requiring concentration and physical effort. This is because darts may be seen more as a fun game or a game played in social settings. Secondly, to examine if there would be a difference in accumulated number of hours engaged in various facets of practice in relation to levels of professional/amateur ranking. Moreover, whether the accumulated number of hours engaged in various facets of practice correlates with actual dart performance, namely single dart averages (as previously explained). The final aim is to examine whether various facets of practice could also account for gender differences in dart performance and professional ranking. If the latter is true it does imply that at least one factor accounting for the male superiority effect in dart throwing is practice related. If, however, male and female dart players do not show any obvious differences on accumulated hours in facets of practice, it might imply that perhaps something of a more fundamental nature (e.g. biological differences) play a key role.

Method

The sample targeted in this study were twelve professional male dart players, mean age 41.7 years, twelve amateur level male dart players, mean age 41 years, six professional female dart players, mean age 36.6 years, and six amateur level dart players, mean age 42 years. All participants were right-handed throwers. Handedness was determined on the basis of which hand the participants claimed to be their dominant hand for dart throwing. The criteria for both male and female professional level players was as follows; i) to have attained international level of performance, ii) to have professional status recognized by the sports governing body, iii) at least one singles win at World level and five singles wins at International Open Championship level, and iv) to be ranked in the top 16 of the World rankings for at least 75 percent of their playing career. The criteria for both male and female amateur level players was as follows; i) no attainment of international level of performance, ii) to have amateur status as recognized by the sports governing body and iii) to have played county darts for a duration of at least 15 years. Due to the strict nature of selection criteria for the group of professional level players it was difficult, if not impossible, to select more than six women dart players. This determined that 6 women amateur level players were selected to provide the appropriate match.

Procedure

The data collection procedure for all four groups of dart players was identical and covered a span of three years from 1998 to 2001. All data was collected during personal interviews with participants. Information was recorded and included up to the end of the 1998 dart-playing season, hence ensuring the same finishing point of data collection for all participants. Appointments were made with each participant and information regarding the nature and purpose of the impending interview was given to the participant by the author. This enabled each participant to gather relevant information regarding their dart playing careers and gave them a timeframe whereby they could best recall the timing and nature of activities in which they had engaged during this period. The framework of the interview was similar to that employed by Ericsson et al (1993) in their interviews with musicians.

Materials

The main materials for the present study consisted of a rating sheet for practice and an activity chart. The subjects were asked to rate using a scale of 0–10, where 0 was low, 5 was average and 10 was high as to how much they considered practice to be enjoyable, how much it requires concentration and how much physical effort is required. The activity chart was designed to enable each participant to record the weekly number of hours spent in engaging in those activities most relevant to dart playing performance. The activity chart was similar to the one used by Ericsson et al (1993), but was modified to incorporate activities related to dart players. The activities listed were as follows: Playing in competitions, playing for fun, playing in a league, total deliberate practice, solitary practice, and practice with a partner. Total deliberate practice is solitary practice and practice with a partner added together.

Results:
Ratings and practice

Means and standard deviations for the rating of three aspects of practice, namely physical effort, concentration, and enjoyable for men and women dart players across two levels of skill were documented. There does not seem to be significant differences between participants in their rating of various aspects of practice i.e. physical, concentration, and enjoyable. Pillais criterion indicated no significant main effect for level of skill (i.e. professional vs. amateur), gender, and no significant interaction.

Results of activity chart

For clarity the results of the activity chart were documented to include the facets of practice related to competitions, playing for fun and playing in a league. The facets of practice related to total deliberate practice, solitary practice, and practice with a partner were also documented. Each facet of practice was analyzed separately in relation to gender, professional ranking (professional-amateur), and in four distinctive years of the players career namely (3, 5, 10, and 15) using Multivariate Analysis of Variance (MANOVA). Pillais Criterion was also employed, as there were unequal groups (men vs. women). Post-hoc analysis was also employed by way of Roy-Bargman step down F-tests (applying Bonferroni correction), as this method addresses the problem of dependent variables, which are correlated. This is done by a method analogous to the testing of several Independent Variables in Multiple Regression via Hierarchical Analysis. The Highest priority Dependent Variable is tested in a Univariate Anova (using the appropriate adjustment for alpha) and the remaining Dependent Variables are tested in a series of ANCOVA's. Furthermore, Pearson's Product Moment

Correlation Coefficients were used to examine the relationship between single dart averages with accumulated number of each facet of practice.

Playing in competition

There were no significant main effects for number of hours engaged in playing in competitions for gender, or for level of skill (professional vs. amateur), and no significant interaction, all p values greater than 0.05. There was also no significant relationship between the number of accumulated hours spent playing in competitions and single dart averages.

Playing for fun

There were no significant main effects for number of hours engaged in playing for fun for gender and for level of skill (professional vs. amateur), and there was no significant interaction all p values greater than 0.05. There was also no significant relationship between the number of accumulated hours spent playing darts for fun and single dart averages.

Playing in a league

There was a significant main effect for number of hours engaged in playing league for gender (i.e. women have played more in league than men). There was also a significant interaction between gender and level of skill (professional vs. amateur). However, there was no significant main effect for level of skill. This implies that professional men have played less in a league (and more in competition) than amateur men, but the same is not true for women. Post-hoc analysis by way of Roy-Bargman step-down F tests, applying Bonferroni correction, found significant interaction effects at year 15 into career and a significant effect for gender at year 15 into career.

There also was a significant negative relationship between the number of accumulated hours spent playing league darts and single dart averages at year 3, at year 5, and year 10, into career. This negative interaction is expected as the higher a person has a dart average (e.g. professionals) the less he/she is likely to play in a league (more preference to play professionally).

Total deliberate practice

There was no significant main effect for number of hours engaged in total deliberate practice for gender, however, there was a significant main effect for level of skill (professional vs. amateur). The interaction between gender and skill was not significant. Post-hoc analysis by way of Roy-Bargman step-down F tests, applying Bonferroni correction, found a significant effect for level of skill with professional players reporting a higher number of hours engaged in deliberate practice at year 10 into their career.

Pearson's Product Moment Correlation Coefficient revealed a significant positive relationship between single dart averages and the number of accumulated hours spent engaged in total practice (solitary deliberate practice and practice with a partner) at year 3, at year 5, year 10, and year 15 into career. Significantly, the relationship between single dart averages and total deliberate practice becomes stronger as career span progresses.

Solitary practice

There was no significant main effect for solitary practice for gender, and no significant interaction between skill and gender. However there was a significant main effect for level of skill (professional vs. amateur). Post-hoc analysis by way of Roy-Bargman step-down F tests, applying Bonferroni correction, found a significant effect for level of skill with professional players reporting a higher number of hours engaged in deliberate practice at year 10 into their career. There was a significant positive relationship, by way of Pearson's Product Moment Correlation Coefficient, between single dart averages and the number of accumulated hours spent engaged in solitary deliberate practice at year 3, at year 5, year 10, and year 15 into a career.

Practice with a partner

There was no significant main effect for deliberate practice with a partner for gender, and no significant main effects for level of skill (professional vs. amateur), and for interaction between level of skill and gender. There was no significant relationship between single dart averages and the number of accumulated hours engaged in deliberate practice with a partner.

Discussion

The key research questions were as follows:

-Is there a difference in professional and amateur men and women dart players ratings of practice as being enjoyable, effortful, and requiring concentration?

-Is there a difference between accumulated facets of practice between professional and amateur men and women dart players?

-Is there a relationship between accumulated facets of practice and single dart averages (a measure of professional ranking)?

The ratings on various aspects of practice showed no significant differences. This was somewhat surprising, as playing darts seems to be a sport whereby, for amateurs at least, the main aim is enjoyment and social interaction. It thus appears that for men and women professional and amateur players there is no significant difference in how much they rate practice as enjoyable, or requiring physical effort or requiring concentration.

Generally, all ratings (0–10) were accumulated on the higher end of the ratings (above 5) and this may have accounted for lack of significant within category differences.

Similar trends in these ratings have also been found in previous research; for example, the requirement of high concentration for practice was strongly supported by martial artists, musicians, figure skaters, wrestlers, soccer, and field hockey players. More recent work by Young and Salmela (2002) reported that, according to runners, the most effortful activities were also viewed as the most enjoyable. These findings have been viewed as contrary to the tenets of Ericsson et al's (1993) Theory. Nevertheless, the critical issue is whether the superior players would view solitary deliberate practice activities as more enjoyable than other players, which might explain the professionals' more extensive engagement in deliberate practice.

However, the current study did not find higher enjoyment ratings for the professionals compared to the amateurs, if anything, the amateurs' ratings tended to indicate higher enjoyment. The engagement of the dart-related activities differed between groups for three types, namely playing in league darts, solitary practice, and total deliberate practice. The latter two findings were in line with prior expectations namely; the more an individual engages in deliberate practice (particularly solitary practice) the more proficient their performance is likely to be. This finding supports one of the main tenets of Ericsson et al's (1993) theory whereby expertise is acquired through a vast number of hours spent engaging in activities purely designed to improve performance, i.e., deliberate practice. However, the fact that no gender differences or interactions were found for accumulated amount of practice was further evidence in line with Duffy, Baluch and Ericsson's findings that the *magnitude* of gender differences in accuracy of dart throwing is the same for university students and professional dart players regardless of years of training. It does seem to be the case that explanations other than total amount of practice must account for gender differences in dart throwing (Duffy 2002, Duffy, Baluch, & Ericsson).

Returning to the significant finding for playing league darts, these results indicated a reliable interaction with gender. For female dart players there was no difference between professionals and amateurs, but male amateurs reported having played more in this environment than male professionals from the beginning of their respective dart careers. In fact, accumulated number of hours playing league darts showed a reliable negative relationship with single dart averages. Indeed, mere engagement in many types of activities does not automatically improve performance (Ericsson, 1996, 2003), which may be, in part at least, an explanation for the lack of relation between dart performance and accumulated participation in several activities, such as playing in competitions, playing for fun or practicing with a partner. This lack of relations between participation and dart performance does not imply that the players, especially the professional players, do not gain any benefits from participating in certain activities. It is possible that professional and amateur players engage in these activities with different attitudes and level of concentration. For example, in the case of playing in competitions, both professional and amateur level dart players would engage in this activity on a regular basis to compete for trophies and/or prize money. However, differences in the level of competition are crucial factors. For example: Professional players would play in predominantly world ranked international competitions and fewer national, regional or local competitions, whereas for amateur players, the reverse would be the case. In view of many of the professional players' attitudes towards competitive play, and its contribution to improving performance, this could be argued to have a significant effect on overall performance. However, it is also possible that participation in competitions might have an indirect influence. Preparations for upcoming competitions for professionals might increase the amount of quality deliberate practice and reviews of their competition performance might motivate professionals to engage in additional solitary practice to make corrections and further improvements. Hence, deliberate practice might be the real cause of the better performance of the professionals.

In relation to playing for fun, again it is not surprising that no significant differences were found between groups. Darts has its roots firmly embedded in a social context. Professional dart players are typically introduced to playing darts in an informal social environment, whilst professional performers in other domains, namely music and most sports, may have their first point of contact with a particular activity in a specifically designed domain-related environment, i.e., a music school, gymnasium or an athletics track. Therefore, professional dart players spend several years, prior to becoming professional, playing darts within a "social type" framework.

Arguably this could go some way toward explaining why there were no differences between groups for practicing with a partner. When dart players decide to make a conscious effort to improve their performance beyond their current levels, their preferred method is to become isolated, thereby distancing themselves from the social context to engage in solitary deliberate practice. In short, the present study revealed that the single major factor contributing to professional level dart playing performance is deliberate practice. Moreover, differences in the total amount of solitary practice were unable to explain the differences in dart playing performance for men and women. Future research will be necessary to identify the nature and locus of these gender-based differences.

APPENDIX B:
BATTLE OF THE SEXES

When it comes to performance standards, there have been noticea-
ble differences in the competitive levels between men and women.
While it is often said that darts is a game where there are nonphysical
limitations and differences in size, shape, and gender do not matter, there
has never been any credible studies done on these differences until long-
time English player Linda (Batten) Duffy chose the topic while working
to obtain her PhD in Sports Psychology. Linda completed a very thorough review of the differences and has graciously shared her published
paper regarding the subject.

Abstract

It has been very difficult to determine whether differences in perceptual-
motor performance between males and females reflect differences in experience or biological/genetic endowment. This study examines the effect of
extensive training on one of the largest sex differences, namely accuracy
in dart throwing and found that physical differences in height and reach
could not explain sex differences in a combined sample of highly experienced male and female regional/national level dart players. A second
study rejected accounts of sex differences based on participation rates by
showing that male dart players recruited from a small pool of club players were superior to the best female players selected from a large pool at
international level. Alternative accounts of the source of sex differences
in darts, based on male and female players' differential development and
practice histories, are discussed.
Research on perceptual-motor abilities has predominantly studied the
performance of representative samples of children and adults with standardized tests. The presented tasks have typically not been practiced during
development in everyday life, although many tasks, such as running, throwing, and catching, have counterparts in many leisure and sport activities,

such as baseball, basketball, and soccer. When scientists identify factors that are related to performance on a particular task, it is typically difficult to determine whether the factors reflect virtually un-modifiable biological factors, such as individual differences in genetic endowment, or differences in prior practice and experience or interactions between genetic endowment and experience. This discussion has been particularly active in the interpretation of differences in performance related to sex differences. Although there is broad consensus of the existence of sex differences in performance during the life span, there is limited agreement as to the

In Search of Differences Between the Sexes in Throwing: The Effects of Physical Size and Differential Recruitment Rates on High Levels of Dart Performance.

nature of these differences and their potential implications. Performance on many tasks is influenced by experience and there is evidence from meta-analyses that the performance of females can be improved by practice. Moreover, there is compelling evidence for "catch-up" in some cases whereby females improve more than males as a function of practice. In spite of comprehensive studies of the effects of biological and experiential factors on throwing performance in children, most of the variability associated with sex differences cannot be explained. Many researchers agree that current evidence has not allowed an identification of the loci of the sex differences. In this article, we examined the perceptual motor activity that has been proposed to reflect the largest biological differences between the two sexes, namely dart throwing. Watson and Kimura (1989, 1991) demonstrated a clear superiority for males where physical size or amounts of sports activity were unrelated to individual differences in performance. In their original paper, Watson and Kimura (1989) also found a relationship between dart throwing with the right hand and previous sporting activity amongst female participants. The current study examined the effects of sex differences, physical attributes, and participation rates by reviewing evidence on the performance of male and female sports performers, such as dart players, who compete at club, regional/national and international levels and have engaged in play and practice for hundreds and typically thousands of hours.

Physical Size Advantages for Dart Throwing and Levels of Participation

The participation of women in public competitions in sports and games is a relatively recent phenomenon that evolved primarily during the latter part of the twentieth century. Female athletes have, in the main, competed against other females, therefore, hardly ever competed directly alongside male athletes. One reason for separating competition for males and females concerned the advantage that physical size plays in superior performance. In fact, males are grouped into classes based on their weight in many sporting events, such as wrestling, weight lifting, and boxing, to assure competition between individuals of comparable size. In events without weight classes, such as shot putting, discus and basketball, the best male athletes are significantly taller, thus providing indirect evidence for the advantages of increased height and body size. In domains of expertise that employ gross and fine motor skills, and where physical differences in size and strength shouldn't be directly relevant (such as snooker and archery), the best men's performance still may often exceed that of the best women, but this advantage arguably does not reflect any general superiority of skilled motor performance. For example, many women match and surpass the achievements of the best men and are generally considered to have attained more advanced levels in many activities requiring fluidity of movement, such as figure skating, gymnastics and ballet. Unfortunately, in such activities, men and women are not consistently evaluated by the same standards; moreover, completely objective measures of performance are not employed. There are several domains where motor performance is evaluated without regard to sex and where the best women are able to compete alongside the best men. Women compete directly with men in equestrian events and in some shooting events, such as skeet and trap and are highly competitive with men in archery and other shooting events. The superiority of men's performance is, in many sporting domains, closely related to men's higher levels of participation. Generally, males are much more interested in sports, thus, one could argue more likely than females to engage in these activities as children. It is shown that the larger size of the population of participants is associated with superior performance of its best performers. Hence, it is important to examine if the higher participant rates of males can explain their superior performance in sports.

In this paper we examined sex differences in skilled motor performance in representative samples of female and male dart players at club, regional/national, and international level, thus investigating if the sex differences found by Watson and Kimura (1989, 1991) would extend to dart players with various amount of practice and training. First, we investigated whether sex differences exist and, if so, assessed whether they could be influenced by differences in body size and the individuals' ability to reach (arm length). In the sport of darts, where the playing environment is static and consistent for all competitors, it may be that a height and/or reach advantage could facilitate superior performance. This is due to the opportunity of being able to "train" oneself to lean toward the target when throwing, therefore effectively be closer at the point of release of the dart. In a second study, we examined the possible effects of greater participation rates for men compared to women; the ratio of dart players is 4:1 in favor of men (British Darts Organization 2003). We also compared the performance of female and male dart players at different levels of expertise, namely club, regional/national and International level. Given that the size of recruitment pools, for both female and male dart players, will increase proportionally as the levels of competition increase, such as from club to regional/national level and from regional/national to International level, it will be possible to measure the effect of the recruitment pool and assess its potential interaction with sex differences in performance.

In the first study, we assessed whether differences in body size or reach could explain at least part of the differences in dart performance between men and women playing at a national level of expertise. Players were selected from a population of County A team players representing teams from England and Wales currently participating in the Premier Division of British Inter-County Darts Championship (regional/national level of performance). In order for players to be included in the current study, they must have participated in at least eight matches during the current season (nine being the maximum possible), including the last match. Once these criteria had been met, the top forty male and forty female dart players, based on their single dart average, were selected as participants. Each selected participant was contacted by the first author and interviewed about their age and the length of their dart playing experience at this competitive level (measured in months). Furthermore, the first author also measured the participants' height and arm length in inches. Height was measured with a measuring stick secured against the flat surface of a wall. Participants were asked to stand in their stocking feet against the instrument to be measured. Arm length was measured from the top of the throwing arm at the humerus (shoulder bone) to the tip of the middle finger. The participants' dart performance was based on the official records for British Inter County Dart Championships kept by the British Darts Organization. Our study relied on data from the final match played in the Premier division. We recorded the number of darts that each participant threw in a game of 501 during that match. For all officially recorded legs during this final match, we used the single dart average as a measure of each participant's dart performance. Means, together with their corresponding standard deviations, illustrating age in years, height in inches, length of arm in inches, previous experience in months and single dart average for men and women were documented.

An analysis of the two samples of female and male dart players revealed that both groups had played darts for a comparable period, on average over ten years, and did not reliably differ in their ages with a grand mean of around 35 years of age. As expected, the heights and reach were greater for men than women and the dart performance of men was superior to that of women. To assess whether differences in height and reach could explain the difference in dart performance, we conducted a regression analysis. Participants' height and reach reliably predicted their dart performance. However, these two variables did not explain all the variation associated with sex differences because adding sex differences to the regression equation led to reliable improvement in prediction. Most importantly, height and reach did not contribute any systematic information independent of sex differences because when these variables were removed from the regression equation the reduction in R^2 was not reliable. The findings from the regression analysis show that the relation between height and reach on the one hand and dart performance on the other is fully explained by normal sex differences in these variables rather than direct influences on performance. In further support of that conclusion, we found no reliable correlations between dart performance and height, reach, previous experience or age when the data for men or women were analyzed separately.

In a second study, we evaluated the hypothesis that differences in the size of the recruitment pool through differential rates of participation by males and females at a given level of expertise could explain sex differences in dart performance. We compared the effects of size of recruitment population by analyzing the performance of dart players at the club level with players at regional/national and International level. Fifteen male and fifteen female dart players at three different levels of expertise participated. The best players consisted of those recording the top 15 single dart averages for each sex selected from three International teams (England, Wales, and Scotland). Slightly less skilled players at the regional/national level consisted of a sample, based on the top 15 single dart averages for each sex from the players analyzed in Study 1. The least skilled players at club level contained selected players from the London Super League, based on the top 15 single dart averages for each sex. Each participant's dart performance was extracted from official data recorded by the British Darts Organization. The performance of international level players was calculated by averaging their scores during the Three Nations International series. The performance for regional/national and club level players was averaged across a complete season.

Means, together with their corresponding standard deviations for single dart averages by level of skill (International, Regional/National, and Club) and sex were documented, along with minimum and maximum scores for each level and by sex. An ANOVA with sex differences and level of expertise as the two main factors revealed a significant interaction between sex differences and level of expertise, as well as a main effect of level of expertise and sex differences. As expected, the performance of players at the higher level of expertise (selected from a larger recruitment pool) performed at a reliably superior level for both females and males, as evidenced by separate analyses for men, and for women, Post-hoc comparisons of the group means of expertise within each sex showed that higher levels of expertise were associated with reliably higher levels of dart performance with only one exception. Female dart players at the International level did not perform at a reliably higher than female players at the National level.

An analysis of simple effects of sex differences found a large advantage in favor and International level. The effect sizes of sex differences were estimated for the club, regional/national and International levels, respectively. These very large effect sizes for sex differences in skilled dart players exceed even the largest sex differences in throwing for children and amateurs. Although the effect sizes are numerically smaller with higher levels skill and accumulated practice, the only reliable aspects of these differences are the increases in the pooled variance as a function of level of skill. The pooled variance was reliably larger for the International level players compared to those at the club level, and compared to those at the regional/national level.

The ranges of dart performance for both sexes as a function of level of skill (International, regional/national and club) were documented and showed that the performance of all male players exceeds the performance of the best female dart player. A post-hoc analysis confirmed that all three groups of male dart players performed at a reliably higher level of performance than any of the three female groups. In fact, the least accomplished male players (i.e., those at club level) were reliably superior to the female dart players at International level and all three categories of male players had higher scores than all three categories of female players.

Our two studies replicated Watson and Kimura's (1989, 1991) findings of large sex differences in throwing accuracy even after control for physical differences and selection biases. Most importantly, our study showed that after thousands of hours of practice, the differences were not eliminated, nor even reduced, but rather the sex differences for International dart players was two to three times larger—the effect size was 5–10 standard deviations—than those observed for American undergraduates. Our study found that the least accomplished group of male competitive dart players, who played at the club level, were superior to the female dart players at the International level—the distributions of male and female competitive dart players did not even overlap. Given that our samples differed both in age and skill from Watson and Kimura's studies, we collected information on the best female and male dart players, who were below the age of 21 from the British Inter-County Youth Dart League 2004–2005, Southern Section. The single dart average of the top 15 female players was 15.6 with a 2.46 standard deviation. The best fifteen male players averaged 22.9 with a standard deviation of 2.12, which is statistically different and the male with lowest score in the sample was higher than the best female. This difference in highly skilled dart players corresponds to a Cohen's effect size for sex of 3.17, which is similar to those observed for typical college students by Watson and Kimura (1991). It is not immediately obvious how these very large sex differences in adult dart performance can be reconciled with much smaller sex differences among elite athletes in other sports with related motor performance. In the target sport of rifle shooting, the sex ratio is far greater in favor of men (10:1) (National Rifle Association of GB, 2002) than in darts, yet women's performance is comparable to that of men. There are similar findings showing that women remain competitive with men in clay pigeon shooting (14:1 ratio between number of participants, Clay Pigeon Shooting Association, 2002) and pistol shooting

(16:1 ratio, Great Britain Target Shooting Federation, 2002). In some sports such as bowling, archery and croquet, it is possible to find samples of women and men that are matched for equivalent performance. In ten-pin bowling, female professionals can successfully compete on equal terms with the best male professionals. The large sex differences in performance in many sports other than dart playing that were observed several decades ago have decreased toward their current levels as women have increased their participation and adopted the training regimen and practice methods of their male counterparts. However, recent research on the development of expert performance has shown that the effects of training and practice extend well beyond the training supervised by coaches during adolescence and early adulthood when dart players typically initiate their practice. There is now compelling evidence that early exposure to an activity is essential for elite performance in many domains of expertise, especially activities involving perceptual-motor coordination, such as skating, skiing, and golf. Furthermore, engagement in practice and other domain-related activities at young ages is associated with altered range of joints, such as in dancers' hips and in shoulder's of baseball pitchers. Moreover, previous research examining musicians has shown that early start of music training (frequently well before age 7) is associated with changes in the structure of the developing brain, which is linked to the superior ability of these musicians to coordinate their hands, control their fingers on the non-dominant hand and detect absolute pitches.

It is interesting to note that in the domains of music and ballet, the elite performers started their supervised training at very young ages—often between 4 and 7. In the domain of music, boys and girls start with supervised training at around the same age and reach a comparable level of adult music performance, as reflected in the mixture of male and female musicians in international orchestras. In ballet, girls tend to start at younger ages than boys and, arguably, reach as high or perhaps even higher levels of mastery of the technical aspects with dance on Pointe. Certainly, those abilities mentioned previously in relation to musicians, such as finger control and hand coordination, are essential to acquisition of expert performance in dart throwing. In many of the arts and sports, training by teachers and coaches is initiated during childhood, typically between 4–7 years of age. In contrast, most dart players take responsibility for their own training and start practice around age 18–20. At those mature ages, people have already acquired most of their abilities and there are large individual differences between the sexes at that age among college students and competitive dart players. These adult differences (prior to practice) must reflect normal development. It is well known that there are large differences in the preferred play activities of boys and girls. Studies of the normal development of motor skills and abilities show that sex differences may be explained by the differential engagement in associated motor activities.

More recent studies have analyzed these differences by careful longitudinal analysis of the development and structure of acquired throwing skills. Moreover, the effects of designed training interventions have identified important non-genetic factors that appear to mediate the differential development of sex differences in overhand throwing. Analysis of individual differences among boys—between 7 and 10 years of age—show that differences in movement patterns are established at surprisingly young ages. It is becoming increasingly clear that the development of motor skills, in particular bilateral transfer to the non-dominant arm, is mediated by complex mechanisms that are not fully understood. Until there is a comprehensive account of the development of skilled throwing that explains both the evidence on training effects as well as the evidence on influences of sex hormones and evolution of sex differences, it will be difficult to assess the degree to which the observed large differences between male and female international dart players can be altered by different developmental pathways.

New research on the development of the detailed mechanisms mediating expert dart performance and their development during childhood and adolescence will allow us to differentiate these alternative accounts. The lack of overlap between performance of competitive male and female dart players will make case studies of females informative. If girls from an early age (2–3 years) received focused training in overhand throwing in darts, would this training allow them to attain the performance of male players at the international level? A similar case study in chess has radically changed beliefs about women's ability to play games involving spatial reasoning and planning. For a long time, it was believed impossible for female chess players to compete successfully with male players at international level due to genetic sex differences in cognition. However, the Polgar family decided to challenge this dogma by home schooling their three daughters and training them to play chess from an early age. Two decades later, all three daughters attained a ranking among the top twenty female chess players in the world. Moreover, their youngest daughter became the youngest ever player, male or female, to reach the status of International Master after successful competitions with male chess players in tournaments at the International level. She was consistently ranked among the top twenty male players in the world and considered a contender to become a world champion. Only future research will tell whether early training in throwing for girls would similarly lead to increases in the attainable level of dart performance for female adult players. In sum, we believe that extended intense training in sports offer very important evidence on the adaptability and improvement of performance. Our findings on the preserved sex differences in dart performance will similarly provide essential evidence for our increasing understanding of the importance of development during childhood and adolescence for enhancing, as well as possibly limiting, adult potential.